OUT OF THE BLUE

D1412282

September 11 and the Novel

OUT OF THE BLUE

KRISTIAAN VERSLUYS

Columbia University Press **NEW YORK**

Columbia University Press
Publishers Since 1893
New York   Chichester, West Sussex

Copyright © 2009 Columbia University Press
All rights reserved
"A Poem for America" quoted on p. 10, is printed by permission of the author,
Jennifer Bhardwaj Ruigrok.

Library of Congress Cataloging-in-Publication Data
Versluys, Kristiaan
Out of the blue : September 11 and the novel /Kristiaan Versluys.
p. cm.
Includes bibliographical references and index.
ISBN 978-0-231-14936-5 (cloth : acid-free paper) — ISBN 978-0-231-14937-2 (pbk. : acid free paper) —
ISBN 978-0-231-52033-1 (e-book)
1. Fiction—21st century—History and criticism. 2. September 11 Terrorist Attacks, 2001, in literature.
3. September 11 Terrorist Attacks, 2001—Influence. 4. Psychic trauma in literature. I. Title

PS374.S445V47 2009
809.3′935873931—dc22   2008052348

Columbia University Press books are printed on permanent and durable acid-free paper.
This book is printed on paper with recycled content.
Printed in the United States of America

c 10 9 8 7 6 5 4 3 2 1
p 10 9 8 7 6 5 4 3 2

References to Internet Web sites (URLs) were accurate at the time of writing. Neither the author
nor Columbia University Press is responsible for URLs that may have expired or changed since the
manuscript was prepared.

For Annie, Helen and Dries, to whom I have been promising this dedication for years.

CONTENTS

ACKNOWLEDGMENTS

THIS STUDY was started during a wonderful sabbatical year at the Netherlands Institute for Advanced Study in 2004 and 2005. I want to thank the rector, the staff, and the fellows of the institute for creating, in the midst of the sand dunes of Wassenaar, an atmosphere that was conducive to scholarly work and in which earnestness mingled with congeniality and good cheer. I also want to thank my colleagues (junior and senior) at the English Department of Ghent University in Belgium and especially the members of the Ghent Urban Studies Team and of the Centre for Literature and Trauma.

On the other side of the ocean, I owe a great debt of gratitude to Andrew and Dawn Delbanco for the more than thirty-five years of close friendship and for encouraging us to make of New York our second home. Another enthusiastic New Yorker, Stacey Olster, could be called the godmother of this book. Without her constant support and scholarly vigilance, the project would never have come to fruition. To Judy Rosenthal I am indebted for coming up with the title of this book.

The constructive criticism of my editor, Philip Leventhal, was instrumental in improving the text and finalizing it for publication. His assistant, Avni Majithia, was the cicerone, who led me through the unfamiliar procedures of American publishing. The manuscript and production editor, Michael Haskell, currycombed the text with great accuracy and unfailing linguistic sensibility. Also the comments of the anonymous readers were helpful in revising the manuscript and strengthening the argument.

My various intellectual debts are acknowledged in the notes. I want to single out, however, the writings of Dominick LaCapra, which have been a constant inspiration. The volume of essays, *Literature After 9/11*, edited by Ann Keniston and Jeanne Follansbee Quinn, was published after the manuscript of this book was completed and thus came too late to be fully taken into consideration. Several of the essays in the volume offer valuable insights that are complementary (and sometimes contradictory) to mine.

In a slightly different and abbreviated form, chapter 2 was published as "Art Spiegelman's *In the Shadow of No Towers: 9/11* and the Representation of Trauma" in *Modern Fiction Studies* 52 (2006): 980–1004. In a slightly different form, chapter 4 was first published as "Frédéric Beigbeder's *Windows on the World*; Or, 9/11 as the End of Irony" in *CinematoGraphies: Fictional Strategies and Visual Discourses in 1990s New York City*, ed. Günter Lenz, Dorothea Löbbermann, and Karl-Heinz Magister (Heidelberg: Universitätsverlag Winter, 2006). A few paragraphs from the introduction and the epilogue first appeared in "9/11 as a European Event: The Novels," *European Review* 15, no. 1 (2007): 65–79. Permission to reprint in all cases is gratefully acknowledged.

The persons to whom I owe everything are the ones mentioned in the dedication.

OUT OF THE BLUE

INTRODUCTION

9/11: THE DISCURSIVE RESPONSES

ON AUGUST 9, 2006, *World Trade Center*, the long-awaited 9/11 movie by Oliver Stone premiered in New York City and it became an instant dud. Even on opening night the theaters were half empty. The public, clearly hostile to the commercialization of a wound still so fresh, in large part stayed away. Those who went to see the movie were lukewarm in their reception. In his review, the influential *New York Times* critic A. O. Scott promised that the film, while offering an "astonishingly faithful re-creation of the emotional reality of the day," also evokes "the extraordinary upsurge of fellow feeling that the attacks produced" (Scott, "Pinned"). But the actual movie falls far short of the mark. The story of the miraculous rescue of two Port Authority policemen buried seven meters under the rubble turns out to be a mere disaster movie. In spite of some spectacular shots of Ground Zero—realistically recreated on some Hollywood back lot—the movie has a generic quality. It could just as well have fictionalized the rescue of miners trapped in a collapsed pit or unfortunate passengers caught in the debris of a train wreck.[1] The grief and especially the shock caused by the events of that day do not seem exceptional, and the rescuers and trapped victims all look flaccid as heroes. If the individual case of the Port Authority cops is meant to stand for the larger tragedy, the synecdochic imagination does in no way do justice to the scale of the events or to their symbolic reverberations.

In a way, of course, Stone's failure was predictable. In the instantaneity of its horror and in its far-flung repercussions, 9/11 is unpossessable. It is a limit event that shatters the symbolic resources of the culture and defeats the normal processes of meaning making and semiosis. As Donna Bassin, a psychologist who went with the first family members to visit Ground Zero, puts it: "The rubble screams the collapse of individuality, security, and mastery that is impossible to represent. Words don't suffice, because the experience taps into helplessness known before words can be uttered to represent and contain experience. It is all gray at ground zero. Life becomes not a range of colors but only its absence" ("Not So Temporary," 198). September 11—for all the physicality of planes impacting on giant skyscrapers and for all the suffering caused to victims and their near and dear—is ultimately a semiotic event, involving the total breakdown of all meaning-making systems. The writer Star Black calls the collapse of the buildings "a sight without reference" ("Perfect Weather," 47), while Dori Laub, a psychoanalyst well known for his work with Holocaust survivors, states that "September 11 was an encounter with something that makes no sense, an event that fits in nowhere" ("September 11," 204). Similarly, James Berger declares: "Nothing adequate, nothing corresponding in language could stand in for it" ("'There's No Backhand to This,'" 54). For Jenny Edkins, 9/11 is a traumatic event that "is outside the bounds of language, outside the worlds we have made for ourselves" ("The Absence of Meaning"). In Don DeLillo's estimation, the downfall of the towers is "a phenomenon so unaccountable and yet so bound to the power of objective fact that we can't tilt it to the slant of our perception" ("In the Ruins," 38–39). In a moving prose poem, composed two days after the events, Toni Morrison writes, addressing a victim: "knowing all the time that I have nothing to say—no words stronger than the steel that pressed you into itself; no scripture older or more elegant than the ancient atoms you have become" ("The Dead," 1). Most extensively, Jacques Derrida explains that what collapsed that halcyon morning was not so much two "strategic urban structures" as

> the conceptual, semantic, and one could even say hermeneutic apparatus that might have allowed one to see coming, to comprehend, interpret, describe, speak of, and name "September 11." . . . [W]hat is terrible about "September 11," what remains "infinite" in this wound, is that we do not *know* what it is and so do not know how to describe, identify, and even name it.   (qtd. in Borradori, *Philosophy in a Time of Terror*, 93–94)

Yet name it we must. There is no way to wrap one's mind around what happened that day. There is no stylistic device, no trick of the imagination, no amount of ingenuity or inventiveness that can even begin to render the "primal terror" (DeLillo, "In the Ruins," 39), the horror of people burning alive, in desperation jumping from the towers hand in hand, or being crushed to death. And yet, as again Don DeLillo contends, "living language is not diminished" ("In the Ruins," 39). To the observation that 9/11 is unpossessable must be added the countering truism that somehow in some way it must be possessed. Even to say that the event is unnameable is a form of naming it. There is no way even something as indescribable as what transpired on that sunny Tuesday morning can stay out of the reach of symbol and metaphor. Willy-nilly, the event gets absorbed into a mesh of meaning making. This most real of all real events—220 stories crashing down, thousands of tons of steel collapsing—demonstrates, if not the primacy, then at least the inevitability of discourse. The event would not exist and could not exist outside the interpretative schemes that are imposed upon it. These schemes are at the same time limiting and yet empowering. For some observers, all the pabulum that gets attached to 9/11—the full accretion of commentary in the media and the almost instantaneous political recuperation—constitutes a new and very insidious form of terrorism and indoctrination (Derrida, qtd. in Borradori, *Philosophy in a Time of Terror*, 108). For others, the commentaries, ranging in their diversity from the rudimentary expletives heard all around Ground Zero that morning to the most sophisticated poetry, are an act of resistance, opposing the single-mindedness of ideology and of ideologically inspired terror.

Simply in order to cope, people have no choice but to rummage through the symbols that the culture puts at the disposal of the distraught individual. Trauma leads to numbness, flashbacks, or nightmares. These intrusive symptoms can only be dealt with when a traumatic memory gets situated within a series of events. Trauma must be given a place within one's recollection in order to be (se)cured. In other words, as the French psychiatrist Pierre Janet puts it, traumatic memory must be turned into narrative memory (*Médecine*, 23–24). Trauma makes time come to a standstill as the victim cannot shed his or her remembrance and is caught in a ceaseless imaginative reiteration of the traumatic experience. Narrativizing the event amounts to an uncoiling of the trauma, an undoing of its never-ending circularity: springing the time trap. The discursive responses to 9/11 prove, over and beyond their inevitability, that the individual is not only made but also healed—made whole—by the necessary mechanisms of narrative and semiosis.

As the critics E. Ann Kaplan and Bang Wang put it: "While it shatters the culture's symbolic resources, trauma also points to the urgent necessity of reconfiguring and transforming the broken repertoire of meaning and expression" ("From Traumatic Paralysis," 12). If trauma is the collapse of the network of significations, a narrative is needed to restore the broken link. Even if according to some theories trauma is unrepresentable, there is the need on the part of the traumatized to relieve anxiety through telling, a feeling on the part of the victims that they have the duty to testify and the desire on the part of the listener to learn more about trauma in order to reintroduce it into a network of signification. The latter need can be exploited: sensationalized, neutralized, abused for political or commercial purposes. It can also lead to a better understanding, to compassion, even to agency (the urge to change the world so that the traumatic event does not repeat itself). Above all, the need to understand, the need to "place" the event, is shared by victim and mere bystander. In a time of globalized witnessing and shared vicarious experience, an event like 9/11 is a rupture for everybody. As a consequence, there is a globalized need to comprehend, to explain, and to restore.

In this effort, Oliver Stone and the movie industry in general may be at an ironic disadvantage. Any number of commentators have pointed out that the experience of 9/11 was already "pre-mediated and de-realized" (Houen, "Novel Spaces," 428) by Hollywood extravaganzas such as *Towering Inferno* and *Independence Day*. In his reaction to 9/11, Slavoj Žižek writes: "the unthinkable which happened was the object of fantasy, so that, in a way, America got what it fantasized about, and that was the biggest surprise" (*Welcome to the Desert of the Real*, 16). In his essay on 9/11, Jean Baudrillard offers this typically hard-hitting chiasmus: "The spectacle of terrorism forces the terrorism of spectacle upon us" (*Spirit of Terrorism*, 30). In his view, the events of September 11 have vanished completely into the realm of hyperreality, the ethereal world of simulacra. The factual data of 9/11 do not add up to a reality that resembles fiction (in particular the fiction of Hollywood disaster movies), but, the other way round, they consist of a fiction that resembles reality. The fact that the terrorist attacks verifiably happened, that the buildings did collapse in real time and people actually died by the thousands, provides "an additional *frisson*" (29) to a perception that is predetermined and fore-coded by popular culture in a quasi-totalizing way. In this light, it may be that what Oliver Stone and future 9/11 filmmakers are up against is the simple fact that what was so indelibly precoded cannot be recoded. If Hollywood preempted 9/11 and thus what happened in Lower Manhattan was a Hollywood movie only better because real, it is not surprising that the public, fully remembering the horrors of five years before, balked at celluloid fakes, no matter how cleverly reenacted. The relative lack of success of the Stone movie proves that, pace Baudrillard, the public knows full well the difference between the real and the hyperreal. Out of piety and a sense of common decency, it rejects the latter in an attempt to hold on to the former. This may well be the reason why the most gripping visual representation of 9/11 is not Paul Greengrass's *United 93* or Oliver Stone's *World Trade Center*, nor the Hollywoodized real-life footage of the Naudet brothers,[2] but the straightforward, no-frills-added PBS documentary by Ric Burns. The events need no claptrap or heroization. It is enough to let them speak for themselves.

The simplest forms of discursivization and the most direct ones derive an aura of authenticity from being close to the events. Nothing is more poignant or gripping than the telephone messages sent from the towers minutes before the speakers were crushed to death. This is the closest we have to something like a firsthand account. The messages to the emergency services were taped and released to the public, at least in part, some time ago. To protect the privacy of the victims, their voices have been edited out and what one hears are the calm voices of the dispatchers. Even though their mettle was put to the severest of tests, their training served them in good stead, and most show remarkable grace under extreme pressure. In spite of their unfazed professionalism, though, the chaos and the pathos of those 102 minutes of agony are clearly audible. Operators, in no way well informed about the extent of the unfolding disaster and out of touch with the reality on the ground, often advised desperate callers to stay put rather than to flee, unwittingly causing their deaths.

People trapped on the upper floors of the towers also tried to reach their relatives by phone or e-mail. In tones that are sometimes calm, sometimes frantic, they relate their losing battle against the heat and the smoke and, in turn, ask their interlocutors for information (often the relatives watching television knew more than the people in the midst of the imbroglio). Many, realizing the desperateness of the situation, say their last farewells, often in the simplest of words: "I love you" (Dwyer et al., "102 Minutes," 24).We know of the case of Edmund McNally, who called his wife as the floor of his office started to buckle. In the words of a newspaper report:

> Mr. McNally hastily recited his life insurance policies and employee bonus programs. "He said that I meant the world to him and he loved me," Mrs. McNally said, and they exchanged what they thought were their last goodbyes.
>
> Then Mrs. McNally's phone rang again. Her husband sheepishly reported that he had booked them on a trip to Rome for her 40th birthday. "He said, 'Liz, you have to cancel that,'" Mrs. McNally said.
>
> ("102 Minutes," 22)

In his introduction to *11 septembre mon amour*, his book on 9/11 (part autobiography, part fiction), the French author Luc Lang evokes, in the most touching of manners, the voices of those about to die in the towers as they try to reach their loved ones on the telephone for a final adieu. In the epilogue to the book he comes back to these voices and shows how even these simple and direct discursivizations are ensnared in multiple loops. On the one hand, there is the relentless repetition of the images of the collapse of the towers on television—an endless loop accompanied by media chitchat. Simultaneously, the forfeited lives of the victims are recuperated by the president, whom Lang insists on calling "Double V Bouche" ("*bouche*" is the French word for mouth), thus indicating how the authentic words of love of the victims minutes away from their deaths contrast with the deceitful doubleness of the official propaganda. Caught in that loop, the voices of the soon-to-die are instrumentalized and betrayed, "abandoned to the political mercantilism of the cynical and calculating powers that be, which are already recycling them in their false thirst for vengeance" (247).[3]

There is, however, another loop, symbolized by the novel bending backward on itself and ending where it began, the first and final chapters both being devoted to words of love, the love of the victims for their near and dear, the affection of the writer for his own beloved. That loop delineates how "for the first time perhaps in the history of humanity, we were all contemporaries" (244). Modern communication technology makes us part of the tragedy, live and in real time, so that all of us, individually, are appealed to "in the intimacy of our lives" (246). Such solidarity creates a "sonorous space of ethics" (247), in which the voices of the dying resound and loop us in. From beyond the grave, they enjoin us to give sense and permanence to their despair. They beg to be delivered from the political-commercial media loop that ensnares them and to be adopted into a worldwide community that does not preach hatred or revenge. It is in the name of these innocents that Lang makes a sharp distinction between, on the one hand, what he calls "l'empire You Esse Eïe," Double V Bouche presiding, which he loathes and detests, and, on the other hand, the true America, which consists of, among others, those who died on September 11, to whose urgent and ardent voices we are tied by virtue of our common humanity.[4]

Another form of instant discursivization that marked the immediate aftermath of 9/11 comprises the innumerable missing-person signs that were put up all over New York City after the collapse of the buildings. These signs made what Jay McInerney termed a "makeshift gallery... —the faces of the missing glancing back hopefully and artlessly in photographs taken at weddings and graduation ceremonies, now hanging above impromptu shrines of flowers and candles" (*The Good Life*, 144). The architecture critic Mark Wigley highlights the special significance of these posters. He points out that the "World Trade Center was a hyper-development of the generic postwar corporate office tower," which typically features an anonymous façade, representing the corporation as an open network and serving as "a screen that conceals the body" ("Insecurity by Design," 75). The layout of the buildings conspired to relegate the workers inside to anonymity at the service of a centerless multinational.

"When the façades [of the World Trade Center towers] came down," however, "the faces of the invisible occupants who were lost came up" (82). The signs posted all over the city "formed a new kind of façade, a dispersed image of diversity in place of the singular, monolithic screen" (83). The architecture of the megatowers (two minimalist glass boxes) suggested the endless replicability of the industrial process and thus blotted out the uniqueness and variegation of their occupants. Only in death did the World Trade Center workers acquire the individuality that, as cogs in a nameless mechanism, they had been denied during their lifetime. As Marshall Berman puts it: the missing-person signs "dramatized one of the central themes of modern democratic culture: *life stories*." Life stories show "how heroically extraordinary... ordinary life can be" ("Bad Buildings," 5).

The 1,910 short biographies of the victims that appeared in *The New York Times*, first under the heading "Among the Missing," but soon, as of the second day of reporting, under the title "Portraits of Grief," are offshoots and continuations of the improvised fliers. They, too, derive their poignancy from the portrayal of ordinary lives. Or, more precisely, they consist of anecdotes that are striking because they describe daily routines and habits that have been rudely broken off. They flesh out lives that should never have been lost. Unlike the typical *New York Times* obituary, which memorializes the acts of public or notorious persons, the miniprofiles of not more than 300 words emphasize the importance of everydayness and thus glorify the common man. They are a tribute to what Berman calls "Plainmanism" ("Bad Buildings," 5). Like the missing-person signs, they give a face to the faceless. Coming from all walks of life, all social classes, all ethnicities and religious backgrounds, the victims constitute a representative cross-section of the city, and their serial portraits helped to provide a collective identity to New York in its hour of need. Moreover, in their variation and comprehensiveness, the portraits—which were published as a book (*Portraits*) but which are also freely available to this very day on the *New York Times* Web site as a sort of electronic shrine—embody the utopian moment of solidarity right after the attacks, when the unity of the population, transcending the usual dividers of gender, race, and class, was also concretized in candlelight vigils, small-scale classical concerts, and the more mournful than defiant flying of the American flag.

The profiles themselves are wonders of miniaturization. With one soft touch, through the skilful introduction of the characteristic anecdote, the portraits individualize the massive loss. As Nancy K. Miller indicates, "their effective economy" involves "a paradox of scale: the loss is so great that the only way to bring it to language is to think small, cutting it down to size" ("'Portraits of Grief,'" 122–23). The synecdochal imagination is better served by the few lines offered in the portraits by immediate relatives—evocations of the way the deceased lives on in memory—than by the hackneyed Hollywood clichés warmed over in Oliver Stone's uninspired version of the events. The advantage of scale of the big-budget disaster movie is rendered null and void by the directness of true and authentic testimony.[5]

A conspicuous part of the discursive response to 9/11 was the spontaneous outpouring of poetry—most of which was published online at Web sites set up for that purpose. The well-known poet and essayist Dana Gioia, who also happens to be the former head of the National Endowment for the Arts, sees in this unprecedented use of poetry as a vehicle of public sentiment proof of the "media's collective inadequacy to find words commensurate with the situation" ("'All I Have Is a Voice,'" 164). "The media may have provided information and commentary," he writes, "but it was still left for poets to present language equal to the historical moment" (166). His findings are borne out by the Dutch cultural critic Liedeke Plate, who, in an incisive analysis, asserts that in the wake of the terrorist attacks "poetry emerged as an aesthetic form to counter the anaesthetic effect of television" ("The *Poethic* Turn," 24). For her, poetics is a form of ethics, and she coins a new phrase—"the poethic turn"—to indicate how poetry functioned as "a means to engage moral values of right and wrong and inquire in codes of political conduct and media practices" (40). Her claims, though, need to be qualified. While the events gave rise to significant poems by Galway Kinnell and the Polish Nobel Prize winner Wislawa Szymborska, large quantities of amateur versifying amount to nothing more than eerily comic doggerel. This, for instance, is one characteristic example, plucked from a Web site called poetry.com:

A Poem for America

America the Beautiful
America the great
If this is true
Why was this our fate?
Was it something we did?
Was it something we said?
Even if so
Do all those people deserve to be dead?
We are going through horror
We are going through pain
Yet we are not to worry
For justice we shall gain
We must pray and stick together
Pray and be strong
Finding the one responsible will not take too long
And when we do find them
We will make them pay
And that my brothers and sisters
Will be the most glorious day!   (Jennifer Bhardwaj Ruigrok)

The striking naivety of these verses and their technical clumsiness are only outdone by the thoughtless way in which the lines evoke the horror of the day, slightly examine the underlying causes of the events, and end with a resounding revanchist exclamation. The poem testifies to the confusion caused by 9/11, but its general tenor in no way questions the consensual response in the media or in political discourse. That it sounds so false in all registers proves, ex negativo, that authenticity is an "effect" gained when language cuts a path through pregiven linguistic structures and thus reveals a corner of human experience that otherwise goes unexplored. This is the true "poethic turn": when language, charged to its utmost potential, manages to say something that is nearly unsayable and that, if it weren't for the exact wording of the poem, would remain unsaid. Only a few among the thousands of poems written on the occasion of September 11 attain that level of discursive precision and human expressiveness.

It is against this background of local efforts at discursivization that the novelists and prose writers launched their own more ambitious attempts to come to terms with 9/11. In an article entitled "Art and Atrocity in a Post-9/11 World," the Jewish American author Thane Rosenbaum asks himself, "Is there a proper role for the artist, and specifically the novelist, at this time in our nation's history? Can we make art in a time of atrocity? Does the imagination have anything to say when it has to compete with the actual horror of collapsing skyscrapers?" (130). He himself has a categorical answer to these questions. "As a novelist," he writes, "I wouldn't touch the World Trade Center, and the looming tragedy around it, as a centerpiece for a new book. . . . I'm not ready to write, or talk, about it yet" (135). According to him, in the aftermath of September 11, "silence might be the loudest sound of all" (132). He pleads for a "collective numbness" as the only proper response to "the horror of what happened" (132).

His reaction is strongly reminiscent of other caveats that have been sounded in connection with the narrativization of collective trauma. (The warnings of Theodor Adorno, Lionel Trilling, and others in connection with the Holocaust immediately come to mind.)[6] As trauma is deemed to be unsayable, any saying of it may be seen as a cheapening, a reduction of its irreducible atrocity to something less threatening, more controllable. Moreover, the question arises of how much time has to elapse before one can take enough critical and meditative distance to deal with an event such as 9/11. As every invented story about that tragic day is in a sense an appropriation of the event, who has the credentials to speak about it with authority? And how long does it take before such narrativizing becomes permissible or at all possible? In a short story that came out soon after the terrorist attacks, the novelist Lynne Sharon Schwartz indicates in the form of a parable how, in the wake of 9/11, it was literally impossible for a writer to move on to the "next sentence." She describes how writers were stuck in an endless repetition of those things they "know for certain": "I would have been in there except I slept late . . . I had a toothache . . . I got caught in traffic" ("Near November," 261). The reason for this refusal to go beyond simple utterances of actual facts is that "grief, at an infernal temperature, had burnt knowledge out of us" (261). It is impossible to know what to think: "What is the just path? Revenge is tempting, but also loathsome and useless" (261). In other words, beyond mere facticity (the mentioning of where one was and what one was doing at the time) the event does not yield any meaning. "We long to hear an intelligent word," Schwartz writes (261). But right away she understands that this an impossible yearning: "No, we long for silence. Enough words have been spoken" (261).

Schwartz's story—in that it is a telling of 9/11 or at least about 9/11—is oxymoronic. She talks about the impossibility of talking about 9/11 and thus talks about it. Novelists arrogate to themselves a certain power of explanation, comprising not systematic knowledge but a kind of affective and empathic understanding. In their ongoing mission to interpret the culture and to provide points of view from which to approach it, they have no choice but also to confront the signal event that reorients the culture and marks it in its deepest substratum. This may be the reason why Schwartz concludes her little parable by stating: "We will do what is needed; we will write the next sentence" ("Near November," 262).

In fact, in the immediate confusion after the attacks, writers were often solicited to express their opinions in newspapers and magazines, as if they possessed oracular insights or at least enough clarity of thought or power of the imagination to explain what had happened. The need to "explore the possibilities of language in the face of gaping loss" (Baer, "Introduction" 1) was so imperative that quickly after September 11, short story collections appeared with such titles as:

- *110 Stories: New York Writes After September 11* (ed. Baer)
- *September 11, 2001: American Writers Respond* (ed. Heyen)
- *September 11: West Coast Writers Approach Ground Zero* (ed. Meyers)
- *To Mend the World: Women Reflect on 9/11* (ed. Agosin)

Most surprising of all, while voices such as Thane Rosenbaum's were initially heard stating that, confronted by mass death and unprecedented terror, dignified silence was the only proper response, to date nearly thirty novels have been written that deal directly or indirectly with the events on that bright September morning, and that is not counting juvenile or detective fiction.

This substantial body of 9/11 fiction, which is growing by the day, ranges from the absolutely inane to the interesting and probing. Many of the novels deal with the events of September 11 only tangentially: as a tragic moment that punctuates other, more mainstream (mostly love) interests.[7] There is also no shortage of novels that, just like a great deal of the poetry, express raw outrage and revanchist feelings. These—often patriotic or Christian-revival novels—sell in large numbers but have little or no literary merit. In their treatment of 9/11, they are characterized by what, in a totally different context, Eric Santner has termed "narrative fetishism." "Far from providing a symbolic space for the recuperation of anxiety," Santner writes, "narrative fetishism directly or indirectly offers reassurances that there was no need for anxiety in the first place" ("History," 147). The formulaic plots of the narratively fetishized 9/11 novels are always the same. The attack on the homeland is the occasion for a conversion: from a sinful or worldly attitude to a religious and pious one or from lukewarm citizenship to flag-waving patriotism. The terrorist attacks, in other words, are shamelessly recuperated for ideological and propaganda purposes. The ultimate aim is to suppress the trauma of 9/11. Tragedy is turned into triumphalism without proper mourning or working-through.[8]

Those few novels that succeed in engaging the full range of the imagination, beyond patriotic clichés and beyond the pabulum of the talking heads, resist such premature closure. They affirm the humanity of the befuddled individual groping for an explanation, express the bewilderment of the citizen as opposed to the cocksureness of the killers, give voice to stuttering and stammering as a precarious act of defiance. In gingerly working their way around the unsayability of the events, they are able to substantiate a true "poethic turn": that is to say, their poetics is a form of ethics. Through formal means they suggest the impact of shock—the immediate shock that causes panic or the slower realization that things have been altered beyond repair. These works testify to the shattering of certainties and the laborious recovery of balance.

To put it differently: in a gesture that is familiar to therapists and writers alike, the novels affirm and counteract the impact of trauma (Gilbert, "Writing Wrong," 262). At one level, they register the moment of *anamorphosis*, the moment the subject loses its foothold in a world of objects, the moment the everyday sense of security and mastery is shattered, objects reveal a malign intention of their own, and the human subject—deprived of its superiority vis-à-vis the world outside—is revealed in its utter vulnerability (Sass, "Lacan and 9/11"). But at another level, the novels also provide a context for what seems to be without context. They contain what seems uncontainable and reconfigure the symbolic networks that the terrorist attacks destroyed. In transcending jingoistic discourse or media insipidities, the full engagement of the imagination reveals how, at the moment of traumatic impact, the known world dissolves in a flash and all that remains is bafflement and pain. By the same token, the plots are informed by the mental mechanism of recovery and repair. Language is the first healer. Expression counters obsession. Telling the tale is the first step in getting on with life, integrating what happened into a meaningful narrative.

The extreme difficulty of tackling trauma, while avoiding cheap sensationalism or fetishization, shows itself in two respects. First of all, the best 9/11 novels are diffident linguistically. On the whole, the narratives shy away from the brute facts, the stark "donnée" of thousands of lives lost. As an event, 9/11 is limned as a silhouette, expressible only through allegory and indirection. Second, there is a marked tendency for the compensatory imagination to counteract the impact of September 11. This concentration on the recuperative powers of the mind was anticipated by Don DeLillo when, in his meditation on 9/11, he alluded to the void left by the vanished towers and wrote: "There is something empty in the sky. The writer tries to give memory, tenderness, and meaning to all that howling space" ("In the Ruins," 39). In his practice as a writer, DeLillo has given abundant proof of discursive savvy. His novels are steeped in postmodernist irony. Official lingo is debunked, and the vernacular serves as a means to undercut pretension and make-belief. Nonetheless, in the immediate aftermath of September 11, he stresses the healing potential of language. He defines the task of the writer as that of giving meaning, while at the same time indicating the full extent of the emptiness the discursive practice is meant to fill. "The writer," he states, "wants to understand what this day has done to us" (39).

Given this humanistic imprint and this tendency towards moral uplift in the magazine article, which DeLillo wrote shortly after September 11, it is surprising that DeLillo himself has written the most devastatingly pessimistic novel among all the 9/11 narratives. As I explain in chapter 1,

DeLillo's *Falling Man* is a portrait of pure melancholia without the possibility of working-through or mourning. As the account of an endless re-enactment or acting-out of a traumatic experience that allows for no accommodation or (symbolic) resolution, it stands in sharp contrast to Art Spiegelman's comics series or graphic novel *In the Shadow of No Towers* (see chapter 2). Spiegelman opts for a different kind of 9/11 "counternarrative." His graphic novel consists of a narrative sequence that does not preclude agency and, in the presence of an all-absorbing fixation, does not succumb to unrelieved pessimism. In other words, *In the Shadow of No Towers* balances collapse and resurgence. The unknowability of the event and the absence of a cognitive or emotional structure that can contain it, rather than standing in the way of testimony, inspire the author-protagonist's creativity and fire his political imagination.

Central to all the 9/11 novels under consideration is the question of language: how can words be found that are capable of naming the unnameable? How can this be done without nudging the events into a reified interpretative scheme? Chapter 3, in discussing Jonathan Safran Foer's *Extremely Loud and Incredibly Close*, focuses on the struggle of trauma victims to bring their various losses to language. Honesty and authenticity, in this context, become a function of how language manages to expose its own limits and to suggest that a traumatic event such as September 11 is ultimately incommensurate and beyond full comprehension. Pain is related to the impossibility of utterance. The three narrator-protagonists of the novel are faced with an ineffable trauma, an unspeakable truth, which they try to reveal through language. In this effort, Foer explores the outer reaches of language, where it borders on silence and where saying nothing and saying everything are virtually synonymous.

Chapter 4 deals with the French writer Frédéric Beigbeder's novel *Windows on the World*. Though a novel of minor literary merit, the text is crucial in any consideration of the discursive responses to the terrorist attacks, in that, from an outsider's point of view, it sketches 9/11 as an occasion of universal and lasting pain and thus as an event that, transgressing its own time frame, leaves behind ghostly presences and spectral after-imaginings. September 11, as an apocalyptic event, has seeped into the international collective unconscious. The absent towers are present all over as symptoms of a half-buried trauma, which yet, through a dialectic reversal, rejuvenates Western culture. September 11 is made meaningful in an overarching biblical analogy, whereby New York stands for the postmodern episteme in general and as such is both Babel and Babylon. September 11, as an "unrelatable" occurrence, involves the disintegration of language, and thus it is staged as a discursive dispersal, a Babel-like linguistic brokenness. At the same time, it is an apocalyptic event in which *chronos* (mere "passing" or "waiting" time) is turned into *kairos* (the fullness of time). While putting an end to an age of frivolity, the destruction of the Twin Towers ushers in an era of new seriousness, where the mores of the West, as exemplified by those of the protagonist, take a turn away from sensual indulgence and toward gravitas and fidelity.

The crucial text in the final chapter of this study is John Updike's *Terrorist*. The centrality of this novel is related to the fact that, alone among several attempts by novelists to deal with the question of alterity in the context of global terrorism, it seeks fully to illuminate the viewpoint of the Other. As the title of the novel indicates, Updike has tried to write from the perspective of the ultimate Other, whose mind-set—to quote the psychologist Ruth Stein—is completely "discordant with our Western ideals and humanistic values of morality and compassion" ("Evil as Love," 396). In that effort, Updike brings to a conclusion an exploration of the complex notion of alterity, which includes not only his own short story "Varieties of Religious Experience" but also his short piece that appeared in the *New Yorker* immediately after the attacks. The problem Updike wrestles with can be formulated as follows: how to avoid a dichotomizing discourse, whereby, under the pressure of extreme circumstances, the world is simplistically divided into "us versus them." It is a question that, within the broad context of 9/11, has also exercised other writers, such as Paul Auster, Nicholas Rinaldi, Martin Amis, and Michael Cunningham.

In speculating about the future of 9/11 fiction and briefly looking at two novels in which the events of that day are touched upon obliquely or allegorically, the epilogue to this study confirms that these indirect treatments of 9/11 are also pervaded by an effort to see the terrorist attacks as an event that, rather than enforcing a logic of revenge, appeals for an ethics of responsibility. In both Anita Shreve's *A Wedding in December* and Ian McEwan's *Saturday*, common decency is the first and foremost response to terrorist rage. While extreme circumstances strain the bonds of solidarity and communality, self-sacrifice and compassion serve to reassert one's humanity. At stake in this search for a triangulating discourse that avoids the bland polarity of "us-versus-them" is the very nature of the art of the novel itself. The novelistic practice of viewing a situation in its full complexity entails the denial of the reductive logic of terrorism, the black-and-white ideological view that legitimates indiscriminate violence. It equally goes against the simplifications of patriotic rodomontade and revanchist rhetoric. In embracing the viewpoint of the Other (including the terrorist, the ultimate Other), novelists employ an ethics that gainsays binary thinking and that, *in potentia*, proffers a way out of the deadly spiral of violence and counterviolence that the planes, coming out of the blue, initiated.

1

AMERICAN MELANCHOLIA

DON DELILLO'S *FALLING MAN*

IN AN ESSAY ENTITLED "In the Ruins of the Future" published in the December 2001 issue of *Harper's Magazine*, Don DeLillo writes that, in the aftermath of September 11, the "sense of disarticulation we hear in the term 'Us and Them' has never been so striking, at either end" (34). The context clarifies what this cryptical phrase means: the 9/11 attacks pit a (Western, American) vision of the future against the wish of the terrorists to return to "medieval expedience, to the old slow furies of cutthroat religion" (37). The terrorists, who have pledged themselves to a destructive ideology and fail to recognize the humanity of their victims, dedicate themselves single-mindedly to one purpose: "Kill the enemy and pluck out his heart" (37). They want to go back to "what they used to have before the waves of Western influence" (38). To reach that goal, they narrowly conform to "a morality of destruction" (38).

DeLillo sharply observes how the events of 9/11 have ruined the future; that is, they have damaged American self-confidence and exposed an hitherto hidden vulnerability. But above all, he makes clear where his sympathies are. In the struggle between past and future, he sides with "modern democracy" (40), whatever its shortfalls, and he opposes the "global theocratic state, unboundaried and floating and so obsolete it must depend on suicidal fervor to gain its aims" (40). While the terrorist "pledges his submission to God and meditates on the blood to come" (34), democracy fashions a counternarrative. Redemptive words and gestures prove the "daily sweeping taken-for-granted greatness of New York" (40) and provide even "a glimpse of elevated being" (34). By furnishing a panoramic view of all the stories that circulate around 9/11 (the "stories of heroism and encounters with dread" [34], stories of good luck and bad), by relating in detail the story of his cousin Marc, who lived two blocks away from Ground Zero, by demonstrating how the diversity of New York accommodates and even welcomes milder versions of Islam, DeLillo creates a communion of telling, which somehow fills the void caused by the attacks and offsets the murderous intents of the terrorists.[1]

Melancholia

Given the humanistic imprint of the December 2001 essay, it is surprising that, of all the 9/11 narratives, DeLillo's novel *Falling Man* is, without a doubt, the darkest and the starkest. Unlike the *Harper's* essay, it describes a trauma with no exit, a drift toward death with hardly a glimpse of redemption. In a way, *Falling Man* is the narrative that takes 9/11 most seriously, and, for that reason, it is the most gloomy of the 9/11 novels. In psychoanalytical terms, it describes pure melancholia without the possibility of mourning. The endless reenactment of trauma presented in *Falling Man* allows for no accommodation or resolution.

In a 1917 essay, Freud makes a vital distinction between melancholia and mourning. While the latter represents an active working-through of a traumatic loss, the former is characterized by inertia and self-hatred. The melancholic, Freud writes, is "apathetic, ... incapable of love and achievement"(*On Murder*, 206). Totally possessed by the past, the melancholy mind is dead to the surrounding world. In the words of Dominick LaCapra, Freud "saw melancholia as characteristic of an arrested process in which the depressed and traumatized self, locked in compulsive repetition, remains narcissistically identified with the lost object" (*History*, 44–45). Or as LaCapra, elaborating Freud's concept, puts it in a different essay: "Melancholia is an isolating experience allowing for specular intersubjectivity that immures the self in its desperate isolation.... [I]t is a state in which one remains possessed by the phantasmatically invested past and compulsively, narcissistically identified with a lost object of love" (*History*, 183).

Falling Man sets itself the task of articulating such a condition of total immurement. Dwelling without letup on a state of apathy in which individuality is rubbed out, willpower attenuated, and language barely functional, the novel illustrates how history claims lives and swallows up a whole culture. One of the ways in which the polysemous title reverberates is that *Falling Man* has the ambition of being an updated, early-twenty-first century version of the fall of man. The (post)modern condition evoked in the novel is one of drift. The aspirational culture, the characteristic American drive and can-do mentality have come to a grinding halt. More trenchantly, humanity, as it is traditionally defined, has vanished. The characters are so thin that their whole existence boils down to mere nomenclature. Personality has disintegrated into a mere semiotic mark, while the great achievements of modernity (romantic love, technology-driven prosperity, the small-group dynamics of happiness) are nullified by angst and mental paralysis.

In the opening scene of the novel, the main male character, Keith Neudecker—having survived the terrorist attacks—is staggering north just after the first tower has come down and minutes before the second one will collapse. Dazed and disoriented, he is entering a landscape of "rubble and mud" (3). Immediately setting the prevailing tone, the very first sentence of the novel describes a postlapsarian world of lost innocence: "It was not a street anymore but a world, a time and space of falling ash and near night" (3). At Ground Zero, where streets have disappeared as part of recognizable reality and darkness has descended at noon, the confusion and the mayhem immediately convey the sense of the irremediableness of the situation, its utter finality. Keith's confusion, widened to encompass all of time and space, is generalized into a symbol of the *condition améri-caine*.[2] September 11 is figured as the collapse of everything that is familiar, and, in its familiarity, comforting. The impersonal voice of the narrator intones : "This was the world now" (3). The terrorist attacks punctuate an era characterized by brokenness and unrelieved melancholia.

As an utterly aporetic and deliberately antiredemptive narrative, *Falling Man* figures acedia or tedium as the main characteristic of the post-9/11 time frame. The terrorist attacks in no way precipitate a cleansing or catharsis. Instead, the shock following the collapse of the Twin Towers acts as a catalyst, exposing modernity and its many discontents. Modernity is defined as existential emptiness, as a state of irremediable, total, and immutable mental immobility and numbness.

Death, as the ultimate form of this melancholy stasis, hovers over the novel as a grim certainty. To an unusual extent, the novel is death-driven.

Keith's father-in-law, Jack Glenn, committed suicide at the first signs of early dementia. Keith's mother-in-law, Nina Bartos, a feisty former professor of art history, loses her zest for life after knee-replacement surgery. Her formidable energy falters. Self-indulgently, she settles into old age. Smoking too much, overmedicating herself, not following her physical fitness regimen, she deliberately courts death: "She was finally and resolutely old. This is what she wanted, it seemed, to be old and tired, to embrace old age, take up old age, surround herself with it" (9). Keith's wife, Lianne, holds "story line sessions" (29) with Alzheimer patients in the early stages of the disease. They, too, are bound to slip into oblivion and finally death.

Most significantly of all, the novel is named after a performance artist, who, tethered to a primitive safety harness, jumps from buildings and viaducts. Having heard about these stunts, Keith's wife, Lianne, thinks: "He brought it back, of course, those stark moments in the burning towers when people fell or were forced to jump" (33). More in particular, the fictional performance artist in DeLillo's novel replicates the many falls taken by the real-life artist Kerry Skarbakka, whose 9/11 imitations mayor Michael Bloomberg of New York called "nauseatingly offensive."[3] The performances by Skarbakka, in their turn, allude to a famous photograph by Richard Drew, which shows a man plunging head-first down along the shimmering columns of the World Trade Center towers on September 11. In an article published in *Esquire*, the journalist Tom Junod discusses this picture and gives it the name by which it has come to be known ever since and which DeLillo borrowed for the title of his novel: "The Falling Man." "In most American newspapers," Junod writes, "the photograph that Richard Drew took of the Falling Man ran once and never again" (Junod, "The Falling Man"). The reason for this act of self-censorship is that, though tens and maybe hundreds of people had no other choice but to escape the flames through the windows, "from the beginning, the spectacle of doomed people jumping from the upper floors of the World Trade Center resisted redemption" (Junod, "The Falling Man"). Quickly, the newspapers ran pictures not of the victims but of the survivors and, more emphatically, of the rescuers. As James Berger puts it, "it was astonishing ... how quickly the media's focus was on triumph: of the nation's spirit, New York's spirit, our resolve, our community, our political system, the president's oratory, our policies, our strategies, our weapons, our soldiers, our way of life" ("'There's No Backhand to This,'" 55). Or in the words of Susan Faludi: "By September 12, our culture was already reworking a national tragedy into a national fantasy of virtuous might and triumph" (*The Terror Dream*, 289).

Illustrating the true horror of the day and resisting heroization, Drew's photograph—just as Skarbakka's "nauseatingly offensive" performances—had no place in the instantaneous recuperation of the events by politicians and the media. By choosing an image of irredeemable death as the iconic moment that indicates the true place of 9/11 in the cultural repertoire of the nation, DeLillo indicates how his novel provides a counterdiscourse to the prevailing nationalistic interpretations. The falling man, standing in for the people who had no choice but to submit to their fate, is the symbol of the dark underside of 9/11, its enervating effect that the mainstream media tried to crush. As the critic Frank Rich puts it in a review of the novel: *Falling Man* "touches the third rail of 9/11 taboos" (Rich, "The Clear Blue Sky"). Says Lianne about the spectacle of the falling man: "There was the awful openness of it, something we'd not seen, the single falling figure that trails a collective dread, body come down among us all" (33).

In thus relentlessly focusing on September 11 as the symbol of irreclaimable melancholy, *Falling Man* unfolds as a series of ineffective holding actions against death and despair. If, in the normal course of events, death is feared because it is the negation of life, here life is defined as a state of near death or a state of barely escaping the condition of death. The characters are minimally alive in that they are numbed and they labor under the shadow of an overwhelming sadness that they cannot throw off. In article entitled "A Humanistic Approach to the Psychology of Trauma," Ilene Serlin and John T. Cannon write: "From a humanistic perspective, a traumatic event is a disruption so serious that it threatens our existence, shaking the foundation of who we are and who we once were. It makes us face our basic helplessness and mortality. Trauma confronts us with the reality of death, ripping through our sanitized lives and our monumental denial of death" (314). Serlin and Cannon add that since the experience of trauma questions our ordinary perspective on life, it may allow us to grow. Victims can become survivors, and, by the grace of true grit (and some expensive psychoanalysis), survivors may become "thrivers." In *Falling Man*, no such working-through or mourning takes place or is even possible. The "falling man" (standing for the fall of man) demonstrates the irresistible pull of gravity, the overpowering might of the downward plunge. Since the fictional performance artist uses primitive, backbreaking equipment, which causes spinal injuries and leads to "chronic depression" (222), and since he made "plans for a final fall, [which] did not include a safety harness"(221), his performances signify death on the installment plan (see Mars-Jones, "As His World"). As such, they are but the extensions of the other characters' vaguely self-destructive lives.

Noninvolvement

After staggering out of the burning north tower, Keith Neudecker does not go back to his nearby apartment. Instead, for reasons he himself cannot fathom, he goes to the apartment, much farther north, where his estranged wife and his seven-year-old son are living. Instinctively, in the rush of events, he goes back to Lianne, looking for the shelter of the family. Soon he finds out, however, that the family idyll cannot be restored and the home does not function anymore as a safe haven. The passion between the spouses has long since disappeared, and it cannot be rekindled. They reconnect sexually but otherwise remain strangely aloof. Even moments of great intimacy indicate the distance that has opened up between them :

> After the first time they made love he was in the bathroom, at first light, and she got up to dress for her morning run but then pressed herself naked to the full-length mirror, face turned, hands raised to roughly head level. She pressed her body to the glass, eyes shut, and stayed for a long moment, nearly collapsed against the cool surface, abandoning herself to it. Then she put on her shorts and top and was lacing her shoes when he came out of the bathroom, clean-shaven, and saw the fogged marks of her face, hands, breasts and thighs stamped on the mirror. (106)

After having given herself away, Lianne feels the need to make a weird gesture of self-repossession. She embraces her mirror image, as if to make sure she can hold on to herself. Keith, in turn, is made privy only to the quickly disappearing traces of her act of narcissism. He may have enjoyed access to her body, but his corporeal attentions are unable to alleviate her loneliness or break the spell of her lingering egotism.

The only moment of true intimacy occurs when the spouses jointly watch a rerun of the events of September 11 on television (134–35). But though Lianne is obsessed by the events of 9/11, steeping herself in the newspaper reports and the daily obituary profiles of the victims, and though she wakes up at night full of hatred for the attackers and indulging in dreams of revenge, she has no firsthand knowledge of the trauma that Keith suffered and, for that reason, she cannot begin to understand what he went through. They talk little about what they feel deep down, and, when they do, they talk at cross purposes. They want "to sink into [their] little lives" (75), but world events have made such retrenchment into the comforts of the home impossible.

Keith's relation to Lianne is complicated by the fact that, shortly after their reunion, he starts an adulterous relationship with Florence, a black woman living on the other side of town and a fellow survivor of the terrorist attacks. Florence, who barely got out of the north tower herself, is in a position to provide the solidarity of the comrade-at-arms, which Lianne is unable to offer. Yet when Keith and Florence meet, "the sense of ill-matched people was not completely dispelled" (107). In an attempt to come to terms with the horror they experienced and witnessed, they talk extensively about what happened to them on the fatal day. In these exchanges, Keith is merely a sounding board for Florence. She wants to talk to "a person who might confirm the grim familiarity of the moment" (91), yet, in his presence, she basically talks only to herself. The company of Keith is a pretext for an act of auto-projection: "She was talking to the room, to herself, he thought, talking back in time to some version of herself. . . . She wanted her feelings to register, officially, and needed to say the actual words, if not necessarily to him" (91). Obviously, their growing intimacy comes from her need to hold forth about the day of the disaster and his willingness to listen: "This was their pitch of delirium, the dazed reality they'd shared in the stairwells, the deep shafts of spiraling men and women" (91). Even so, he grows tired of her; the mutual witnessing does not succeed in healing their wounded selves. Florence sees Keith as an actor (88). There is something stagey about his behavior, as if he were always playing at reality. Conversely, Keith calls his affair with Florence "unreal" (166). Neither of the interlocutors is fully present to him- or herself. Lacking a rock-bottom sense of identity, they cannot express themselves fully or authentically. Their feelings are articulated through clichés, borrowed mostly from the media or the movies. It is not that genuine declarations are proven to be false. It is genuineness itself that has become a staged condition. The characters are playing their own lives, as if they were actors on a movie set.

Throughout, the affair is characterized by a melodramatic quality and an eerie sense of déjà vu. When the relationship is sexually consummated, the seduction scene has an air of staleness to it and inevitability: a man and a woman find themselves in the same bedroom and one thing leads necessarily and dispassionately to another. The predominant feeling is not one of ardor but of lassitude. Similarly, when Keith arrives at her apartment, he is already anticipating the moment of leaving:

> Later she would say what someone always says.
> "Do you have to leave?"
> He would stand naked by the bed.
> "I'll always have to leave."
> "And I'll always have to make your leaving mean something else. Make it mean something romantic or sexy. But not empty, not lonely. Do I know how to do this?" ...
> She said, "Do I know how to make one thing out of another, without pretending? Can I stay who I am, or do I have to become all those other people who watch someone walk out the door? We're not other people, are we?"
> But she would look at him in a way that made him feel he must be someone else, standing there by the bed, ready to say what someone always says. (137–38)

The passage deserves to be quoted at length as a perfect illustration of the indirectness that characterizes human relationships in the novel.

Ostensibly, the leave-taking of lovers is a moment of intimacy. Yet even such a highly personal and private occasion is predetermined by collective experience. People's lives are prelived in the movies and so are shorn of a personal quality. Their experiences have the air of belatedness, of having been lived through before by others. Keith and Florence both have the sense that they have been expropriated, that their own lives have their centers somewhere outside themselves, somewhere distant and out of control.

This feeling of self-othering is supported by the diction of the passage. The many conditionals indicate that the sentences reflect not the exchange as it actually takes place but as Keith, knowing beforehand what predictably will happen, imagines that it will take place. The words express not what the lovers say but what, given the impossibility of authentic utterance, they are doomed to say by the ambient culture. Moreover, the meandering style—the one-sentence paragraphs in close succession, the uncertainty of reference in the personal pronouns, the bewildering use of conjunctions—is a function of indeterminacy, of marking time. The incoherence of the diction mirrors lives that are out of whack and relationships that have lost their focus.

The psychoanalyst Dori Laub has established that witnessing—in which the interlocutor becomes a coparticipant in the healing—is vital in the restoration of the mental health of trauma victims (Felman and Laub, *Testimony*, 57–68). By talking to someone who lends a willing ear, one is able to get control over one's memories and thus to avoid painful flashbacks or nightmarish intrusions. No such recuperation takes place in the novel. The family idyll falters because Lianne, in spite of her obsession with 9/11, remains alien to Keith's most fundamental, behavior-altering experience. Similarly, Florence and Keith, though fellow survivors, cannot truly communicate with each other. After the terrorist attacks, in which she lost many friends and coworkers, Florence sinks into a deep depression. When, by coincidence, Keith appears at her doorstep and they strike up a relationship, the relief initiated by their conversations is such that she confesses to him : "You saved my life" (108). Conversely, Keith, too, profits from talking to her. The knowledge they share—"what they knew together" (137)—more than erotic pleasure, is what keeps the liaison going. Yet, for reasons that are not so much specific as they are the expression of the general listlessness of the times, the incipient redemption plot fails to mature. By a significant choice of nontelling as communicative strategy, the text apprises the reader of the end of the affair only indirectly and in passing, in a few summary sentences that primarily deal with Keith walking his son home from school (157–58). Keith's final thoughts on the matter, his appraisal of how Florence will cope with the situation (and the *style indirect libre* in which these thoughts are rendered) are typical of the sort of noninvolvement that makes up the sum total of his reaction to the people around him: "This was the old undoing that was always near, now come inevitably into her life again, an injury no less painful for being fated" (158).

In the 9/11 fictions of Art Spiegelman, Frédéric Beigbeder and Jonathan Safran Foer, the effects of the day on children play an important role. Parental solicitude serves as the ultimate antidote against the blind destructiveness of terrorism. In caring for their children, parents affirm their humanity against the inhuman thrust of homicidal ideologues. In *Falling Man*, that conventional source of comfort is denied to the main characters. Keith and Lianne not only fail to rebuild their relationship and thus to provide a safe haven for their son Justin but also prove incapable of protecting him from the direct fallout of 9/11 and the more indirect damage caused by the strains in their marriage. Justin, who seems to be a strange kid to start with, vaguely suffers from symptoms of PTSD such as angst, dissociation, and withdrawal. He eats bread covered with mustard and nothing else (200). At inappropriate moments, he starts imitating a bloodhound (185). In "his mood of somber opposition" (166) there are times he refuses to speak in anything but monosyllables. These acts of unmotivated recalcitrance point to the disturbed relationship of the son with his parents. As nothing is normal in the Neudecker household—neither the disappearance of the father, who abandoned mother and son, nor his sudden and unannounced reappearance on the day of the disaster—Justin shows signs of inner distress and enduring suspicion.

The events of September 11, rather than drawing the family together, are the cause of further alienation. In developing an idiosyncratic way of coping with the terrorist attacks, Justin seeks peer-group support rather than adult guidance. He and his friends become secretive and slip out of parental control. They spend their days scanning the sky for planes. In a classic case of dissociation, they construct an alternative universe, in which the towers have not come down. Most of all, they are obsessed by a man they call Bill Lawton. The anglicizing of Bin Laden's name by the children proves the extent to which they, too, are gripped by the collective paranoia. Normally, the solecisms and malapropisms of small children are endearing and a source of mild humor. Here the mishearing is ominous, making Lianne fulminate against the "damn kids with their goddamn twisted powers of imagination" (72).

It is not that Keith and Lianne do not try to be good parents. As part of his education, Lianne takes Justin along to an antiwar rally (182). She engages him in conversation about what he learned in school (186), and she has an almost morbid concern for his physical safety (127). In addition, she implores Keith to resume the family routine (75). Surprisingly, in the aftermath of his traumatic experience on September 11, Keith is susceptible to her reasoning. As part of his newfound sense of responsibility, he takes up a new job, and, in order to change his unhealthy ways, he makes plans to join a fitness center (143). He also pays more attention to his son, trying to make conversation when he collects him from school (157). But the futility of these efforts proves the extent to which Keith is distraught and preoccupied. He is nearing forty and asks himself: "How is it possible that he was about to become someone of clear and distinct definition, husband and father, finally, occupying a room in three dimensions in the manner of his parents?" (157). That kind of maturity, it turns out, is not for Keith. To be clearly defined by one's daily routine and one's station in life is an ideal he cannot live up to. He is averse to Heideggerian *Sorge* (concern or responsibility) not out of a sense of freedom but because he is basically too morose to concentrate, too shackled to his backward-looking trauma, and too scattered to fulfill his familial or occupational duties.

In her book on the cultural impact of 9/11, *The Terror Dream*, Susan Faludi points out, citing many instances in the media, that there was a "post-9/11 fixation on male protectors at work and mommies at home" (139). Searching television programs, magazines, and newspapers, she found that in the wake of the terrorist attacks, there was a concerted effort to restore the family idyll and to reaffirm "the illusion of a mythic America where women needed men's protection and men succeeded in providing it" (118). That neither Keith nor Lianne manage to form a conventional family or react to the cataclysm with suitable and socially approved nesting instincts proves once again that, in stressing the paralyzing effects of September 11, *Falling Man* is a novel contrary to the national trend and subversive of nationalistic imperatives.

Dystopia

In *Falling Man*, trauma is not healed; it spreads like a contagious disease. No aspect of life remains untouched by melancholia. The material world itself is contaminated and characterized by general dispiritment. No transcendence is to be found anywhere, not even in art. As a retired professor of art history, Lianne's mother, Nina, regularly goes to the Met to look at three or four pictures: "She looked at what was unfailing . . . in its grip on the eye and the mind, on memory and identity" (11). For Nina, art is redemptive and provides anchorage in a flawed world. For the same reason, Lianne likes her mother's living room. She perceives it as "a space that was serenely self-possessed" (12). The paintings in it give it a "timeless quality" (9). In particular, Lianne admires two Giorgio Morandi still lifes, which "held a mystery she could not name, . . . some reconnoiter inward, human and obscure" (12). Lianne experiences art as something oracular, as a perfection beyond words, containing "latent meanings," that "turn and bend in the wind, free from authoritative comment" (12). Soon, however, the events of September 11 demonstrate how also art is infected. It cannot stay out of the reach of either public (49) or private catastrophe (209). Morandi's arrangement of simple household objects—"groupings of bottles, jugs, biscuit tins" (12)—loses its air of composure and innocence. Two "dark objects, too obscure to name," (49) inevitably evoke the silhouettes of the fallen towers. In the 9/11 aftermath, art can no longer work its transformative magic. When Lianne later goes to a Morandi exhibition, she ruefully remarks that there is "nothing detached in this work, nothing free of personal resonance" (210–11). Art can no longer provide a realm of the imagination, outside of space and time and free from the urgencies of the moment.

The topography of New York, which, as a hyperdynamized environment, is often deemed to have a redemptive propulsion all of its own, is equally shorn of all restorative power. September 11 has turned the streets, usually bustling with life, into a militarized, dystopian landscape. When Keith goes back to his old place near Ground Zero to pick up a few of his belongings, he has to wangle his way through several checkpoints. Moving through New York has been stripped of all fun and excitement. Instead, in a downtown that is desolate and deserted, the individual must assert himself against an anonymous bureaucracy and the far-reaching tentacles of the state apparatus. After having arrived at his apartment, by working "his way through the frozen zone, south and west, passing through smaller checkpoints and detouring around others" (24), Keith is moved to state: "'I'm standing here,' and then, louder, 'I'm standing here'" (27). This affirmation of his precarious *Dasein* is inspired by surprise: the surprise that, against the odds, the individual can hold his own against the forces of massification, at least for a moment.

The profound change that has come over the city is neatly summarized by Lianne, who, half remembering a classic Japanese haiku, ponders: "*Even in New York—I long for New York*" (34). The essence of New York, as it used to be, has vanished. "State troopers in tight clusters or guardsmen with dogs" (32), watching over Grand Central Station, violate the liberal propensity of the place. Moreover, the Falling Man, whose performance Lianne witnesses shortly after reaching Grand Central, embodies the repetition compulsion of the whole city. He brings back to vivid and painful memory the haunting images that will not go away. Later in the story, Keith and Justin decide to meet Lianne in the city. The setup of the passage is cinematographic, with lots of crosscutting between Lianne, walking south after a writing session with her Alzheimer patients in East Harlem, and Keith and Justin walking north from the latter's school. Given the many opportunities the city grid offers to choose alternative itineraries, the odds of actually running into each other are rather slim. Nonetheless, the family members, usually so dispersed and mutually alienated, manage to meet up. This surprising coming together might be rife with redemptive symbolism if the occasion were not thoroughly spoiled and turned, once again, into an emblem of melancholy. When Keith and Justin reach Lianne, she has just witnessed another appearance of the Falling Man and she finds herself in total shock. Claimed, as it were, by the spirit of the times and perturbed by the re-enactment of an unmasterable tragedy, she is unable to regain a sense of belonging.

The melancholy that pervades *Falling Man* is a consequence of September 11. But 9/11, as a cataclysmic event, is equally the indicator of a more general imbalance that reaches deep into the roots of the culture and manifests itself as a personal pathology in the lives of the characters. Keith's visits to the hospital, to have his wounds and lacerations treated, are a case in point. The first thing he is required to do upon arrival, in a routine that immediately impresses upon him his station as a mere cog in a bureaucratic machinery, is to fill out and sign a series of forms. After this first administrative hurdle is taken,

> [d]octors in scrubs and paper masks checked his airway and took blood-pressure readings. They were interested in potentially fatal reactions to injury, hemorrhage, dehydration. They looked for diminished blood flow to tissues. They studied the contusions on his body and peered into his eyes and ears. Someone gave him an EKG. Through the open door he saw IV racks go floating past. They tested his hand grip and took X rays. They told him things he could not absorb about a ligament or cartilage, a tear or a sprain. (15)

The remarkable thing about this paragraph is that the description of the efficiency in a twenty-first century state-of-the-art hospital implicitly contains its own condemnation. Modernity is tantamount to anonymity and alienation. The administrations of the medical staff may be competent and effective, but they are also impersonal and partial (concerned with only the corporeal aspect of the person). The examination of the body involves its segmentation, as the diagnostic process—carried out according to protocol—is characterized by piecemeal probings and a nonholistic approach. Keith's experience in the hospital, while yielding results, is an encounter of the vulnerable "I" with an anonymous and overpowering "they." By an arithmetic that illustrates the paradox of modernity, the more help that is provided by the hospital staff and their powerful machines, the more Keith is made aware of his essential helplessness. This is equally the case when he has to undergo a brain scan, which is extremely unpleasant and can only be endured because Keith entertains himself with reminiscences about a drunk woman he once had sex with. The hospital episodes illustrate that there is no medical (i.e., technological) solution for what is essentially a spiritual crisis. Keith's wounds can be treated and healed. Similarly, Lianne keeps insisting she is in good health (in contrast to her mother, who suffers from strokes). But at a deeper level, both Keith and Lianne are ailing.

Their true condition is revealed in the small details of their daily lives. In Lianne's case, her professional activities as an editor are a source of irritation more than satisfaction. Within the general disorientation that characterizes her days, the meticulous screening of a text for imperfections gives a semblance of structure to her life: "There was serious work to do on the book she was editing, for a university press, on ancient alphabets, deadline approaching. There was definitely that" (22). The painstaking combing through the text provides a goal to reach and a routine to cling on to. Yet the book she is editing, written in English by a Bulgarian and dealing with ancient alphabets, indicates that globalization—cultural transmission across different cultures—comes with its own sort of frustrations: "The joke, at her expense, is that the work in question was typed on an old manual machine with textual emendations made by the author in a deeply soulful and unreadable script" (23).

Thus finding no anchorage either in her professional or domestic life, Lianne is prone to fits and irrational behavior. Even something as simple and routine as taking a number in a store and waiting for one's turn becomes expressive of the ennui of modernity and what one could call culture fatigue (38). Similarly, when her friends call up and, guessing that after his ordeal Keith requires special attention, they thoughtfully inquire "Is this a bad time?" she experiences this act of considerateness as an imposition and an irritant (20). She is most annoyed by a neighbor who insists on playing Middle Eastern music. At one point, Lianne takes out all her pent-up rage on the poor woman. Her patriotic feelings and her hatred of the Muslim terrorists take the form of a symbolic revenge when, unceremoniously, she thrusts her hand in the woman's face (120). This eruption of violence is mirrored when Keith, demonstrating that he, too, is going around with a short fuse, randomly punches a man in the face (132). These outbreaks of bad temper, giving the lie to metropolitan tolerance, prove that both Lianne and Keith are mentally distressed to the breaking point and struggling with unassimilated feelings of anger and frustration.

In her search for anchorage, Lianne holds on to the little chunks of everyday reality that remain recognizable: "And there was this, the taxis in broad ranks. . . . There was that, and Keith in the shower this morning, standing numbly in the flow, a dim figure far away inside the plexiglass" (22–23). Summing up, by way of anaphora, the little sensory bits her life consists of, Lianne testifies how, lacking a larger interpretative framework, she has to hold on to scattered observations. The ambient personal and public world is characterized by juxtaposition without convergence, a jumble of disparate impressions that fail to cohere.

Alzheimer

In different circumstances and in a less gloomily inflected narrative, the enumeration of the metropolitan epiphenomena—there is this, there is that—could give rise to a Rimbaudian high (derangement of all the senses) or, more specific to the place, to a Whitmanesque "barbaric yawp." Instead, "the taxis in broad ranks, three or four deep, speeding towards . . . [Lianne] from the traffic light one block down the avenue as she paused in midcrossing to work out her fate" (22) are expressive of a ubiquitous threat, indices of a life in disarray and therefore in danger. The historical trauma caused by the terrorist attacks reveals a structural trauma that has to do with the conditions of modernity as well as with the human condition in general.

For that reason, effecting the switch from melancholia to mourning is almost an impossibility in the narrative. The characters' efforts at working through remain either ineffective or riddled with traces of indelible acedia. Lianne's commitment to her Alzheimer patients is a case in point. She regularly conducts "a gathering of five or six or seven men and women in the early stages of Alzheimer's disease" (29). These writing sessions, in which the patients jot down bits of their autobiographies or dwell on everyday occurrences, are a way of resisting the inevitable decline into dementia and incoherence. In spite of their fading awareness, the patients try to hold on to the world through writing and language: "They worked into themselves, finding narratives that rolled and tumbled, and how natural it seemed to do this, tell stories about themselves" (30). The delving into the past, while the mind flickers and slowly disintegrates, provides "a chance to encounter the crossing points of insight and memory" (30). The writing is "a gathering against the last bare state" (156), a kind of holding action against the inevitable slip into oblivion.

The Alzheimer patients "approached what was impending, each of them, with a little space remaining, at this point, to stand and watch it happen" (94). Theirs is the endgame, the ultimate time before, a period of growing dimness before the curtain comes down. As such, they epitomize the tenor of the novel. Synecdochically, they stand for the entropic drift of society, where things tend to come apart. The presence of Alzheimer's disease is so insistent in the novel that, next to the image of the falling man, it provides a secondary icon of unavoidable downward motion. In the last analysis, the writing sessions with Lianne do not provide a stay against confusion. To the extent the writing sharpens the awareness of the patients, it sharpens their awareness of the gathering gloom. The true horror of Alzheimer's as a condition is not only that the mind slides "away from the adhesive friction that makes an individual possible" (30) but that interstitially the mind is in a position to observe its own unraveling.

September 11 is again the catalyst that brings out this state of nonrecuperable loss. Like the children (Justin and his friends), the Alzheimer patients have been affected by the cataclysmic news. When they start writing about it, the group, as *communitas*, falls apart. Everybody is obsessed by his or her own line of thought. The events, filtered through their faltering minds, turn into a quick succession of increasingly unidentifiable one-sentence snippets of noncommunication (60–64). As a result, we never get to know the patients. The deindividualization they will undergo when their memory vanishes and they no longer exist as coherent human beings is anticipated in the way they are written about. Lightly sketched, known only by first name and initial, they remain shadowy presences, partly rubbed out already, getting more and more vague as time goes by.

It is this flimsiness of existence that inspires Lianne to compare the patients to figures on old passport photographs. These old photographs are part of a work of art that is displayed in her mother's living room. The faces in them are "looking out of a sepia distance, lost in time" (141). The pictures demonstrate the transitoriness of everything. The faces stare out of the past, signifying lives that have been forgotten totally. The papers that once attested to the holders' individuality and that allowed them free travel and movement (away from old tyrannies and toward the land of the brave and the free) are now null and void. In Lianne's mind, the fate of these dead strangers gets connected somehow to the fading lives of her Alzheimer patients. What they share is that they are locked into history. They speak to Lianne's obsession with demise, slipping into the abyss, the disappearance of direction and cohesion.

Rather than being an escape from the self, the meetings with the Alzheimer patients take an inward turn for Lianne. They are something to keep her busy, a way of coping with her divorce and, especially, a way of coming to terms with the untimely death of her father, who killed himself with a rifle rather than submitting "to the long course of senile dementia" (40). At one point she realizes that it "was possible that the group meant more to her that it did to the members" (61). She is in danger of appropriating the sessions, becoming emotionally dependent on the group and using it for her own ends. This proves that even the compassionate gesture can be selfish. Above all, it proves that Lianne finds herself in a closed universe from which there is no exit. Every session—far from freeing her from her present preoccupations—is a return to that moment her father "fired the shot that killed him," to "the day that has marked her awareness of who she is and how she lives" (218). If, as LaCapra puts it, melancholy "is a state in which one remains possessed by the phantasmatically invested past and compulsively, narcissistically identified with a lost object of love" (*History*, 183), then Lianne is fully immured in the melancholic fixation on her dead parent. Her effort to shed him as a memory (by committing herself to her Alzheimer patients) is marked by the very impossibility of escaping her doomed filial connection. Running away from her father ends up being a return of the repressed. His death "by his own hand" (218) is her foundational moment, the one act from which her life takes its flavor and destiny.

From him, too, she inherits an obsession with religion. Her father was a nonobservant but believing Catholic who was convinced that "human existence had to have a deeper source than our own dank fluids" (231). She identifies her father as "a sad man" (232) and his religious fervor as the result of "the kind of sadness that yearns for something intangible and vast, the one solace that might dissolve his paltry misfortune" (232). In an effort to distance herself from her father and to establish "clarity of thought and purpose" (65), Lianne in later life resists the pull of these religious stirrings. She "wanted to disbelieve.... She wanted ... to snuff out the pulse of the shaky faith she'd held for much of her life" (64–65). Nonetheless, in her college years, she eagerly read Kierkegaard, who "made her feel that her thrust into the world was not the slender melodrama she sometimes thought it was" (118). Kierkegaard propounds the leap of faith as the central fact of life, that gives meaning to an otherwise absurd universe. Thus from her own reading and from her father's example Lianne learns that the presence of God, infusing "time and space with pure being" (232), fulfills the longing for an exhaustive explanation, provides wholesale coherence and, therefore, puts an end to melancholy.

In the aftermath of 9/11 the God question asserts itself more urgently than ever before. Her patients feverishly argue the point, asking themselves: "Did God do this or not?"(63). Seeking enlightenment, Lianne ends up attending the Catholic church of which one of her patients is a member. Or more precisely, she goes to a church, which she thinks (on very slender evidence) to be her patient's church. The fact that that patient has entered the irreversible stage of the disease in which she loses her bearings is of a piece with Lianne's lingering religious doubts. The expressions of her faith take the form of a series of self-enclosed paradoxes: "She was stuck with her doubts but liked sitting in church" (233); "She thought that the hovering possible presence of God was the thing that created loneliness and doubt in the soul and she also thought that God was the thing, the entity existing outside space and time that resolved this doubt in the tonal power of a word, a voice" (236). The looplike dilemma in which she is caught finally boils down to this: "God is the voice that says, 'I am not here'" (236). Her sense of the deity is that of the *Deus absconditus*, who manifests himself mainly as absence and lack.[4]

Playing Poker

For reasons that have to do with the overall imprint of melancholy on the novel and for linguistic reasons that I will discuss below, the narrative leaves little room for a resolution. Lianne's religious experience, marked by the persistence of doubt and the tantalizing nearness (i.e., nonpresence) of the sublime, is more an expression of melancholia than an escape from it. Similarly, her engagement with the Alzheimer patients comes to an end when one after the other they lose their ability to write. Nonetheless, at the very end of the novel, Lianne achieves a fleeting moment of self-reappropriation, a moment at which she is at ease with the mystery of herself: "She was ready to be alone, in reliable calm, she and the kid, the way they were before the planes appeared that day, silver crossing blue" (236). This return to her responsibility as a mother represents a working-through of sorts, a temporary accommodation with the vicissitudes of the times, a recovery from shock and trauma.

That Keith is unable to share this restoration of the family idyll demonstrates the extent to which the novel is dedicated to the portrayal of enduring loneliness and unresolved melancholy. Keith abandons New York, where neither wife, child, nor mistress can keep him. He runs away from the memory of that awful day in September, away from "the chaos, the levitation of ceilings and floors, the voices choking in smoke" (40). He runs away almost as far as the continent will allow, and, in memory of the poker group to which he belonged before 9/11 and partly as a kind of tribute to his poker buddy Rumsey, who died in the terrorist attacks, he ends up as a semiprofessional poker player in Las Vegas. Keith spends his time there in a half-world of stunted human contacts, seeking numbness and oblivion. The gambling ritual provides him with "standard methods and routines" (197)—just what he needs to lose himself: "He was fitting into something that was made to his shape.... These were the times when there was nothing outside, no flash of history or memory that he might unknowingly summon in the routine run of cards" (225). So deeply is he attached to his traumatic memory, that self-loss seems to be the only feasible strategy for self-rescue.

As depicted in the novel, the casinos in Las Vegas are among the most disconsolate places in the United States, especially at eight A.M., when the tournaments are over and only the most addicted players still linger in a halo of stale smoke: "The whole place stank of abandonment" (189). The casinos are a world in suspension. For Keith they provide the opportunity to mark time: "Days fade, nights drag on, check-and-raise, wake-and-sleep" (226). The gambling is a soothing ritual, a powerful symbol of a state of numbness, of withdrawal, nausea, and constriction: "There was nothing outside the game but faded space" (189). Living inside a bubble and outside of time, Keith dissolves into his environment. The anonymity of Las Vegas—"the mingling of countless lives that had no stories attached" (204)—fits his mood. He only knows the other players as "the man in the surgical mask" or "the blinking woman" or "the dwarf" (205). Every meeting he has (even with a member of his former poker group) is the occasion for further estrangement and isolation. He becomes so desensitized that he begins to wonder "if he was becoming a self-operating mechanism, like a humanoid robot"(226). The starving of his emotions and the numbing of his rational faculties have only one cause and one ulterior motive: "The point was one of invalidation" (230). He wants to forget. Although for the longest time we have no clue as to what it is that is ailing Keith, and though the novel springs this secret on us only at the end, it is obvious that the empty poker ritual constitutes a desperate attempt to find a source of comfort and assuagement. His state of suspended existence is summarized in one sentence: "He was becoming the air he breathed" (230).

The Evaporation of Meaning

Much of the eeriness that is the hallmark of *Falling Man* follows not only from the incidents of the plot but also and equally from the steady application of an unsparingly fragmented style, the point of which is to suggest corrosive despair and its attendant disarray. The novel, James Wood writes, "seems to drift in a stunned, meaningless void" ("Black Noise," 48). According to Frank Rich, "Disconnectedness is the new currency. Language is fragmented. Vision is distorted" ("The Clear Blue Sky"). For Adam Mars-Jones, the novel is characterized by "alternating crispness and indeterminacy" ("As His World"), while Laura Frost speaks of the novel's "dispersed style" ("Precarious Balance"). All commentators agree that what Stephen Abell calls the "self-conscious manipulation of prose" ("Moments of Truth," 21) is in large measure responsible for the effect of mental distance. The characters are not able to fully focus on their lives; they exist in a state of suspension. That state is not simply a function of the plot (the result of numbing and constriction) and it is not just stated as a theme. The very texture of the prose itself reflects the raggedness of experience, while the splintered composition of the novel is the most telling proof of the indelibility of trauma and its shattering impact.

The attenuation of coherent novelistic form is such that it prompts James Wood to state: "Don DeLillo's new book is not a 9/11 novel but a 9/11 short story, or perhaps a 9/11 poem. It is not a synthesis or an argument or even, really, a sustained narrative, but an arrangement of symbolically productive elements" ("Black Noise," 47). It is certainly the case that the novel is riddled with interruptions and that, as a result, the reader ends up feeling, in the words of James Wood again, "that a lot of white space on the page is glaring at him beseechingly" (47). First of all, the chapters are not arranged in a strictly chronological order. The plot progresses by leaps and bounds, but, at unexpected moments, it also regresses so that the reading experience itself mimics the violent lurching back and forth between the (imperfectly engaged) present and (the vividly relived) past, which is typical of traumatic memory. In addition, no narrative momentum is allowed to develop, as the novel is chopped up into many small, discrete, and mostly tenuously related parts. Also contributing to the fractured nature of the narrative is the fact that the focalizers change incessantly, with Keith and Lianne usually taking turns but not always. Unexpected metaphors and the use of indirect discourse further wrong-foot the reader, while in dialogues one quickly loses sight of who is saying what. Most chapters have a number, but three of them (which also stand apart thematically) have a title. One conversation ends on page 49 and is taken up again in medias res and without any form of introduction or transition on page 111, more than sixty pages later.

The novel comprises three parts, entitled: "Bill Lawton," "Ernst Hechinger," and "David Janiak." While this neat ternary division seems to suggest an overall patterning or intent, each of the names used in the headings is enigmatic or problematical. Bill Lawton is the children's distortion of Bin Laden's name; Ernst Hechinger is the real name of Nina Barton's lover, who, not wanting to be reminded of his terrorist past, goes now by the name of Martin Ridnour; and David Janiak is the real name of the Falling Man. This play with names and pseudonyms is indicative of a slippery sense of identity, the pitfalls of language, and the misleading nature of appearances. As eponyms the names are equally treacherous (red herrings, really). The three persons are tangential to the plot, and their marginal importance in no way justifies the prominence of their names on separate pages introducing the three parts of the book. Their role as headings is more deceptive than deictic. The very inappropriateness of the choice highlights a world that is out of kilter, where names, in one way or another connected with terrorism or its effects, have an all-absorbing resonance and therefore function not so much as guiding posts than as what James Wood calls "symbolically productive elements"—items that create a sense of unease rather than anchor the narrative.

The disjointedness of experience speaks not only from the structural elements of the plot but equally from the smallest textual details. The accumulation of slight shifts in linguistic patterning adds up to a general upset of expectations and thus accounts for the "dispersed style" (Laura Frost's term) of the novel. This is a typical paragraph from the beginning of the book, when Keith is walking away from Ground Zero right after the attacks: "He heard the sound of the second fall, or felt it in the trembling air, the north tower coming down, a soft awe of voices in the distance. That was him coming down, the north tower" (5). This passage obviously owes a lot to the stream-of-consciousness technique. External observation seamlessly flows into internal impressions. At the same time, description gives way to suggestion and groundless metaphor. "[A] soft awe of voices in the distance" is an enigmatic phrase, totally unexpected in the context of hundreds of tons of steel crashing down and unspecific in what it points to. (What is a "soft awe of voices" exactly?) The expression also has a vaguely aestheticizing effect, at odds with the rawness of the experience it describes. Equally askew is the last sentence. What seems grammatically incorrect—the use of the pronoun "him" to ostensibly denote a tower—points to a reordering of reality, a shift in reference. At the end of the tale, 230 pages later, it will become clear that what seems an unimportant grammatical slip is the indicant of a repetition compulsion, an obsessive fixation, and, since the referent of the personal pronoun remains cryptic, it also indicates the repression of the traumatic memory, the refusal to remember. In the flow of the narrative and this early in the tale, this seemingly misplaced pronoun is but a small bump, easily overlooked. Yet an accumulation of such minor divergences points to the forging of an idiosyncratic language, slightly out of sync with common parlance, the result of the personal upset that changes everything, including one's means of expression. Ordinary language collapses together with the tower.

Often it is unrelieved parataxis that conveys the sense of a world no longer hanging together. The lack of experiential integration finds its grammatical equivalent in the juxtaposition of phrases that, instead of cohering, seem to repel one another. The "white space" glaring at the reader, which James Wood mentions as a conspicuous feature of the novel, is a result of the little gaps that separate sentences, not connected by any conjunctions or not entering into any larger syntactical arrangements. This long paragraph, toward the end of the novel, describes Keith's interest in the poker games:

> The money mattered but not so much. The game mattered, the touch of felt beneath the hands, the way the dealer burnt one card, dealt the next. He wasn't playing for the money. He was playing for the chips. The value of each chip had only hazy meaning. It was the disk itself that mattered, the color itself. There was the laughing man at the far end of the room. There was the fact that they would all be dead one day. He wanted to take in chips and stack them. The game mattered, the stacking of chips, the eye count, the play and dance of hand and eye. He was identical with these things.

> (228)

The bleakness of the paratactic style mirrors the bleakness of experience as Keith's identification with the game is reflected in a paragraph that, apart from one conjunction and two simple relative clauses, features nothing but asyndetic coordination. The frequent repetitions (often in the form of anaphoras, which makes the novel more resemble a poem) underscore Keith's zombielike absorption in the game, while the blatant non sequitur in the middle of the paragraph betrays what is really going on: the hypnotic obsession with the poker paraphernalia is a desperate ploy to escape the traumatic awareness of death. In suppressing his 9/11 experience, Keith demonstrates the inadequacy of the suppression. Stunting his life and steeping himself in a meaningless routine, he has not been able to move beyond 9/11 and recover his balance. He lives his life haltingly, in little fits and starts, which are mirrored in the broken-up syntax, the concatenation of loosely assembled impressions and tattered phrases.

Keith's self-willed stupefaction is given further shape three paragraphs later (after one of the intervening paragraphs has taken us away from the casino scene in yet another momentum-destroying deviation or non sequitur). On this occasion, syntax has shrunk into mere verbless enumeration. The minimal connective tissue that is provided by the asyndetons in the passage quoted above has disappeared. We are submerged into world of total stasis and pure sensation: "Forty tables, nine players a table, others waiting at the rail, screens high on three walls showing soccer and baseball, strictly atmospheric" (229). Reduced to random observations, Keith's life is grammatically shorn of resilience and determination. His mind, adrift in mere atmospherics, undergoes reality passively. The syntax, which in its tight packing of nouns without conjugated verbs takes away agency and direction, is further compressed in the next paragraph, which consists of exactly three words: "SHEER and BULK" (229). The words echo a small incident that has happened before, but in the present context they have lost all relevance. The nonsense phrase stands for the evaporation of all meaning. "Sheer and bulk" is mere antithesis without reference. Like "tick-tock," it indicates the passing of time, the completely contentless seesaw that dominates the vacant mind.

Geopolitical Stalemate

Alluding to DeLillo's great works *Libra* and *Underworld*, Adam Kirsch writes in his review of *Falling Man* that the Kennedy assassination and the atomic bomb seem "to demand proliferating narratives, conspiratorial in their restless sweep." He adds that "perhaps the most striking thing about 'Falling Man' is the way September 11, a far more intimate and frightening eruption of history, drives Mr. DeLillo to the opposite extreme" ("DeLillo Confronts"). In many ways, *Falling Man*, as a narrative of retreat (Joseph Dewey's term [Dewey, *Beyond Grief*, 17]), is not the kind of 9/11 novel that DeLillo watchers had anticipated or expected. Jesse Kavadlo, for instance, sees in the figure of Abu Rashid in *Mao II* a foreshadowing of Osama bin Laden (*Delillo*, 76), and at the beginning of his study he writes: "We live in DeLillo-esque times. In the aftermath of September 11th, 2001, America is experiencing a dizzying convergence of Don DeLillo's most frightening themes" (1). Along a parallel line of thought, Harold Bloom mentions that "*Mao II* is the way we live now, in the Age of George W. Bush, John Ashcroft, and Osama bin Laden" (Bloom, *DeLillo*, 11). Given DeLillo's penchant for grand, history-driven narratives and his interest in conspiracy as a feature of world politics, one could have expected a 9/11 novel on the scale of *Mao II*, *Underworld*, or *Libra*. *Falling Man*, however, is at the opposite end of the spectrum from such epic novels. In the words that Peter Boxall uses to describe muted and foreshortened DeLillo narratives such as *Body Artist* or *Cosmopolis*, *Falling Man* takes place "in a kind of evacuated time which has lost its narrative quality" (Boxall, *DeLillo*, 216). That a historic event of such enormous sweep and influence as the terrorist attacks is treated on the scale of a domestic drama is indeed, as Kirsch puts it, a "most striking thing."

Nonetheless, *Falling Man* contains the 9/11 epic that some had predicted, albeit in a very much reduced form. Among the many estranging features of the novel is the fact that the narrative is not limited to Keith and Lianne and their immediate next of kin. Interspersed with the interrupted family idyll and the account of the main characters' bouts of melancholia is the story of Hammad, a fictional character who figures as one of the "muscle men," assisting Mohamed Atta in hijacking American Airlines 11. Several reviewers find this interposition about the terrorist's doings jarring (Frost, Kirsch, Mars-Jones, Wood). But that may well be the point. By opposing the enervation of his American characters to the evil intent of the Islamic terrorists, DeLillo indicates that September 11 can only be understood geopolitically as the clash of two opposing frames of reference, two world visions on a collision course.

Hammad himself (unconsciously echoing Jean Baudrillard [*Spirit of Terrorism*, 16]) summarizes the defining difference between East and West: "We are willing to die, they are not. This is our strength, to love death, to feel the claim of armed martyrdom" (176).[5] In his role as henchman to the leader of the hijackers, Hammad becomes a function of the conspiratorial scheme: "Plot closed the world to the slenderest line of sight, where everything converges to a point" (174); "the plot shapes every breath he takes" (176). He feels claimed by fate (174). The sense of mission, the sense of being God-directed, gives him purpose and bestows manhood. From that perspective, his "life had structure. Things were clearly defined" (83).

This directionality stands in sharp contrast to the drift that characterizes Lianne's and Keith's lives. But it is equally, if not more, death-oriented. The price Hammad pays for his strict, ideological perspective is a willed dehumanization. The plot forces him to resist ordinary human aspirations (food, sex, tenderness): "He had to fight against the need to be normal" (83). Individual desire, too, has to give way to group solidarity: "They were strong-willed, determined to become one mind. Shed everything but the men you are with. Become each other's running blood" (83). Above all, the terrorist must learn to ignore the humanity of the other. As Atta tells him in a particularly chilling paragraph: "There are no others. The others exist only to the degree that they fill the role we have designed for them. This is their function as others. Those who will die have no claim to their lives outside the useful fact of their dying" (176). In order to serve their cause, the terrorists feel entitled to instrumentalize human life. They have no respect for the integrity of their own bodies and even less for that of their innocent victims.

The sharp division between East and West also manifests itself as a difference in the experience of time. Lianne and Keith are anchored in the past. Their foundational moments (the suicide of Lianne's father, the terrorist attacks for Keith) are behind them, and by the mechanism of traumatic memory they are either inexorably drawn back to that moment or they try to suppress its vitiating proximity. In contrast, Hammad lives in the fullness of time: "He flew through the minutes and felt the draw of some huge future landscape opening up, all mountain and sky" (82). He lives in the awareness that the "time is coming" (82). He is driven by a forward-projecting teleology. His acts are inspired by the certain knowledge that his martyrdom will gain him paradise and eternal bliss.

At a crucial late juncture in the novel the two chronologies (Keith's backward-looking and Hammad's forward-looking ones) meet in mid-paragraph. The end of the hijacker's forward propulsion (the reaching for the future that is part of his strict ideology) curves into the beginning of Keith's backward drift, the draw of the past that keeps haunting him and that he cannot get rid of. The moment Hammad's plane hits the north tower is the moment the narrative suddenly switches from the terrorist's perspective to that of his victim (239). This moment of cataclysmic contact is the mysterious meeting of two opposites ways of life. Globalization is one of DeLillo's signature themes (Annesley, *Fictions*, 60–76), and here the interdependence of human fates takes on an especially disheartening, mutually destructive form.

In including the synoptic story of Hammad's actions, DeLillo has extended his narrative to include both the cause and effect of the terrorist attacks. The paradox is that the cause, necessarily predating the attacks, involves a future-oriented inclination, whereas the effect, postdating the attacks, consists mainly of an unbreakable cathexis to the past. Cleverly, the structure of the novel embodies this paradox. The last scene of the novel is a graphic description of Keith's foundational moment. It reveals in full detail the trauma that has been lurking underneath the surface all along. As a scene of revelation, it goes back to the origin and thus provides closure, but of the claustrophobic kind. The novel turns back upon itself, mimicking the mental development of the main character, who remains enclosed in endless reenactments of this originary scene. The end is the beginning in the vicious circle of melancholia.

Unrelieved Gloom (and Its Discontents)

In thus relentlessly focusing on September 11 as an aporetic event that leads to the destruction of both perpetrators and victims alike, DeLillo has given shape to a kind of U.S. melancholia. The title of the book summarizes this inflection. "Fall" as a metaphor recurs throughout the novel, gathering a variety of meanings. It is applied not only to the desperate efforts of the 9/11 victims to escape the raging fire by jumping, to ash falling from the sky (3, 103), or to the backbreaking plunges of the performance artist. It equally serves to indicate the failing memory of an Alzheimer patient (94) or the fizzling out of Keith and Lianne's marriage (104).

The gamble DeLillo took with this book is that he tries stylistically and narratively to suggest the enervating effect of this multiple fall. In order to evoke the sense of attrition and lassitude that characterizes clinical melancholia, he has gutted his style sentence by sentence, has continuously broken the narrative momentum, has tethered his characters either to their murderous, humanity-denying beliefs or, more prominently, to their future-denying traumas. Such a submersion in unrelieved gloom may well run counter not only to basic narrative schemata, which ask for a resolution and even a happy ending, but, more importantly, also to the basic human need to work through grief, to counter melancholia with mourning.[6] As Tom Junod puts it in his review: the novel is "a portrait of grief, to be sure, but it puts grief in the air, as a cultural atmospheric, without giving us anything to mourn" (Junod, " The Man"). Among 9/11 novels, *Falling Man* stands out because it staunchly refuses to be a narrative of redemption. In taking us far outside the comfort zone, it pictures September 11 as an enduring condition for which there is no remedy.

Ultimately, the novel is marked by the confusion between what Dominick LaCapra has termed historical and structural trauma (*Writing History*, 76–85). Structural trauma is a feature of every life. As a general condition, it takes a great variety of forms: separation from the mother, the transition from the presymbolic to the symbolic, the entry into language, and so on (*Writing History*, 77). In contrast, historical trauma "is specific, and not everyone is subject to it or entitled to the subject position associated with it" (*Writing History*, 78). While the first and last scenes of *Falling Man* are attempts to render imaginatively what happened on September 11 and thus anchor the experience of melancholia in a definitive historical context, the general purport of the novel seems to consist of an expansion of the mood of that specific event to include the whole human condition. The danger involved in such a conflation of historical and structural trauma is not only the arrogation of surrogate victim status. (Not everybody has been truly affected by 9/11 as a victim.) The insistent characterization of melancholy without letup and the absence in the novel's possible world of any valid alternative to melancholy also brings to mind LaCapra's caveat that "the preemptive foreclosure of any and every modality of closure is as doctrinaire and open to question as the quest for definitive, totalizing closure" (*Writing History*, 194). Nonclosure can be as formulaic as closure. Moreover, while in *Falling Man* the melancholy universe has no exit, LaCapra has pointed out that the subsumption of historical trauma as a generalized condition often leads to utopian or totalizing schemes of redemption. "It is important," LaCapra writes, "not to hypostatize particular historical losses or lacks and present them as mere instantiations of some inevitable absence or constitutive feature of existence" (*Writing History*, 65). The danger lurking in DeLillo's portrait of transcendent grieving, which allows for no proper mourning or working through, is that it can serve as a prelude to, or be used as an excuse for, wholesale, reactionary and even totalitarian movements of redress and moral restoration.

2

ART SPIEGELMAN'S *IN THE SHADOW OF NO TOWERS*

THE POLITICS OF TRAUMA

IN HIS DECEMBER 2001 ESSAY in *Harper's Magazine* Don DeLillo, in indicating that September 11 left "something empty in the sky" ("In the Ruins," 39), also points out the need for a "counter-narrative" (34). His own novel *Falling Man* provides such a counternarrative in the form of an exitless recounting of the events, the enactment of an unabating repetition compulsion, and the emplotment of intransitive melancholia. In making each detail of the tale expressive of ennui, DeLillo has met a self-imposed challenge: how to prevent articulation from becoming redemptive, how to express an obsession that disables without the expression itself putting an end to the obsession. In his comics series or graphic novel *In the Shadow of No Towers*, Art Spiegelman has opted for a different kind of 9/11 counternarrative. His graphic novel consists of a narrative sequence that does not preclude agency and, in the presence of an all-absorbing fixation, does not succumb to unrelieved pessimism. In other words, *In the Shadow of No Towers* balances collapse and resurgence. It describes 9/11 as a limit event, that is to say, an event that is so traumatic that it shatters the symbolic resources of the individual and escapes the normal processes of meaning making and cognition. At the same time, it reintroduces trauma into a network of signification, without, however, normalizing or naturalizing the event.

Crucial to an understanding of this uneasy accommodation is the fact that Spiegelman is the son of two Holocaust survivors and that in an earlier, Pulitzer Prize–winning graphic novel, *Maus*, he has succeeded in rendering the horrors of the concentration camps through the use of the comics medium, usually associated with "the very unserious, unsacred world of Loonytoons" (Gordon, "Surviving," 84). As David Hajdu wrote in the *New York Times Book Review* : "Spiegelman clearly sees Sept. 11 as his Holocaust (or the nearest thing his generation will have to personal experience with anything remotely correlative), and in 'In the Shadow of No Towers' [he] makes explicit parallels between the events without diminishing the incomparable evil of the death camps" ("Homeland Insecurity," 13).

What is equally crucial to the shaping of this comics series is that Spiegelman witnessed the collapse of the Twin Towers from a "ringside seat" (2). As a result, he speaks with great passion both about the imprint the attacks left on his mind and about the immediate political follow-up, which, in his opinion, amounts to nothing less than a betrayal of the true meaning of 9/11. In order to compact personal experience and public outrage, Spiegelman has altered the usual comics format. *In the Shadow of No Towers* is not a sequential narrative in graphic form, as *Maus* is. Instead, the author—who appears *in propria persona* in the story and thus also functions as narrator-protagonist—has conveyed his impressions in a series of ten large (nine-and-a-half-by-fourteen-inch), brightly colored plates or pages, which are themselves further divided into irregularly spread frames or panels. About half of the material deals with the actions of Spiegelman and his immediate family on that bright September morning. The other half consists of a savage satire on the doings of the Bush administration up till the end of August 2003. The plates are preceded by a two-page (but unpaginated) prose introduction, in which the author explains at length the circumstances in which the comics series came to be composed, and they are followed by a two-page (equally unpaginated) "comic supplement," which contains a cameo history of newspaper comics in the United States, illustrated by reprints of original cartoon strips and plates.

September 11 and the Holocaust

Spiegelman's reaction to 9/11 is shaped in part by the fact that he was a direct witness to the terrorist attacks and that, through hearing and recording the tales of his father, he was the indirect or secondary witness of the Holocaust. It is no wonder, then, that he viewed one event through the conceptual screen of the other. He was walking north from his Soho home when a few blocks behind him the first plane smashed into One

World Trade Center. He and his wife were on their way to vote in the mayoral Democratic primary election held that day. Immediately they changed course and hurried to the Stuyvesant High School on Chambers Street, a short distance away from the Twin Towers, to retrieve their teenage daughter, Nadja. Spiegelman actually did not see the planes hitting the towers, nor did he see the South Tower crumble. But when from close up he saw "the bones of the [North] tower glow and shimmy in the sky" (4) just before the building collapsed upon itself, he knew that—just like his parents before him—he had stumbled upon "that faultline where World History and Personal History collide" (introduction).

It is, of course, not with relation to the scope, the cause, or even the nature of the event that the Holocaust analogy is of service to Spiegelman. In all respects, the death camps and the terrorist attacks are singular and irreducible historical facts. Both are instances of the mass slaughter of innocents. But in one case the death immersion was institutionalized as a permanent condition; in the other it was acute and momentary. Moreover, Spiegelman's tale is not a tale of horrors and only partially a tale of physical survival. He was not in one of the towers. Nor did he suffer personal injury. This absence of direct involvement prompted the critic Adam Begley to accuse Spiegelman of narcissism and to state that "he has no access to the desperate terror of the people actually *in* the towers, and no words or images to communicate the aching grief of that day" ("Image of Twin Towers"). In the same vein, Wyatt Mason goes so far as to state that "*In the Shadow of No Towers* is not a book about September 11. Rather, it is an essay in comics that attempts, through its form, to exhibit Spiegelman's fractured state of mind during the weeks and months he spent unmoored in the catastrophe's wake" ("The Holes"). In other words, the comics series zooms in on the mental processes of the autobiographical narrator-protagonist. It records his fear and panic and stages the seesaw between melancholia or acting out, on the one hand, and mourning or working through, on the other. In that sense, it *is* a book about 9/11. It is the record of a psychologically wounded survivor trying to make sense of an event that overwhelmed and destroyed all his normal psychic defenses.

Spiegelman, as the narrator-protagonist of the tale, has a name for this condition. He calls it a "state of alienation" (7) and clinically he diagnoses it as "Post-Traumatic Stress Disorder" (2). It would be more accurate still to speak of a syndrome that is doubled or aggravated by personal precedent. In reading 9/11 through the Holocaust, Spiegelman suffers a primary trauma that resuscitates the secondary one. There are plenty of indications in the graphic novel itself that 9/11 reactivated the Holocaust memories he had imbibed from his parents, starting with the title and with an oblique reference to his situation on the flyleaf. The children of Holocaust survivors often refer to themselves or are referred to as living in the shadow of the tragedy their parents were part of. This is the case in Aaron Hass's classic study *In the Shadow of the Holocaust: The Second Generation*. The same metaphor with the same meaning also occurs in the introduction to *Second Generation Voices*, a volume edited by Alan L. and Naomi Berger. They write about second-generation witnesses: "Although they were *not* in Auschwitz, their lives are lived in the shadow of death camps" (1; italics in the original). In resorting to an oxymoronic expression and, like the Bergers, making use of a conspicuous negative particle, Spiegelman indicates in the very title of his graphic novel that the events of 9/11 reinforced in him the "presence of an absence" (Berger and Berger, *Second Generation*, 1, A. Berger, *Children*, 2, 61). The absence is the familiar sight of the Twin Towers, overshadowing the neighborhood. The presence is that of transmitted memory and pain.

The flyleaf—a reprint of the September 11, 1901, front page of the New York newspaper *The World*—similarly points to a tragic legacy. The headline that day, exactly a century before 9/11, concerned another, now largely forgotten (but repeatedly reenacted) collective American trauma: the shooting of a president, in this case William McKinley. The relevant part of the headline reads: "President's Wound Re-opened." Literally, the report deals with the fact that the surgeons had to remove a number of stitches in order to clean the president's bullet wound. But figuratively, it indicates how Spiegelman interprets history as a concatenation of shocks, as a never-ending series of wounds that will not heal and that keep festering. Seeing September 11 as the latest manifestation of this ongoing trauma and especially seeing it as a Holocaust analogue exacerbates the effect of the event and leads to "hysterical fear and panic" (introduction). At the same time, it also colors Spiegelman's urge to testify; it accounts for the dramatic and dynamic form of the tale and, ultimately, for his fierce partisanship and political commitment.

One feature of Spiegelman's Holocaust tale, *Maus*, that has been widely commented upon is the cross-cutting between past and present and more precisely the way the traumatic past not only possesses the Holocaust survivor (Spiegelman's father) but also holds the second-generation witness (the son hearing the father's tale) in a stranglehold (Orvell, "Writing Posthistorically," 125; LaCapra, *History*, 154; Huyssen, "Of Mice," 70–71; McGlothlin, "No Time," 177–98). Given that for Spiegelman the Holocaust acts as the unwritten intertext or hidden substratum for his 9/11 interpretation, it is possible to see how the transmission of trauma extends far beyond the immediate circumstances of its causes and blends in also with non-Holocaust experiences or memories. That is the reason the attacks on the World Trade Center are framed by or give rise to manifestations of the narrator's Jewish identity and thus illustrate his direct implication in both the tragic history of his parents and the larger historical destiny of the Jews in general. If one sees *Maus* and *In the Shadow of No Towers* as episodes in a continuing family saga, one can go even one step further. While the narrator of the first graphic novel is only occasionally seen to be overwhelmed by what he hears and by his responsibility as bearer of the tale, it is in the 9/11 narrative that it becomes clear how, at one remove, he has been affected by the Holocaust, how it has undermined his self-confidence and made him jumpy and angst-ridden, as well as artistically innovative and politically committed.

In his work with second generation Holocaust survivors, the psychologist Aaron Hass found that "almost three-quarters of [his] participants, a generation once removed from the Holocaust, responded affirmatively to the question: 'Do you believe there could be another attempted Jewish Holocaust?'" (*In the Shadow*, 127). "The continuous exposure to survivor parents," Hass explains, "provokes an insecurity from which it is difficult to escape" (128). In the very first paragraph of the introduction, Spiegelman indicates that his apocalyptic sensibility ("The Sky is Falling!") is indeed a family heirloom, passed on by his parents, both Auschwitz survivors, who, thoroughly imbued with the uncertainty of fate and the whimsicality of history, taught him "always to keep [his] bags packed," that is, always to expect and be prepared for the worst. It was common in the early hours and days after the attacks to feel that the destruction of the World Trade Center was but the beginning of a widespread terrorist offensive and that further disasters were to follow.[1] With Spiegelman this fearful anticipation became a virtual certainty. The attacks pushed an alarm button in the psyche of this son of Holocaust survivors. His instant and unabating panic is born from the conviction that history is in the process of repeating itself, that the sky is falling once again and that he is reliving or on the verge of reliving his parents' experience.[2] As part of his complex reaction to the trauma, the author allows the past not only to color the present but also to shut down the future. This overriding anxiety is expressed in two different ways in plate 1 of the series. In a newspaper-like comic strip the author explains the mock etymology of the expression "waiting for the other shoe to drop" by cleverly and humorously literalizing the metaphor. (His medium, after all, is the "funnies.") It is, however, only toward the end of the plate that the full weight of the expression is brought to bear on the present circumstances with deadly seriousness. A big panel (overriding the gridlike structure of the page and given further emphasis by the fact that it is circular while all the other panels are rectangular) shows through expressionist distortions how the New York population is turned into a terrified and stampeding mob. This haunting picture, which in a different format also appears in the pages of the introduction, sets the tone for the whole series and indicates that the attacks on September 11 did more than destroy part of the physical infrastructure of the city. More importantly, they unraveled civil order and disturbed personal equipoise. In rendering this extreme terror, Spiegelman reverts significantly to Holocaust iconography. While the style of the image reminds Michiko Kakutani of "the noirish pulp fiction art of the 1930's and 40's" ("Portraying 9/11"), it is also possible to see in it a visual echo of Holocaust documentaries. Referring to footage showing the newly liberated concentration camps, Joshua Hirsch writes: "Close-up shots of individuals showed bodies and faces apparently stripped of everything that the Western imagination associates with meaningful human existence: individuality, personality, reason, dignity, kinship" ("Post-traumatic," 97). Such vacant expressions, rendered in a low resolution painterly style, are also typical of the New Yorkers as Spiegelman depicts them in that particular panel: terror-stricken and dehumanized by angst.

The Holocaust inheritance shows itself equally in the pose that is struck by Spiegelman as the autodiegetic narrator of the tale, who self-reflexively dramatizes his own actions. He uses his own case as an exemplum to demonstrate what these attacks meant to the ones undergoing them and what they meant collectively to a traumatized city. He tells us in detail about the frantic rush to collect his daughter from Stuyvesant High School and his waxing sense of anguish and panic. The details bring home what it was like to be in the middle of a cataclysm, how from one moment to the next one is thrown into a new realm of experience for which there is no preparation or training and for which there is no fitting name. In many other—also comics—accounts of 9/11, the event setting off the tale is an anguished phone call from someone urging the protagonist to switch on the television.[3] In contrast, Spiegelman was walking in the streets of his neighborhood when the first plane crashed into the tower. Even though he had his back to the scene, he was close enough to hear the enormous roar of the impact and thus he has the special perspective (and suffered the horrors) of the first-hand observer and witness.

There are many panels in the story in which the narrator takes stock of his own situation. A continuing theme is that Spiegelman becomes totally unhinged. As a Jewish person, pretraumatized and bringing to the scene a Holocaust sensibility, he completely falls to pieces, while his hands-on and pragmatic wife, who is French, keeps her cool and is "out impersonating Joan of Arc—finding shelter for Tribeca friends who'd been rendered homeless" and "sneaking into the cordoned-off areas to bring water to rescue workers" (introduction).[4] The role Spiegelman adopts for himself is that of the neurotic and paranoid Jew whose ineffective jitteriness is the object of self-ridicule. Throughout the series the author slouches through the pages like a victim of circumstances beyond his control—but also like the schlemiel of traditional Jewish fiction, the victim of his own unworldliness.[5] He is a nervous wreck, perennially puffing at a pathetic cigarette, spending whole nights pursuing his paranoid obsessions, no longer able to distinguish his "own neurotic depression from well-founded despair" (8). This ironic self-portrait has precedents in Jewish self-representation predating the Holocaust, as it is an expression of survivor's wit—the Jews having been survivors for as long as the Diaspora has lasted. As such, the narrator's attitude is the result of transmitted lore as well as of secondary and primary trauma. Tradition, family history, and personal experience all combine into one culturally determined icon.

There are a number of instances in which the issue of the protagonist's Jewishness breaks through the surface rather than lingering in the ethnic substratum of the tale. In each case, there clearly is a Holocaust subtext or intertext. The narrator mentions both in the introduction and on page 8 how certain Arab Americans claimed that the Jews were responsible for the attacks, the proof being that supposedly no Jews were in the Twin Towers that fateful morning. This one example of blaming the victim is of a piece with another, more private instance of Jew baiting that is worked out on page 6 of the series. That plate consists mostly of the story of the protagonist's daily encounter with a deranged, homeless lady, who routinely curses him when he is on his way from his home to his studio. It takes him a while to realize that, inspired by the neofascist politician Vladimir Zhirinovsky, she is hurling anti-Semitic invective at him in Russian. (Her crazy, racist notions also extend to African Americans, for at one point she disappears from the street after having assaulted a black woman.) After September 11, she all of a sudden starts cursing him in English, blaming the "damn kikes" for what has happened to the city and threatening to hang every "dirty Jew . . . from the lamp posts one by one!" (6). Not only is this scene reminiscent of the humiliations and the threats Jews had to undergo in Nazi Germany leading up to the systematic roundups and Hitler's Final Solution, the brightly colored midsection of the plate also indicates that on 9/11 the private madness of that one unfortunate woman broke out and took over the city as a whole. The attacks are her invective writ large, a new chapter in the Jews' calamitous history. And even though the virtuoso Hieronymus Bosch imitation (fiery orange, red, yellow and fuchsia colors predominating) that makes up this midsection is more an image of Armageddon than the Holocaust, they both belong to the same apocalyptic category, depicting the demise of all humanity and reason.

Self-reflexively noting the changes 9/11 has wrought upon him, the narrator-protagonist gives yet another twist to the Holocaust analogy.

FIGURE 2.1

Source: From *In the Shadow of No Towers* by Art Spiegelman, copyright © 2004 by Art Spiegelman. Used by permission of Pantheon Books, a division of Random House, Inc.

On page 2, in a number of small, vertically arranged, descending frames (a sort of minitower mimicking the much larger one about to crumble) he pictures his own psychic collapse as he is suddenly transformed from a human being into an anthropomorphized mouse (see figure 2.2). That is to say, he resumes the guise he wore in his earlier Holocaust narrative, *Maus*, in which the Jews are portrayed as having the heads and faces of mice, the Poles those of pigs, and the Germans those of cats. As Andreas Huyssen wrote about the Holocaust narrative: "we see persecuted little animals drawn with a human body and wearing human clothes and with a highly abstracted, non-expressive mouse physiognomy. 'Maus' here means vulnerability, unalloyed suffering, victimization" ("Of Mice," 75). In *In the Shadow of No Towers*, the mouse figure appears seven times and applies only to Spiegelman and his immediate family rather than to the Jews in general. Also for reasons to be explained later, the mouse figures are closer to the cartoon animals from which they descend than in *Maus*. Even so, the animal metaphor, which in the Holocaust narrative is the symbol of the martyred victim, here has a related and only slightly different meaning. It stands for the powerless innocent who finds himself in the hands of uncontrollable forces.[6] That is why in a frame adjacent to the ones depicting the author's psychic collapse, the autobiographical stand-in (in the guise of a mouse) is surrounded by Osama Bin Laden wielding a bloody scimitar, on one side, and by George W. Bush brandishing a gun, on the other. Having lost his brain, i.e. his level-headedness, the protagonist as a mouse feels himself to be "equally terrorized by Al-Qaeda and by his own government."

Picturing himself and his next of kin as mice does not mean that Spiegelman arrogates to himself the role of Holocaust victim. What it does signify is that, suffering a primary trauma as a close 9/11 witness, Spiegelman positions himself within a larger Jewish tradition. His meekness is a token of ineffectuality and disorientation, but it is obvious from the confrontations with the perpetrators of violence and counterviolence that his innocence is also a form of wisdom.[7] This ethical turn becomes manifest in later elaborations of the mouse metaphor. The condition of a self helplessly given up to feelings of abandonment is well evoked in the last frame on page 6, where it is sprung on us as a non sequitur and yet follows logically from the mad woman's anti-Semitic rant detailed on that page. In that panel the author has shrunk to a little mouse that has fallen out of bed, clearly disturbed by a nightmare in which "John Ashcroft pulled off his burka and shoved me out of the window" (6). He is tended to by a solicitous mother figure.[8] Yet, as a token of the general disarray and one more reminder of the Holocaust, she ominously wears a gas mask. One page later the little mouse has tumbled out of bed again. But this time he is scolded by a sharp-beaked, birdlike figure—a permutation of the American eagle—who admonishes him, using bureaucratic gobbledygook and government speak: "You *disembedded* again, young man—now hush before mama *liberates*

FIGURE 2.2

Source: From *In the Shadow of No Towers* by Art Spiegelman, copyright © 2004 by
Art Spiegelman. Used by permission of Pantheon Books, a division of Random House, Inc.

you!" (7). The helplessness of the little wailing mouse stands in implicit contrast and thus forms a counterweight to political doubletalk,
patriotic rodomontade, and belligerent heroism. The refusal to strike
a "manly" pose, the refusal, ultimately, to participate in crusades and
manhunts and to answer aggression with aggression is an expression
of Jewish *Mentshlicheit*, which posits that given a choice between good
and evil, one must choose "what is morally and ethically right" (Knopp,
The Trial, 6).

Mimetic Approximation

Trauma is now widely understood as "the response to an unexpected or overwhelming violent event or events that are not fully grasped as they occur" (Caruth, *Unclaimed Experience*, 91) and, as a consequence of this, "as the breakdown of symbolic resources, narrative, and imagery" (Kaplan and Wang, "From Traumatic Paralysis," 17). That is to say, trauma is a rupture not only in the normal order of things, but, more important, in the meaning-giving apparatus that is responsible for this order. Thus the horrors of the Holocaust have often been seen as causing the breakdown of traditional representational practices. Ernst van Alphen speaks in this connection of "the wide-spread conviction that the Holocaust, in all its uniqueness and extremity, is unrepresentable" (*Caught by History*, 41). Some commentators, therefore, have argued that it should not be represented. Theodor Adorno's and Lionel Trilling's famous pleas to keep silent are well explained by Cathy Caruth, when she remarks that such reticence is inspired by the fear that by speaking of it "the event's essential incomprehensibility, the force of its *affront to understanding*" is in danger of being lost (Caruth, *Trauma*, 154).[9] The fact that a traumatic experience cannot be grasped either immediately or afterward and that it manifests itself belatedly as unmediated flashbacks and nightmares has led poststructurally inflected theories to assume that every presentation of trauma necessarily cheapens it by reducing the cognitive rupture to manageable proportions. Other commentators, however, have pointed out that such one-sided emphasis on the inaccessibility of trauma to imagery and understanding precludes the possibility of witnessing.[10] Caruth herself, who is usually associated with the poststructuralist approach, quotes Schreiber Weitz to good effect: "Elie Wiesel has said many times that silence is the only proper response but then most of us, including him, feel that not to speak is impossible" (*Trauma*, 154). Or as Kaplan and Wang put it: "As trauma consists in the unmaking of the world, the prohibition against representation blocks the way to the re-making of the world. While it shatters the culture's symbolic resources, trauma also points to the urgent necessity of reconfiguring and transforming the broken repertoire of meaning and expression" ("From Traumatic Paralysis," 12).

Spiegelman is well aware of this ambivalence. In a much-quoted sequence in *Maus*, he shows his alter ego, Artie Spiegelman, in conversation with Pavel, his psychiatrist. In the course of this exchange, Pavel, himself a Holocaust survivor, remarks: "Anyway, the victims who died can never tell THEIR side of the story, so maybe it's better not to have any more stories." To which Artie replies: "Uh-huh. Samuel Beckett once said: 'Every word is like an unnecessary stain on silence and nothingness.'" In the next frame, the two interlocutors gaze at each other without uttering a word, until in the next panel, Artie says: "On the other hand, he SAID it" (205). In yet another sequence near the beginning of the second part of *Maus*, Artie is seen to be sick and tired of the commercial and critical success he enjoyed after the publication of the first part of the comics series (201). He is wary of the dangers of commodification and exploitation and wrestles with questions regarding the legitimacy and authenticity of what he is doing. He is aware that he is operating on the cutting edge, where he has to express the inexpressible. On the wrong side of this divide there are forms of expression that amount to betrayal, and there are survival narratives that, in uncritically offering tales of heroism or angling for unearned sympathy, are little more than Holocaust kitsch.

With regard to 9/11, Spiegelman, as the narrator of his own tale, shows less hesitancy. Reticence is replaced by determination. In the seesaw between sacred silence and testimonial speech, he comes out squarely on the side of what Lillian Kremer—in the context of Holocaust writings—aptly calls "the sacred duty to bear witness" (*Witness*, 27). According to his own account, the events of 9/11 made such an impression on him that he felt right away that as an artist he had no choice but to stand up and speak about the event[11]—just as in *Maus* he had given witness to his father's agony in Auschwitz. Such commitment is embedded in the personal need to diminish anxiety. (In an interview Spiegelman indicated that creating the book was a "lifesaver" [Terrell, "9/11"].) After the shock of a violent and unexpected event, narration is instrumental in reconstituting the shattered self.[12] But, as R. J. Lifton states, "carrying through the witness is a way of transmuting pain and guilt into responsibility" (Caruth, "Interview," 138). In other words, telling the tale does more than serve a cathartic purpose. The survivor also has the duty to make his or her voice heard, if only to honor the victims and to make sure that their deaths were not in vain. This may explain why 9/11 and its aftermath spoke so strongly to Spiegelman that he felt, as an artist, he was obliged not only to testify as a witness but also to protest when he saw how the events were misinterpreted and abused for political ends.

This urge to tell the tale deeply involves him in a further difficulty, typical of all writing about trauma. Once the choice in favor of testimony has been made, a way must be found to represent the unrepresentable without blunting the response. Trauma in itself is mute: it lies outside the range of comprehensibility and articulation. In order to speak about it one must find "a kind of textual compromise between the senselessness of the initial traumatic encounter and the sense-making apparatus of a fully integrated historical narrative" (J. Hirsch, "Posttraumatic," 101). Since trauma is that for which there is no language, no discursive practice can ever be adequate in rendering it. Trauma is not transmissible through words or images unless the representation stages the breakdown of referentiality, self-reflexively meditates on its own problematic status, or incorporates traumatic experience not so much thematically (on the surface) as stylistically (deep down in the tensions of style and texture) (Michaels, "'You Who Was,'" 193; Leys, *Trauma*, 268). Successful trauma transmission, which brings the incomprehensible within the range of comprehension with a minimum loss of experiential content, goes by different names. After Edmund Burke, Andrew Slade sees in it a manifestation of the sublime (*"Hiroshima"*);[13] Dominick LaCapra speaks of "muted trauma" (*History*, 45); while Andreas Huyssen, drawing on the insights of Theodor Adorno, deploys the notion of "mimetic approximation" ("Of Mice," 72). The latter concept emphasizes that traumatic experience is inaccessible to language (it maintains its untranslatable aseity, and no full mimesis is possible), yet there are means that witnesses can mobilize so as to avoid the terror of memory while yet reviving the trauma for themselves and their audience. To put it differently: mimetic approximation involves "closeness and distance, affinity and difference" (Huyssen, "Of Mice," 79). Documentary *"authenticity* of representation" (76) is never possible, since language distances, distorts, and adulterates traumatic experience. Yet language itself—properly attuned—can carry within it a force that lends it a kind of mediated *authentication*.

Huyssen has discussed *Maus*—a narrative "saturated with modernist techniques of self-reflexivity, self-irony, ruptures in narrative time and highly complex image sequencing and montaging" (70)—as a convincing example of "mimetic approximation." By staging the narrative as a dialogue with his father and by indicating the many heuristic difficulties such a dialogue across time and space involves, Spiegelman in no way hypostatizes the terrible truth about the death camps. Thus he avoids the impression of false authenticity. At the same time, the poignancy and pointedness of the tale is in large measure the result of his father's interventions. The strong presence of the survivor as witness assures authentication, while yet a great deal of the narrative's self-questioning properties are a result of the intricate interpenetration of past and present that such a dialogue entails.[14] In addition, as Marianne Hirsch ("Family Pictures," 12), Linda Hutcheon ("Literature," 9) and Frank L. Cioffi ("Disturbing Comics," 118) have also pointed out, the animal imagery in *Maus* operates as a distancing device so that there is a productive break between the literalness of the aural "true" testimony of the father and the visual figuration (the invented, cartoonlike characters of mice, cats, etc.) The distance between the two has made for what James E. Young calls a "pointedly antiredemptory medium that simultaneously makes and unmakes meaning as it unfolds" ("Holocaust," 676).

Also, the stylistic means that Spiegelman marshals to approximate mimetically the events of September 11 make it possible to consider *In the Shadow of No Towers* a sequel to *Maus*. The strategic devices Spiegelman has opted for can even be seen as an intensification of those used in the earlier narrative. *Maus* largely traces a traditional linear sequence, whereby one panel follows the next, while in *In the Shadow of No Towers*, different, more complicated and defamiliarizing techniques are used to express a mix of helpless confusion and red-hot political indignation. Rather than a consistent tale, the ten giant cartoon pages—displaying a wide variety of styles—present themselves as modernist collage. According to Spiegelman's introduction, the enormous size of the two-page spread color newsprint plates fits a narrative involving "oversized skyscrapers and outsized events." Beyond that, the garish colors, darkly rimmed panels, dynamic, irregular layout of every page, and the superimposition of panels suggesting a random pile-up of material—all have the effect of giving urgency to the tale and pervading it with a sense of disbelief and panic.

There are at least two reasons for this formal excess. On the last plate Spiegelman mentions that he was horrified by the kitsch that was on sale on the first anniversary of 9/11. He is thinking not only of the crude artifacts that were being hawked on that occasion. His definition of kitsch also includes the mawkish and jingoist memorial programs on television, which commodified 9/11 more quickly and much more thoroughly than the Holocaust. Hence he must have felt the pressure to avoid an easy, unproblematical rendering of the historical facts. Even while attempting to master the events, he wants to make sure they remain far beyond the reach of simplistic comprehension. In addition, and most importantly, the broken-up form of the narrative mirrors his consternation; the fragmentary presentation serves as objective correlative for the author's scrambled state of mind. Unlike in *Maus*, there is no retrospect to structure the events, no mediator to channel them through. *In the Shadow of No Towers* is not a frame tale but a direct, in-your-face impression of extreme perplexity.[15] The sense that the terrorist attacks caused a semiotic rupture (that everything is topsy-turvy and semantically dislocated) is deeply embedded in the images themselves and screams, as it were, from every page.

One very conspicuous feature of the narrative's purposely hybrid and nonnormalizing format is the surprising introduction of cartoon characters, most of them dating from the early days of newspaper comics. In the course of the series Spiegelman explains that browsing through old comic strips provided him with solace in the dark days after 9/11 (10) and that the century-old "Sunday supplement stars" (8) started haunting him and thus became part of his September 11 experience. In the "comic supplement" at the back of the volume, he explains the role of the comics characters in greater detail. After mentioning that in the wake of September 11, New Yorkers seemed to need poetry as balm for their souls but that for him neither poetry nor music brought any solace, he continues, "The only cultural artifacts that could get past my defenses to flood my eyes and brain with something other than images of burning towers were old comic strips; vital, unpretentious ephemera from the optimistic dawn of the 20th century."

At first blush, these comments seem to back up David Hajdu's observation that Spiegelman, while struggling "to come to terms with the losses of Sept. 11, . . . lost himself in nostalgia for an irretrievable era in his art—the Old World of comics—much as his aging father longed for the Europe that had existed before the war" ("Homeland Insecurity," 14). However, a closer examination quickly reveals that the introduction of the comics figures is much more than a mere form of escapism. Their aesthetic effect, while sometimes soothing, is most of the time upsetting. Their appearance is not explicable by one simple parameter. They work to contrary effects and thus contribute to the mimetic approximation of the 9/11 tragedy in that they bring it nearer and at the same time push it away. In that sense, they constitute an extension and intensification of the use of animal figures in *Maus*. According to Andreas Huyssen, "Drawing the story of his parents and the Holocaust as an animal comic is the Odyssean cunning that allows Spiegelman to escape from the terror of memory . . . while mimetically reenacting it" ("Of Mice," 74). Similarly, the comics figures help to express the horror of 9/11 while contributing to its mastery.

There are at least three ways in which the comics figures make an impact. Transposed to the twenty-first century and in the context of a calamity, the early cartoon characters introduce a self-reflexive element. In order to express his inexpressible theme, the author grabs all the means (including the least likely) at his disposal. If, therefore, *In the Shadow of No Towers* is a scream prompted by the outrageousness of the events themselves and the political follow-up to them, the rage that the pictures embody is also a byproduct of the author's assault on the ineffable, the sheer frustration of having to give voice to a deep, unwaning, and ultimately unrepresentable rupture in his experience of space and time.

Introducing characters from the "Katzenjammer Kids," "Happy Hooligan," "Bringing Up Father," "Lovekins and Muffaroo," and "Krazy Kat," among others, also has two further effects. It serves, on the one hand, as a distancing device, as an extra layer of interpretation between the events and the response; on the other, it throws the narrative off kilter by enacting a spirited resistance to the overwhelmingness of the events. Some of the pain caused by 9/11 is so unbearable and some of the anger so raw that it needs the mediation of allegory to gain expression. Simultaneously, the inappropriateness of the quotations (in view of the utter serious-ness of the topic) adds a screwball effect to the collage. Most of the early cartoon characters were born in the newspaper offices of Park Row near where the Twin Towers would stand and fall. Hence the appearance of the classic comics rowdies and ragamuffins, who have not nine lives but ninety-nine and then some, is an expression of the city's unquenchable high spirits. They stand for the raucousness and rebelliousness of the New Yorker. They embody the vernacular protest against self-important official rhetoric, as well as the tenacity of the city when face to face with the most egregious hardships.

In summary, one can say that the cartoon characters account for both distance and resistance. Their impact as stylistic devices is such that, even as the tale progresses, the cartoonizing of the events (or aspects of the events) remains rough-edged and there is no consistent sublation of the cartoon metaphor to a higher narrative plane. The older cartoon characters remain outside the process of mimesis or, more exactly, the mimetic is raised to the level of the figural in a conspicuous, self-reflexive way, mixed with a wryness that befits the occasion and its many paradox-es. In other words, the cartoon figures account for a lasting and major disruption in the texture of the tale. They break the horizon of expecta-tion both temporally and stylistically: temporally because they go back a century; stylistically because they are goofy within a tragic context. Given the utter seriousness of the topic, the frivolity of their appearance keeps its shock value. They are reminders of the fact that the expression of chaos allows no direct approach. They are the special (desperate) means by which the author manages to operate in the area where, in the words of Jacques Derrida, "language and … concept come up against their limits" (qtd. in Borradori, *Philosophy in a Time of Terror*, 88).

The Incandescent Tower

One major difference between *Maus* and *In the Shadow of No Towers* is that the latter contains an explicit political message. *Maus* veers away from object lessons and moral conclusions, whereas the 9/11 narrative is to a large extent an acerbic and at times savage spoof and satire on the

Bush administration. Given that Spiegelman's stance is unambiguously biased and partisan, one might get the impression that his discourse serves a didactic purpose and as such co-opts the meaning of 9/11 in a way not altogether different from the one used in the official political propaganda, which is the object of Spiegelman's scorn. On closer examination, however, it becomes obvious that his political interests are a direct outcome of his experience of trauma. While there is no precedent for this in *Maus*, the ethical turn is of a piece with the testimony of many Holocaust survivors, for whom the Holocaust is a paradoxical source of meaning and solidarity. Spiegelman's political commitment is part of the working through of the trauma. As it remains closely allied to the originating experience, the political positioning is marked by shock and hence stays clear of self-righteousness and stasis.

One possible way of understanding Spiegelman's commitment in connection with his traumatic experience is to look at it in the light of R. J. Lifton's distinction between true and false witnessing. False witness, according to Lifton, is a "compensatory process that is very dangerous" (Caruth, "Interview," 139). It occurs when one's own death anxiety is converted immediately into killing. The example cited by Lifton is that of the massacre in My Lai. But the concept could easily be applied to the U.S. government's reaction to the terrorist attacks (as perceived by Spiegelman). The belligerence of the government (backed in this by a large section of the population) can be conceived of as "a perverse quest for meaning" (Caruth, "Interview," 140), that is, an attempt "to reaffirm one's moral system or sense of self by destroying, violating, murdering another" (141). Lifton indicates that whether one reacts to trauma by giving true or false witness involves "a moral judgment" (140). In addition, the ethical choice necessary to turn trauma into a therapeutic and socially useful form of testimony (temporarily) suspends the open-endedness of semiosis. As true witnessing means taking a stand, it inevitably involves the provisional closure of meaning. *In the Shadow of No Towers* proves that such a reconfiguration need not lead to a frozen subject positioning. Ethical commitment, seasoned by irony and self-doubt, can be staged as a heuristic process that is not dependent on a fixed ego identity or an inflexible ideological vantage point. Moreover, it can serve as part of the healing process—part of the mourning or the working through, whereby the victim or witness succeeds in loosening the coils of the traumatic obsession, gets over the psychic wound, and resumes life as a responsible and participating citizen.

In the introduction to *In the Shadow of No Towers* Spiegelman indicates that his political indignation grew slowly but steadily, as "the government began to move into full dystopian Big Brother mode and hurtle America into a colonialist adventure in Iraq." These political developments hurt him so much that he speaks of "new traumas... competing with still-fresh wounds." What is remarkable, though, is that the new traumas did not leave the protagonist in a state of numbed inaction, as did the attacks themselves. The narrative shows how he shed his fixation with 9/11 or, more precisely, how his fidelity to 9/11 fired his opposition to the Bush administration, which, in his opinion, violated the true meaning of the events and dispossessed their true owners.

The narrator-protagonist's commitment is closely linked to his experience of trauma and represents his victory over it. In order to understand what this process of working through entails, it is necessary to emphasize once again how personally upsetting 9/11 was to the narrator-protagonist of the graphic novel. His experience of trauma is symbolized by the central image in the volume: "the looming north tower's glowing bones just before it vaporized" (introduction). This image of the incandescent tower, moments before its collapse, figures on each and every plate and serves as the leitmotif of the series. As such, it can easily be identified as an essential part of the protaganist's post–traumatic stress disorder.[16] Both in the comics series and in an interview with Kenneth Terrell, Spiegelman indicates repeatedly how he was obsessed by the image of the burning tower, how it would not let him go. He is possessed by it to such an extent that it comes to exist in a sort of eternal present. The moment before the crumbling of the tower, when it stood bathing in an orange glow, is the moment "the world ended" (*In the Shadow*, 1) and "time seemed to stop" (Terrell, "9/11" 1). As Kai Erikson puts it:

A chronicler of passing events may report that the episode itself lasted no more than an instant... but the traumatized mind holds on to that moment, preventing it from slipping back into its proper chronological place in the past, and relives it over and over again in the compulsive musings of the day and the seething dreams of night. The moment becomes a season, the event becomes a condition.[17]   (185)

The incandescent tower—as symbol of an unshakable fixation—is prominent from the beginning of the comics series. On the first plate the roseate image of the tower frames the entire (oversize) length of the right side of the page and part of the left side. Thus the horizontality of the other narrative panels is offset (and overshadowed) by the tower rising (or partially rising) vertically on each side. The traumatic last moment in the life of the doomed skyscraper takes on the scariness of an overwhelming dream vision, real and unreal at the same time. Its dominant position on the page shows that several months after the events—work on the first plate was started at the beginning of 2002—the author is still incessantly reenacting the collapse in his mind. More precisely, he sees a mental afterimage of the glowing tower from different perspectives and distances. Neither on the left nor on the right side of the page, the tower is allowed to keep its physical integrity and to stand tall for a last moment before it sinks upon itself. While the descending frames on both sides of the plate have identical dimensions and are perfectly regular, the pictures in them are skewed in different ways and do not add up to one consistent image. The author zooms in and out and sees the tower from different angles. While the regular frames suggest the solidity of skyscraper architecture (and therefore represent normality), the evershifting views of the tower within the frames indicate how, most frighteningly, that physical soundness was compromised. Spiegelman succeeds in conveying the absolute unthinkability of an event even as it was taking place before his eyes. Thus 9/11 is defined as the moment when the instability of nightmare takes over from the solidity of steel, the normal order collapses, the mind is faced with the incomprehensible, and the whole city is submerged in the uncanny and the surreal.

Page after page, the collapsing tower reemerges in accordance with the protagonist's wish to hold on to the experience, to dwell on and even revel in the cataclysmic event of a lifetime. Typically, the narrator-protagonist of *In the Shadow of No Towers* reports that he begins to feel "nostalgic about his near-death experience" (7). On one plate he states that he "is trapped reliving the traumas of Sept. 11, 2001" (4), while on another he seems to address President Bush directly and exclaims: "Leave me alone, Damn it! I'm just trying to comfortably relive my September 11 trauma but you keep interrupting—" (5). The protagonist wants to hang on to the awesomeness of what he saw on 9/11. Self-absorbed and isolated, he nurses and paradoxically cherishes his wounds, thus experiencing what Dominick LaCapra calls "a fidelity to trauma, a feeling that one must somehow keep faith with it" (*Writing History*, 22). Such unwillingness to let time be the healer and the tendency to relish the repeated acting out of the trauma indicate that the protagonist suffers from repetition compulsion: he cannot break the stranglehold of his memories and is unwilling to get on with his life.

However, the narrative, while stressing the hold the image of the crumbling tower has over the protagonist's mind, also details the various steps by which he manages to shed his initial inertia. To begin with, expression counteracts obsession. Trauma is characterized by "the literal return of the event against the will of the one it inhabits" (Caruth, *Trauma*, 5). That is to say, traumatic dreams and flashbacks remain haunting because they refuse to be integrated into a linguistic or symbolic order. Traumatic memories lodge themselves in the psyche as unprocessable and indigestible traces that come out only in ungovernable hallucinations and nightmares. The fact that the narrator-protagonist can formulate his obsessions and Spiegelman, as an artist, has found a fitting form for them reveals that a process of working through or mourning is taking place, even while the protagonist conveys his yearning to dwell in paralyzing melancholia. Graphically naming the obsession is a form of mastery. Wrenching trauma out of the realm of the inarticulate and nudging it toward expression is a first step in the healing process.

While the representation of painful and hardly utterable memories ushers in the beginning of their transcendence, it is in sketching how mourning leaves the strictly private realm and acquires a public dimension that *In the Shadow of No Towers* turns political. In his self-indulgent and nostalgic mood, the protagonist sees the doings of the Bush administration as an intrusion, distracting him from the narcissistic contemplation of his own wound. In opening up to the world outside, he takes a further step toward fulfilling his obligation as true witness. The complex process of metamorphosis and osmosis such a turnaround entails has been rendered self-reflexively and with a great deal of wry humor on plate 6 (see figure 2.3).

Once again the plate shows on the left-hand side a full-length image of the tower in the last moments before its collapse. As if that in itself were not enough to signify the lasting impact of trauma, a man is seen jumping from it, preferring the freedom of the sky to death by fire— performing, as the text has it, "a graceful Olympic dive as his last living act." The amazing thing is that the author admits that he is "haunted now by the images he *didn't* witness." He did not actually see anybody jump from the tower. Nonetheless, the figure caught in a headlong descent is clearly his autobiographical stand-in. It is the author himself somersaulting toward his death. The caption, explaining this transferential identification indicates that the Spiegelman character "keeps falling through the holes in his head, though he no longer knows which holes were made by Arab terrorists way back in 2001, and which ones were *always* there." The fall is a metaphorical (as well as a literal) one, and, as in other places in the narrative, the protagonist asks himself whether this dizzying tumbling—this upsetting of all familiar notions—is the result of his predisposition as a pretraumatized, secondary Holocaust witness (with holes in his head) or a reflection of things as they have really come to pass after September 11.

The text suggests that the protagonist's obsession with 9/11 is a direct outcome of his prehistory and, most importantly, that such a sensitivity allows him to take into his purview scenes he did not witness but experiences vicariously. Such empathy lands him, literally, on the pavement in front of the tower. By the time the fall ends, the author's lookalike has been transformed into the cartoon character Happy Hooligan, staged here as one of the army of homeless who, in the wake of the many bankruptcies in Lower Manhattan after 9/11, the authorities summarily abandoned. If one wants to read this scene against the grain, one could say that it is riddled with facile linguistic and pictorial linkages, misleading visual and verbal puns. To fall through holes in one's head is not the same as being forced to jump from 110 stories by a raging fire. To be exploded on the pavement in front of the towers is not the same as "landing in the street" as a homeless person. However, metamorphosis and falling are the stock-in-trade of the comics medium. Spiegelman has used some

FIGURE 2.3

Source: From *In the Shadow of No Towers* by Art Spiegelman,
copyright © 2004 by Art Spiegelman. Used by permission of
Pantheon Books, a division of Random House, Inc.

of the conventions of comics to indicate the nature of
his personal involvement in the calamity that hit his
city. His specific accusation to the authorities is that
9/11 was a moment of collective valor that has not been
made use of. Worse, it has been abused. In his last moments, the diving man demonstrates personal heroism, showing grace under extreme pressure. While
9/11 held many examples of such demotic heroism, the
government's behavior—as shown by its unconcern
for the homeless—is graceless, unheroic, irresponsible, harsh, uncaring, and boorish. Such an allegation
is made from a personal viewpoint that remains hesi-
tant and unstable. While the identification with the
9/11 victims diving to their deaths may be seen as facile
empathy and therefore as proof of inappropriate arrogance, the identification with a cartoon character is
deflationary and self-mocking. Even in his ruthless political satire, Spiegelman remains within the realm of
mimetic approximation: the depiction of true despair
and suffering is surrounded by an intricate creative
playfulness, which, in mobilizing various intertexts,
prevents premature closure and categorical, apodeic-
tic statements.

Spiegelman is not the only commentator to look
upon 9/11 as a utopian moment the authorities squan-
dered. John Kuo Wei Tchen writes: "the suddenness
of our loss created a need to reach out, to talk, to pull
together" ("Whose," 33). In the same vein, David Harvey comments: "New Yorkers, faced with unspeakable tragedy, for the most part rallied around ideals
of community, togetherness, solidarity, and altruism

as opposed to beggar-thy-neighbor individualism" ("Cracks," 61). "At first," Spiegelman writes in the introduction, "Ground Zero had marked a Year Zero as well. Idealistic peace signs and flower shrines briefly flourished at Union Square, the checkpoint between lower Manhattan and the rest of the city."[18] This moment of harmony, however, was short-lived. The "usual cleavages resurfaced" (Tchen, "Whose," 33). "Social inequality in the city became more rather than less emphatic" (Harvey, "Cracks," 62). In Spiegelman's own words: "the world hustled forward into our 'New Normal'" (introduction). Peter Brooks explains that the collective experience of trauma and the "impoverishing of our egos" are the result not only of the "horror of the attack itself" but also of the political failure of mourning. He states that the proper mourning "was hijacked by a simplistically militaristic response, a knee-jerk jingoism that substituted for any reflective policy" ("If You Have," 49). Similarly, Spiegelman's anger is fed by the disappointment after his realization that the "post-disaster utopia"[19] cannot be carried forward into a lasting policy. Against the background, once again, of the glimmering tower, a caption on plate 7 reads: "Nothin' like the end of the world to help bring folks together." But while the eyes of the frightened protagonist turn into pinwheels and sweat pours from his brow, the stiles of the tower transform into the Stars and Stripes. The fervor raised by 9/11 is turned into jingoism. What for the protagonist is an indelible image connoting world solidarity is quickly evoked by the authorities as a *casus belli* (see figure 2.4).

For Spiegelman, the trauma caused by 9/11 is not just a moment of personal upheaval. Ultimately, it is a moment of political awakening and heightened public awareness. In the words of James Berger, trauma is "a secular apocalyptic moment: shattering, obliterating, but also revelatory" ("'There's No Backhand to This,'" 52). Spiegelman has stated that he "never wanted to be a political cartoonist" (introduction). But 9/11 forced him into politics, as it forced him into expression. As the view of the burning skyscraper and the views of a whole world out of kilter are imprinted beyond deletion upon his retinas, he wants the reader to be imbued with the same awesome sights and, especially, he wants the reader to draw the same conclusions. The tower's melting, in particular, is the signal event that the author cannot put behind him. At the same time,

FIGURE 2.4

Source: From *In the Shadow of No Towers* by Art Spiegelman, copyright © 2004 by Art Spiegelman. Used by permission of Pantheon Books, a division of Random House, Inc.

it is also the authenticating event. As a firsthand witness and "a denizen of the neighborhood" (8), he has the right and the duty to interpret the catastrophe, and he is entitled to scream at those who make use of it for their own political purposes.

In contrast to his personal upset, however, Spiegelman's political commitment is marked by paradox. While it is a token of his reentering the world (after time stopped and the world came to an end), it is fired by the observation that 9/11 is all too quickly forgotten in public discourse. Shedding his 9/11 fixation, therefore, means insisting that 9/11 be properly remembered. Letting go of the trauma as a personally inhibiting experience is tantamount to converting it into a collective loyalty to the dead. That is the reason the series makes a razor-sharp division between insiders and outsiders. The outrage palpable on every page is a result of the feeling that New York has been attacked twice. Or more accurately, that it has been attacked and then betrayed—betrayed by "the Bush cabal," who hijacked September 11 and "reduced it all to a war recruitment poster"; betrayed by the heartlanders "for whom the attack was an abstraction"; betrayed by the population in general, who, once the initial shock had worn off, went back into the television-fed stupor of the "New Normal" (introduction).

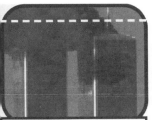

Those crumbling towers burned their way into every brain, but I live on the outskirts of Ground Zero and first saw it all live —unmediated.

Maybe it's just a question of scale. Even on a large TV, the towers aren't much bigger than, say, Dan Rather's head...

Logos, on the other hand, look *enormous* on television; it's a medium almost as well suited as comics for dealing in abstractions.

FIGURE 2.5

Source: From *In the Shadow of No Towers* by Art Spiegelman, copyright © 2004 by Art Spiegelman. Used by permission of Pantheon Books, a division of Random House, Inc.

The narrator-protagonist makes his first appearance in the series as a diminutive and helpless creature sitting in front of an enormous television set into which a plane is crashing (see figure 2.5). This autobiographical stand-in insists that he "saw it all live—unmediated." He experienced the tragedy in its true and full scale, not indirectly, in reduced dimensions, as the television viewers, for whom "the towers aren't much bigger than, say, Dan Rather's head" (1). Even so, millions of people saw the events on television, while only a few thousand were there to live through them on the spot. Hence it is obvious that the voice of the direct witness is no match for the Dan Rathers of this world. The media stars appropriated the event even while it happened. They have reduced first-hand experience to news and cheapened trauma into mere sensationalism. That is, they have immediately expropriated the real owners of the event, those who underwent it personally or watched it from close by. "The media," James Berger writes, "soon spoke more about the heroes of September 11 than of the dead" (" 'There's No Backhand to This,' " 55). Similarly, Spiegelman discovers that the impact of the plane on the TV set turns trauma into the abstraction of the American flag. His first reaction is disbelief, then anger and indignation.

"The literature of testimony," writes Shoshana Felman, "puts into effect, puts into action a question of belonging. To whom do the dead belong? And consequently, on whose side must the living (the surviving) be?" (Felman and Laub, *Testimony*, 116–17). Ultimately, the struggle depicted by Spiegelman is between the proper memorializing and mourning of the event, on the one hand, and its instrumentalization for the political agenda of the government, on the other. That this struggle spans the whole series and remains an ongoing, undecided concern is expressed through a complex chain of visual echoes, which loop from the end to the very beginning of the volume. The last big panel on plate 10 is a reprise in a different form of the big panel on plate 1. While in the beginning of the book the inhabitants of New York anxiously wait for the other shoe to drop, on the last page the other shoe has dropped, not in the shape of a new terrorist attack but in the shape of cowboy boots adorned with dollar signs and American eagles. Manhattan is under siege again, threatened not by Al-Qaeda but by the Republican Presidential Convention of September 2004. Thus the Bush administration transforms "Tragedy... into Travesty" (10). Such a quick political recuperation of trauma—such unearned triumphalism excluding the possibility of proper mourning—does not augur well for the survival of 9/11 as an ethical touchstone. In the last three frames, the glowing tower appears again, but each time the panel is getting darker and darker. Time seems to swallow up the events, and the vanishing of the skyscraper is accompanied by a wry and bitterly ironic "happy anniversary" (10). The narrator is aware of his ineffectualness. His efforts cannot ward off the return of the "New Normal," vanquish the raw power of the Republican propaganda machine, or prevent 9/11 from receding in people's memories.

However, this defeatism is counteracted by yet another visual echo. The panels on the last plate are arranged in such a way that they form the outline of the two vanished towers. Graphically, the artist wills them back into existence. Thus the narrative completes a full heuristic circle, for the cover of the book also features the two towers. In its turn, this initial image carries a further visual echo, bringing us temporally (if not physically) closer to the events of September 11. The picture on the cover is an amended version of Spiegelman's famous September 24, 2001, *New Yorker* cover, which so shortly after the actual disappearance of the towers showed their silhouettes in an ingenious black-on-black painting, suggesting their lingering presence (Spiegelman, "Re: Cover"). The difference with the original is that on the book cover Spiegelman has superimposed on the black towers (roughly at the height at which the planes impacted) a panoramic window, which shows a bearded and turbaned goat (Osama Bin Laden?) kicking the rear ends of the cartoon characters that will appear later in the narrative (Mason, "The Holes"). This touch of levity indicates that the dialectical working out of the narrative (and the working through of trauma) involves a grittiness and endurance that is figured as typical of the protagonist as New York's native son. Bin Laden's attack has unleashed (kickstarted, as it were) the author's creativity. After a long interval, it brought him back to his true medium, of comix (introduction).[20] It allowed him to connect with a vital part of America's popular culture, and it fired his political imagination. *In the Shadow of No Towers* celebrates these acts of resistance. Its ultimate tribute to the fallen towers and to those fallen in them is to set the author's free-ranging ingenuity over against both the violence of the foreign terrorists and the counter-violence of the author's own government.

3

A ROSE IS NOT A ROSE IS NOT A ROSE

HISTORY AND LANGUAGE IN JONATHAN SAFRAN FOER'S *EXTREMELY LOUD AND INCREDIBLY CLOSE*

"TRAUMATIC MEMORIES ... are not encoded like the ordinary memories of adults in a verbal, linear narrative that is assimilated into an ongoing life story," writes the psychoanalyst Judith Herman. Traumatic memories are "frozen and wordless" (*Trauma and Recovery*, 156–57). Thus the relation between trauma and language is a problematical one. Trauma involves an event that cannot be spoken. The traumatic event is a blank, in the face of which words always and necessarily fall short. And yet trauma must be spoken. Trauma leads to numbness, flashbacks, or nightmares. These intrusive symptoms can only be dealt with when a traumatic memory gets situated within a series of events. Trauma must be given a place within one's recollection in order to heal. In other words, traumatic memory must be turned into narrative memory. As Bessel van der Kolk and Onno van der Hart put it, "Traumatic memories are the unassimilated scraps of overwhelming experiences, which need to be integrated with existing mental schemes, and be transformed into narrative language" ("The Intrusive Past," 176).

In no other novel on 9/11 is the relation between trauma and language as explicitly articulated as in Jonathan Safran Foer's *Extremely Loud and Incredibly Close*. The novel derives a substantial part of its originality from the attempt to compose a "writing of the disaster" (the term is Maurice Blanchot's). It does not only explore the etiology of trauma, detailing its various symptoms. It also relates pain to the impossibility of utterance. The three narrator-protagonists of the novel are faced with an ineffable trauma, an unspeakable truth, which they try to reveal through language. Their task is made difficult by the fact that these particular "disasters" are resistant to articulation. One of the destructive effects of trauma is its erasure of the ability to speak. For one of the protagonists, this is literally the case. The two others feel the need to communicate and at the same time the impossibility of doing so. As Judith Herman puts it: "The conflict between the will to deny horrible events and the will to proclaim them aloud is the central dialectic of psychological trauma" (1).

Foer chooses to render his tale in three voices: the voice of Oskar Schell, a precocious nine-year-old boy who lost his father in the World Trade Center attacks, and the voices of his old and mutually estranged paternal grandparents, survivors of the Dresden firebombings. None of these voices is natural or normal. They are cracked and, to a large extent, also crackpot voices. The Schell family is so traumatized by the events of history that conventional utterance is no longer possible. Language is strained to the breaking point. Being forced to its expressive extremes of dense volubility, on the one hand, and ominous silence, on the other, it is barely capable of serving its traditional function as a vehicle of communication between the generations. The characters want to reach out to one another; the novel consists of their attempts to establish contact. Yet the essential experience that permeates the novel is that of ineluctable rupture. Family unity has fallen victim to the vicissitudes of history. This is a tale of people who struggle to stay in touch against the fact that their capacity to relate has been seriously compromised by misfortune. Their family history is so cut through with trauma that their pain, if it is expressible at all, can only be expressed extravagantly. "After a great catastrophe," writes Ulrich Baer, "the destruction might appear so vast that the functions of language and thought necessary for remembrance and reflection seem permanently disabled" (Baer, "Introduction," 4).

The three narratives alternate in an unchanging sequence: Oskar-Grandpa-Oskar-Grandma. The novel goes through this cycle four times and comes full circle with one last chapter by Oskar. This recurrent arrangement may seem contrived or mechanical, but, pivoting upon the tale of Oskar, the novel brings a significant part of the twentieth century within the purview of September 11.[1] Oskar's story is the 9/11 tale proper. To a large extent, the novel is the narrative of his grief. Shorn of much of its direct geopolitical significance, September 11 is imaged on the most intimate scale as a personal brokenness, concretized as the rupture between father and son. Within the economy of the novel, however, the loss of the father comes around as the replay of an earlier rupture between Grandpa and *his* son. As that rupture is embedded in the history of the twentieth century, 9/11 takes its place in a line of historical catastrophes. This seemingly apolitical family novel has history palimpsestically inscribed in every sentence.

History enters the novel emphatically as a series of linguistically encoded events, and September 11, as part of that history, fully participates in the dialectic that connects language to trauma. As an indication of the precarious hold language has over trauma, the linguistic status of 9/11 in the novel is characterized by indirection. The events themselves are described only briefly and at two removes, when Grandma and, separately, Grandpa watch the towers burn on television (225, 272) and when Oskar visits the Empire State Building and imagines what it would be like if a plane were to strike the building (244–45). Otherwise, the novel proceeds by analogy, parable, and metaphor. The special virtue of this technique, not always understood by reviewers who thought the novel's styling was too cute (Kirn, "Everything Is Included"; Updike, "Mixed Messages"; L. Miller, "Terror"; Gathman, "Novelist Trapped"),[2] is that it envelops the events of that Tuesday morning in metalanguage. Such metalanguage shies away from the brute facts, the stark "donnée" of thousands of lives lost. Instead, the creation of a special tone (the crackpot voices of the protagonists) and the mustering of visual, paralinguistic means of communication (photographs, blank pages, illegibly dark pages, pages in cipher) introduce the unsettling nature of the events into the very texture of the prose. The title of Foer's book, *Extremely Loud and Incredibly Close*, signals in and of itself an event that language can barely contain—something so extreme and incredible that it defies description. The disruptions in the texture of the text, the strangeness of its tone, and the pyrotechnic visual devices serve to underscore the incommunicability of experiences of extremity. This novel is full of secrets that cannot be spoken and secrets that are ultimately revealed. More significantly, the novel is full of ploys and devices that hamper the meaning-making process. Simultaneously, however, the interlocking episodes, which are told from several narrative vantage points by the alternating narrators, overlap and dovetail, and therefore the plot development enacts the emergence of meaning in the wake of an event that obliterates the means of creating meaning. In its very structure, the novel stages a radical decoding of reality followed by a significant recoding. While all available linguistic means are mobilized to evoke shock and lasting psychic disablement, at the same time the narrative fulfils the traditional redemptive function of putting things into perspective (LaCapra, *Writing History*, 156–57). In the quest little Oskar undertakes to come to grips with what happened, he finally succeeds in recoding or retranslating the events, which makes it possible to realign reality and allows for what Nicola King terms "the recognition of the past as past" (*Memory*, 31–32).

In the opinion of several reviewers, the tale of little Oskar is imaginatively fully realized, whereas the passages on Dresden are seen as long and unnecessary excursions (Greer, "Disaster Recovery"; Matthews, "9/11 Trauma"; Reese, "'Loud' Narrator"). Such a view loses sight of the dynamics of the novel—the way analogies and contrasts give weight to Oskar's endeavors and serve to demonstrate the full spectrum of possible reactions to trauma. In particular, the failures of his Grandma and especially his Grandpa to cope with their ordeals is a foil to Oskar's own more successfully completed struggle. Moreover, the Dresden episodes problematize the 9/11 terrorist attacks in that they place them outside the reach of facile political recuperation. Given Foer's own antecedents as an American of Jewish origin, and given the fact that his previous (and first) novel, *Everything Is Illuminated*, illustrates the link between language and the Holocaust, and given the fact that the elder Schells are victims of World War II, one would expect the central family in the novel to be Jewish. Yet Grandpa and Grandma are *German* survivors of the firebombing of Dresden by the English and American air forces in February 1945. This book, written by an American Jew, whose family was directly affected by the Holocaust, has *German* victims as its protagonists.[3] As the atomic bombing (again by the American air force) of Hiroshima also obliquely serves as a 9/11 analogue, the novel universalizes grief. Within a highly contentious political context, in which the Bush administration tried to instrumentalize the events of September 11 for its own partisan purposes and in which some commentators regard the terrorist attacks as an episode in a wider clash of civilizations, this book launches a strong plea for tolerance, refusing to take sides. Or, more precisely, it takes the side of the victims, irrespective of their national origin or allegiance. As such, the individualization of pain unsettles revanchist scenarios and speaks loud and clear against the nationalist recuperation of personal tragedies. The novel opposes its indirect, quasi-poetic treatment of 9/11 to a facile, fetishistic narrative that simplistically reduces the issues involved to a pitched battle of "us" versus "them" or good versus evil.

Constriction

The configuration of the novel is such that history, family experience, and the search for an appropriate means of communication are inextricably intertwined. The traumatized people at the center of this novel have experienced an event so shattering that it becomes nearly impossible to put their lives back together again. For that reason, they find themselves frozen in time. Grandma and Grandpa are the only ones in their families to survive Dresden. When by coincidence they meet seven years later in a New York bakery, they recognize each other because Grandma is the younger sister of Anna, Grandpa's fiancée in Dresden. More relevantly, they recognize each other (and quickly get married) because they are both people who have lost everything (30–33). The loss—as well as their shared love for Anna—is their common bond and the shaky grounds of their marriage. They live in their New York present, but they remain completely enthralled to their Dresden past. The dropping of the incendiary bombs and the wiping out of their families signaled the moment time came to a standstill. To say that they are haunted by the past is to understate the case. Every second of their existence is impregnated by horrors they cannot forget. When in the New York bakery Grandma accosts Grandpa, he at first denies that he is Thomas Schell: "But he did not admit to being who he was.   He never did" (81). In fact he is not Thomas Schell anymore, that is, the talkative, amiable and ambitious young man he was in an earlier time on a different continent. In another sense, however, he lives up to the implications of his name: after Dresden, he is only a "shell" of what he used to be (Mason, "Like Beavers," 24).

When Grandma proposes marriage to Grandpa—an "unnatural" reversion already of the "normal" course of events, whereby the man propositions the woman—he initially meets her proposal with laughter of derision (27, 28, 33). Their subsequent marriage is experienced by both of them as a "compromise" (84, 175)—a compromise with reality, fate, and trauma. By uniting their losses, they hope to give themselves a new lease on life and jointly to escape their pain. But Grandpa, in particular, is aware of the futility of the enterprise. The past throws such a long shadow that it voids the present. There is a willed quality to their "compromise," which foredooms the marriage and marks it with unceasing tension. In the old world Grandpa was a sculptor. The coincidental meeting with Grandma in New York jolts him into resuming his activities, and their courtship consists mainly of her sitting for him. He spends a very long time putting her in the right position: "He spent ten full minutes bending and unbending my knee. He closed and unclosed my hands" (84). This posing becomes an elaborate foreplay that leads to the sexual consummation of their relationship. But sex (always performed *a tergo* and without looking at each other [177]) is nothing but a move of desperation. The marriage is fated to fail from the very beginning: Grandma is aware that, in sculpting her, Grandpa is "trying to make me so he could fall in love with me" (84). Moreover, as the sessions proceed, it becomes obvious that Grandpa is not so much sculpting Grandma as the image of her dead sister Anna, his one true love for whom Grandma is but a poor substitute.

The marriage of Grandpa and Grandma is an enactment of the unsuccessful attempt of the protagonists to release themselves from the burden of an onerous and unusable past. They are well meaning toward each other and full of goodwill: "I would get his slippers. He would make my tea" (176). They hope that this reciprocal consideration, plus an elaborate set of house rules, will be enough to reach a modus vivendi. But their very kindness is so deliberate that it becomes a symptom of their pathology: "I would turn up the heat so he could turn up the air conditioner so I could turn up the heat" (176). The present consists of a series of failed attempts to drown the past in the trivialities of the everyday. Beyond that, husband and wife cooperate in a conspiracy of silence. They "never talk about the past," "never listen to sad music," "never watch television shows about sick children" (108). By denying there was trauma in their lives, they hope to escape the worst ravages of memory. The result is a massive case of emotional arrest and what in trauma theory is called "constriction." As Judith Herman puts it: "The effort to ward off intrusive symptoms, though self-protective in intent, further aggravates the post-traumatic syndrome, for the attempt to avoid reliving the trauma too often results in a narrowing of consciousness, a withdrawal from engagement with others, and an impoverished life" (*Trauma and Recovery*, 42). When every aspect of life is permeated by trauma, running away from trauma is running away from life. By throttling their pain, Grandpa and Grandma throttle themselves.

At best, their married life provides a sense of camaraderie (as they are fellow veterans in the struggle against trauma and depression). At worst, it is the cold mockery of a marriage—a lie to protect each other and themselves. They establish strict rules to make the mutual frostiness manageable: "when she gets up to go to the shower, I feed the animals . . . when she gets undressed, I've never been so busy in my life" (109). They cannot cope with marital nudity because they cannot face the unvarnished truth of their estrangement. Early in the marriage they decide to divide the apartment into Nothing and Something Places. A Nothing Place is a spot they are forbidden to look at. As such, it is a place of "complete privacy . . . in which one could temporarily cease to exist" (110). Far from being a place of bliss and oblivion, however, such a Nothing Place demonstrates the devastation history wreaks on personal lives. It is a place of total isolation where, unhampered by human interaction, Grandpa and Grandma are completely absorbed by the past and fully act out the traumas of their existence. First, there is one such Nothing Place in the apartment. Before too long, as grief proliferates and melancholy expands, the newlyweds are surrounded by more Nothing than Something Places. They believe that all the self-imposed and protective regulations, which fix their lives and turn their relationship into "a marriage of millimeters, of rules" (109), will be able to make their existence, if not enjoyable, at least bearable: "Everything was forever fixed, there would be only peace and happiness" (111). But soon they realize they themselves are dwindling into Nothingness (111). As their present is being usurped by their past, their lives turn stale and remain stationary.

The first rule Grandpa imposes—at the very moment Grandma speaks of marriage—is that they will have no children (85). Later we learn the reason for such life-denying injunction. When Grandpa's true love, Anna, was killed in the Dresden bombings, she was bearing his child. After having lost the love of his life and their love child, Grandpa has become basically loveless. He heavily insures all his material property (174). But he is no longer capable of making an emotional investment in people. When, against the terms of their agreement, Grandma, in an attempt to pick up the pieces of her life, feels the need for a child and by a ruse gets pregnant, Grandpa packs up and stealthily leaves, returning to the ultimate Nothing Place, the place from which he has never been able to escape: Dresden. America—very much a highly visible Something Place with a firm grasp on the real—fails to work its transformative magic. In the case of Grandpa, the move to the New World (the absorption into an aspirational culture) entails no second chance or emotional rebirth. Not coincidentally, Grandpa and Grandma meet each other for the first time at the Columbian Bakery on Broadway (28). The name of the bakery and of the street evoke the promise of the American Dream—the hope that life will open up and new discoveries are in store. In their case, the dream fails to take hold and New York, as a place, has no special appeal.

Forfeiting love, Grandpa also forfeits life. His true self died in the firebombing, and only a shell survives. Any number of times he alludes to the "life that [he] didn't want to lose but lost and ha[s] to remember" (109). "Life is scarier than death" (322), he tells his grandson. To his son, he writes: "I can't live, I've tried and I can't" (135). As a self-flagellating mantra he repeats variant versions of the same insight: "I'd lost the only person [Anna] I could have spent my only life with" (33). He indicates that if he had two lives he would have spent one of them "among the living" (133). But he has only one life and he has no choice but to spend it among the dead. He is defeatist about his options and stuck in sterile excuses. Aware of his plight and of his flight from responsibility, he keeps reiterating how sorry he is. At his first meeting with his future wife at the bakery in New York, he writes: "I don't speak. . . . I'm sorry" (30, 81). When he realizes that Thomas Schell Jr.—the son he abandoned before his birth—died in the World Trade Center collapse, he returns to New York after an absence of almost forty years. The first thing he does is to leave a note for his wife with the doorman; it says, "I'm sorry" (233, 274). When some time afterward he finally comes face to face with Oskar, his grandson, his first statement is, again, "I'm sorry" (237, 280). His wish to have more lives than the one he is stuck in, testifies to a longing to put an end to trauma, to give it a place with the rest of his memories and experiences. But such placing proves to be impossible. He realizes he has failed the people around him, but he cannot do more, time and again, than express his regret and lamely apologize. "I'm sorry," he writes to his son, "That's what I've been trying to say, I'm sorry for everything" (132).[4]

In his unresolvable cathexis to trauma, Grandpa is not so much a character as the embodiment of an idea (Greer, "Disaster Recovery"). He has become the impersonation of constriction, and as such he is what E. M. Forster famously called "a flat character" (Forster, *Aspects*, 65–75). Unchangingly, he exhibits in full the long-lasting effects of a historical wound. His flatness as a character demonstrates the diminution of his existence as a result of an unwaning traumatic obsession. Far from being an artistic lack or fault, the flatness of the character of Grandpa proves Foer's acquaintance with and utmost respect for the essence of trauma: its inescapability. The achievement in creating the figure of Grandpa is that, as a character, he is flat and yet irreducibly tragic.[5]

Language

Grandpa's constriction is literalized by the fact that, as a direct result of what happened to him in Dresden, he is struck with aphasia. The affliction grows on him gradually, beginning with his inability to pronounce "Anna" (16). The first word he loses is the name of his fiancée. The second word he is incapable of uttering is "and," probably because it so much resembles Anna's name (16) but also because his falling apart paralyzes the faculty of aggregation (of putting things in a logical sequence). The last word he loses is "I" (17). In step with his contracting verbal universe, his world also shrinks, till he is totally self-centered:

> I would walk around the neighborhood saying, "I I I I." "You want a cup of coffee, Thomas?" "I." "And maybe something sweet?" "I." "How about this weather?" "I." "You look upset. Is anything wrong?" I wanted to say, "Of course," I wanted to ask, "Is anything right?" I wanted to pull the thread, unravel the scarf of my silence and start again from the beginning, but instead I said, "I." (17)

These Beckettian exchanges (Lanham, "Wistful Novel") poignantly illustrate how, robbed of the means to reach out, Grandpa is imprisoned in the puny finality of a reduced selfhood. In a big city the incentives and verbal clues from the outside come fast and furious. But in his case, they are all deadened by an all-encompassing solipsism, sharply and graphically delineated by the word "I." Standing alone in inverted commas and ineluctably followed by a full stop, this marker of identity signals utter loneliness. Grandpa is incapable of making a break with the past and starting again from the beginning. Instead of coming to terms with what happened and then, in a second move, carrying on with his life, he seeks to suppress his memory of "Anna." Thus suppressing his experience of trauma (rather than working it through), he cuts himself off from the world. Step by step, such isolation leads to catastrophic self-absorption.

Grandpa undertakes desperate attempts to stay in touch with the world. But these efforts are so erratic that, rather than diminishing his sequestration, they underscore the damage caused by the loss of language. Once the ability to talk has completely vanished, he communicates by jotting down terse phrases in an endless series of daybooks: "I want two rolls" (19); "And I wouldn't say no to something sweet" (20); "I'm sorry, this is the smallest I've got" (21); "Start spreading the news . . ." (22); "The regular, please" (23). These snippets of language are the thin threads by which he hangs on to a semblance of normalcy. His life is strung out in random, decontextualized phrases, which are emblematic of his foreshortened existence. When he runs out of pages to scribble on, he has to make do with the phrases jotted down before:

> It wasn't unusual for me to run out of blank pages before the end of the day, so should I have to say something to someone on the street or in the bakery or at the bus stop, the best I could do was flip back through the daybook and find the most fitting page to recycle, if someone asked me, "How are you feeling?" it might be that my best response was to point at, "The regular, please," or perhaps, "And I wouldn't say no to something sweet," when my only friend, Mr. Richter, suggested, "What if you tried to make a sculpture again? What's the worst thing that could happen?" I shuffled halfway into the filled book: "I'm not sure, but it's late." (28)

The preused phrases illustrate the bad fit between a severely truncated language and the everyday demands of expression. When even the most momentous decisions—such as those pertaining to his marriage with Grandma (33)—have to be negotiated through the narrowed channel of scribbled-down and recycled words, one realizes the extent to which Grandpa's world and self-expression have shriveled up. Literally, he is a captive in the prison house of his impoverished language.

In order to facilitate communication, Grandpa has the words "YES" and "NO" tattooed on his left and right hands, respectively. Thus he develops a rudimentary sign language, whereby he indicates assent or dissent by lifting one hand or the other. This gesture involves him in an inescapable binary logic that prevents him from situating his ideas somewhere in the large zone between yes and no, where most common opinions are to be found. Trauma has deprived him of more than the capacity to talk; the aphasia also makes it impossible to make considerate judgments (257). Where such a shrinking of options leaves him in the larger scheme of things is expressed through some of the visuals in the novel. The dust jacket of the hardback and the cover of the paperback edition both feature a hand—the five fingers fully stretched out—that is scribbled full of information. In sharp contrast, the photograph of the hand of a skeleton (155) indicates how death manifests itself as a semiotic void. The picture of Grandpa's gnarled hands (260–61)—the "YES" and "NO" clearly visible—shows exactly where he stands: having left a full existence behind him, his half-life is a way station en route to death. The stark logic of yes and no is only one step away from total annihilation (including total muteness).

At one particular point—at the exact point Grandpa feels the tug of family enough to return from Dresden to New York and look up the immediate relatives of his son—Grandpa calls Grandma on the telephone from the airport and, on the spur of the moment, decides to tell her everything: "why I'd left, where I'd gone, . . . why I'd come back, and what I needed to do with the time I had left" (269). He intends to reveal "the sum of [his] life" (269) to her. But this is how it comes out:

6,9,6,2,6,3,4,7,3,5,4,3,2,5,8,6,2,6,3,4,5,8,7,8,2,7,7,4,8,3,3,2,8,8,4,3,2,4,7,7,6,7,8, 4,6,3,3,3,8,6,3,4,6,3,7,3,4,6,5,3,5,7!

And so on, for more than two pages of text. Not being able to speak, Grandpa presses the numbers on the keypad of the touch-tone phone, which results in Grandma hearing nothing but a long series of differently pitched beeps, while the reader is confronted with a long passage, presumably of great import but wrapped in an unbreakable code. (The first numbers can be deciphered as: "my name is." After that, the effort at decipherment is greater than can be expected from even the most assiduous reader). Grandpa is "trying to destroy the wall between [him] and [his] life with [his] finger" (272). But he cannot be heard. His moment of utter forthrightness is also the moment of total incomprehension.

His most elaborate attempt to break out of his linguistic confinement consists of a great number of lengthy letters he writes daily for more than forty years from Dresden between May 1963 and September 2003. These letters are addressed to his son (first unborn, then growing up, then dead), but, although Grandpa holds on to these letters religiously, they are, with one notable exception, never sent. Instead, every day Grandma receives an empty envelope, which she, in her turn, stashes away until one day Oskar finds them. These letters, elaborate but undelivered, form the powerful symbol of a filial connection that is strong, irreducible, renewed daily, and yet empty. The kinship tie between a traumatized and absentee father and the abandoned son is close and emotion-laden, but it does not yield a fullness of affection or experience. It never matures into a dialogue.

The psychoanalyst Dori Laub has pointed out the importance of the sympathetic listener in the therapeutic process. He assigns the listener the role of cocreator in the liberating trauma narrative. It is only in the presence of a listener that the narrative can emerge and "the 'knowing' of the event is given birth to" (Felman and Laub, *Testimony*, 57). Thus the listener is "the enabler of testimony—the one who triggers its initiation, as well as the guardian of its process and its momentum" (58). Without a listener, the trauma remains unuttered and thus unconquered. It is only in the course of a dialogue that the victim or witness can discover the event that he or she has repressed and is not able to acknowledge. The listener is an indispensable part of the heuristic enterprise: without a listener, there is no uncovering of the secret, and thus no cure for the festering wound.

The peculiar nature of Grandpa's letters is that they are written for an audience (his son), but an audience that remains out of reach. For the reader of the novel, the letters are an important source of information. In fact, they make up the sum total of the Grandpa chapters. Grandpa delivers his tale in epistolary form. But as intransitive messages, the letters are put, as it were, *sous rature*. They lead a virtual existence and balance on the cusp of expression. Clearly written under great internal pressure, they express what Grandpa finds incommunicable even to his closest relative. In them, he speaks his secrets, but in such a way that nobody can hear. He admits in yet another unuttered admission to his son (by then deceased) that he created "a trail of things I wasn't able to tell you, it might have made my load possible, but I couldn't" (274). The letters contain the load of memory, misery, and guilt from which Grandpa cannot unburden himself because there is nobody to unburden to.

Without a listener Grandpa cannot truly constitute himself as a witness, and, as a result, he remains deprived of the therapeutic potential of testimony. This becomes obvious when, after his return to New York, he and Oskar exhume the empty coffin of his son and fill it with the unsent letters he has hauled with him from Dresden. At the 9/11 victim's graveside, the three generations—grandfather, father, and son—are reunited. But the reunion is posthumous and more symbolical than real. As it is marked by absence and loss, the improvised ceremony fails to unclench Grandpa's uptight feelings or to bring about a definitive catharsis. After the reburial ritual, even though originally he planned to join his family in the States for good (268), Grandpa wants to go back to Dresden. His is a wound that a deed of symbolic reconciliation will not heal. Burying his secrets does not enable him to renew his married life or make a lasting connection with his newfound grandson. Coming to terms with 9/11 cannot heal what Dresden has destroyed.

The unsent letters themselves bear out Grandpa's cathexis to trauma in every sentence. They illustrate the impossibility of a sustained concentration on the events taking place in the immediacy of the present. The actual circumstances of his existence only set the stage for intrusive memories from the past. The result is a tale that spills onto the page without much rational control or order and with no paragraph breaks. The flow of thought is interrupted here and there by a full stop or, just as frequently, by a question mark. Mostly sentences are strung together by means of commas, which suggest a breathlessness, a great forward surge of emotion, the unleashing of pent-up thought: "The beautiful girl didn't know the time, she was in a hurry, she said, 'Good luck,' I smiled, she hurried off, her skirt catching the air as she ran, sometimes I can hear my bones straining under the weight of all of the lives I'm not living" (113). This particular scene is set in 1963, when Grandpa finds himself in a New York airport about to leave for Dresden. By means of his daybook he asks passers-by, "Excuse me, do you know what time it is?" (112). The question, coyly phrased, is proof of his Old World civility. As there is a big clock in the departure hall (178), it is also a completely unnecessary question—a line Grandpa uses to establish contact with strangers. At the same time it is a symbolic expression of his own confused wavering between past and present. Symbolically, he does not know what time it is. His fixation on the past stands in sharp contrast to the manners of the beautiful American girl, who moves untethered to time yet in a hurry (making the most of time). Her lightheartedness and joie de vivre—"her skirt catching the air as she ran"—asyndetically clash with the crushing weight of his own nonlife. The girl represents the "good luck" he is deprived of. She embodies the carelessness and the promise that he can no longer share.

Grandpa's question—"do you know what time it is?"—also relates to the problem of audience. It carries apocalyptic overtones, as it seems to imply that only someone with Grandpa's experience of history as horror truly knows "what time it is." Part of Grandpa's desperation (and a different kind of muteness) results from the fact that in a happy-go-lucky United States there is no room for tales of woe.[6] He can only address the American girl at the most superficial level of meaning. She responds alertly and politely enough but only because he hides from her his true story. In the superefficient, high-tech environment of a modern airport, there is no way to recall the rain of incendiary bombs. The macabre side of aviation is so far removed from anybody's attention—the airport environment so highly sanitized—that there is no way Grandpa can even begin to communicate what is really on his mind.

As a result, his enduring trauma does not come out in utterance or proclamation. It lives covertly in the interstices of his writing, as every description in the letters has the air of looking back. In Grandpa's case, the "writing of the disaster" takes the form of a phrasing that is claustrophobic, missing the dimension of a possible future. Even when reporting on the narrated present, Grandpa writes retrospectively:

> In this life, I'm sitting in an airport trying to explain myself to my unborn son, I'm filling the pages of this, my last daybook, I'm thinking of a loaf of black bread that I left out one night, the next morning I saw the outline of the mouse that had eaten through it, I cut the loaf into slices and saw the mouse at each moment, I'm thinking of Anna, I would give everything never to think about her again, I can only hold on to the things I want to lose. (113)

Inevitably, Grandpa's thoughts wander back to the experience of lack and loss. His activities in the here and now (filling the pages of his daybook in an attempt to explain himself to his son the moment he is about to desert him) are a function of his memory. The present continuous merely serves to indicate how trauma has left its imprint on every slice of his life. The writing turns allegorical (the little parable of the mouse), it slackens to the point of commonplace and cliché ("I would give everything never to think about her again"), it tautens again and veers towards the apothegmatic ("I can only hold on to the things I want to lose").

But always the focus is on what was and no longer is. Inexorably, the summary exchange with the beautiful American girl, rather than providing a *punctum* of momentary enjoyment, is but a conduit for his pained recollection of Anna and the vanished world she stands for. Grandpa's observations never escape the grasp of repetition compulsion, and even present occupations constitute the acting out of the unclaimable trauma. As LaCapra puts it: "In acting out, tenses implode, and it is as if one were back there in the past reliving the traumatic scene" (*Writing History*, 21).

The most vivid letter Grandpa writes is the one he does send off to his then fifteen-year-old son. It contains a gripping description of the night of the firebombing in 1945—the night that for Grandpa "has no beginning or end" (208). In many ways, this is the central chapter of the book. It constitutes the direct writing of the disaster. But, in a sophisticated and partly hidden way, it also demonstrates the limits of such directness. First of all, the letter establishes a particularly close connection between language and history, in that it is imagined only in part. In composing this chapter of the novel, Foer relies on easily traceable Internet sources, which yet go unacknowledged.[7] While this may raise questions about copyrights and deontological legitimacy, the lifting of phrases and details from the testimony of firsthand witnesses to the Dresden bombing brings the text closer to actual reality. The author has availed himself of his right to use historical sources and embroider upon them. Yet one might have expected Foer to mention his sources not only as a matter of fairness and courtesy but also as an indication of his rhetorical strategy. In a novel in which visual and textual devices abound in an attempt to render desperate circumstances, the merger of Grandpa's testimony with that of real-life victims is one more ploy to defeat muteness and silence. It is not that Foer has simply plagiarized his sources. He has taken snippets of historical language and embellished upon them. His language is an intervention in the historical process and it contends that, in extremis, the historical record does not suffice as adequate testimony. It needs the complement of the writer's creativity, which, in its turn, feeds off the facts as rendered by first-hand witnesses. From a historical point of view, the letter is a fake or rather half a fake. From the literary point of view, it constitutes plagiarism or partial plagiarism. Its ambiguity points to the uneasy relationship between language and history. In order to be fully effective, the directness of first-hand testimony is absorbed into a wider mesh of fictional meaning.

Yet even so, within the fictional universe in which it functions, the letter misfires. It comes to us with the marks of the son's reading upon it. Using red pencil, Thomas Jr. has marked up the letter, indicating misspellings and doubtful punctuation but also phrases that struck him. The numerous markings convey the sense of a letter that has been read and reread and of which every nuance has been scanned and every implied meaning scrutinized. The letter constitutes more than Grandpa's most intense effort at speaking his trauma (and Foer's most arduous attempt to approximate historical reality). It also bears the traces of the obsessive attention that has been heaped upon it by the son (277). Sender and receiver have extended themselves to their utmost ability. From both sides, there is an undeniable longing to reach out and connect. And yet the communication fails. After reading the letter, Thomas Schell Jr. travels to Germany to see Thomas Schell Sr. But the meeting comes to naught: "The room was filled with conversations we weren't having." (278). Words are not able to heal the rift that historical circumstances have created. The son does not even reveal himself as the son but poses as a reporter. The letter is Grandpa's attempt to establish a paternal bond, but the son refuses the identification. As Dori Laub puts it: "The absence of an empathic listener, or more radically, the absence of an *addressable other*, an other who can hear the anguish of one's memories and thus affirm and recognize their realness, annihilates the story" (Felman and Laub, *Testimony*, 68). Grandpa's tale, in a way, is a non-tale: it fails to complete itself in the presence of an interlocutor. For all its vividness (derived from its closeness to the historical record), the letter falls on deaf ears. Though full of affect, it is without effect.

This annihilation of narratable content is given visual proof in Grandpa's last letter. The onward rush of his impressions ultimately ends in total nonarticulation and darkness. In this last letter (which again goes unsent) he repeatedly expresses the fear of running out of space and out of time (276, 279, 280, 281): "There won't be enough pages in this book for me to tell you what I need to tell you" (276). He starts to leave less and less space between the lines till the lines start running into each other. Finally his writing is so compressed—and the urgency propelling him forward so great—that the text becomes illegible and the page turns black. This dark page is the completion of Grandpa's blank voice: muteness and semiotic overload share the condition of incomprehensibility, and for Grandpa, losing his words has the same effect as this overabundance of words. Both result in the erasure of communicability. The darkened page is a visible illustration of the writing of disaster as an impossibility. It represents the dead end of constriction and Grandpa's total isolation. In his blackened page, the writing of the disaster reaches complete aporia: the more he wants to get across on the page, the less gets through. After the writing becomes illegible, Grandpa yet goes on scribbling for a full three pages—each page turning blacker than the previous one. His perseverance underscores what has been obvious all along: he writes only for himself. His intransitive writing is the most negative form of self-absorption. His prose is self-destructive.

The Void

Grandma, like Grandpa, is a prisoner of the past. The gap that separates her from her life in Europe is so large that it has become immeasurable. The seven years that elapsed between the firebombing and her meeting Grandpa in New York "were not seven years. They were not seven hundred years. Their length could not be measured in years, just as an ocean could not explain the distance we have traveled, just as the dead can never be counted" (81). In her mind, Dresden has become an absolute event, so totalizing in its impact that it no longer has a definable place in space or time. So present and pressing is the past that, when she meets Grandpa for the first time in New York, Grandma is suicidal, about to throw herself into the Hudson (82). It is only the hope that his sudden appearance will be restorative that keeps her alive: "His attention filled the hole in the middle of me" (83). Grandpa will inspire her to attempt to readjust to life. From the beginning, this attempt is marked by an effort to find a language capable of lifting her out of her self-imposed confinement. The courtship with Grandpa is carried out in German, but after they have made love for the first time they switch to English: "We never used German again" (85). Grandma realizes the past is irrecoverable. German is a thing of the past. The use of English, however, does not become the significant token of her integration into the New World, as it does for most immigrants. Instead, it becomes the measure of her lasting unhappiness and alienation.

At first, Grandma avidly reads magazines, because she wants "to learn American expressions" (175) and "become a real American" (79). Soon, though, she realizes that she'll never fit in. She gives up on her attempts to acquire a native command of the language, but she has picked up enough slang to give voice to her paradoxical, in-between existence. Over and over again, she repeats: "My eyes are crummy" (30, 81, 119, 124, 176, 179, 233, 307, 309). The often reiterated phrase is a sign of her longed-for, nascent Americanness. Its idiomatic, slangy nature promises or projects a shift in identity away from her burdened European origins and toward an altered and improved existence in the New World. Yet she invokes this colloquial formula not so much to refer literally to poor eyesight as to indicate that in her new place of residence she is disoriented and ill at ease. The clash between the slang of the phrase and its depressing content reflects Grandma's suspension between the future and the past. She cannot fully adapt to the circumstances of the here and now because she remains blinded by what happened to her years before in Europe. There is nothing she can see properly anymore. Even when she watches the events of 9/11 unfold on television, she is occupied with memories of Dresden. The imprint of the past is so strong that even the most spectacular event in the present is not able to absorb her completely (225–28, 232).

At Grandpa's suggestion, she tries out a writing therapy "to relieve the burden" (119). For years on end she withdraws into the guest room, a Nothing Place (119), to work on her memoirs. Grandpa recalls his own exultation at hearing her typing away:

> I was so happy for her, I remembered the feeling she was feeling, the exhilaration of building the world anew, I heard from behind the door the sounds of creation, the letters pressing into the paper, the pages being pulled from the machine, everything being, for once, better than it was and as good as it could be, everything full of meaning.   (119–20)

Foer builds up the expectation that writing will provide a catharsis, that, through the word, Grandma's life will blossom out and she will be able to give a full reckoning of herself. He charges language to the limits of expressiveness only to point out the limits of language. When Grandma shows the finished product of her labors, it is obvious she has delivered nothing but hundreds and hundreds of blank pages. Later she explains: "I went to the guest room and pretended to write.   I hit the space bar again and again.   My life story was spaces" (176). In the terms of Giorgio Agamben, Grandma's life is pure *zoē*, bare living—as opposed to *bios*, which is "the form or way of living proper to an individual or a group" (Agamben, *Homo Sacer*, 1). "We spent our lives making livings" (175), Grandma says. Language has no grip on such mere subsistence, which reveals itself as a blank. The essential ambiguity of trauma is exposed in that for Grandma the past is all-determining and yet cannot be articulated. More precisely, it is all-determining *because* it cannot be articulated. As long as trauma is not narrativized, as long as it cannot be told, it comes across as a blank and keeps obliterating the present. In the words of Anne Cubilié (from another context), the empty pages refer "to the silence that structures the testimony of so many survivors" (Cubilié, *Women Witnessing*, 10).[8]

The blank pages of Grandma's autobiography complement Grandpa's blackened pages. They both illustrate the sterility of expression turned inward, the limits of language and the ineffability of trauma. Yet Foer has gendered the discourse of the two grandparents. While Grandma cannot "relieve the burden" through writing, she is able to overcome constriction in order to fulfill the duties of motherhood. The breakthrough comes when she realizes: "I could compromise my life, but not life after me" (177). She can give herself up to the blankness of existence, but she has a responsibility for the coming generations. That is when she decides to get pregnant. Accordingly, it is the presence of the son and of Oskar, the son of the son, which triggers the ultimate unburdening and, finally, allows her to place trauma within language. While Grandpa's unsent letters dim into illegibility, she finds an interlocutor in Oskar to whom she addresses a long message. Unlike Grandpa, she does not write to someone she has abandoned and from whom she has become estranged but to someone whom she loves deeply and to whom her life is dedicated. Her long message is not intransitive. As such, it adds up not to mere self-release but to significant communication. Grandma has mostly hidden her past from Oskar (105), presumably to spare his feelings. In her letter, she can talk abundantly about her background and thus constitute herself as a subject, since there is, potentially, a sympathetic listener: "The words are coming so easily" (313); "the pages are coming easily" (313).

Her writing style in this long letter to Oskar is characterized by very short (often one-sentence) paragraphs. And she is still inordinately fond of the space bar, as each sentence is separated from the next by a large blank spot. The result is a page that consists largely of whiteness. The page, in other words, is a filled-in emptiness. The conspicuous spaces between the sentences stand for the hiatuses in her life, the voids everything is centered around and the silence out of which she speaks. But at least there is expression (as opposed to darkened pages or a blank autobiography). In addressing her grandson, Grandma has created something out of nothing. The very layout of the page is testimony to the slow, painstaking genesis of the word—the laborious victory of the survivor over the muteness of traumatic experience. The scattered arrangement of the verbal traces of pain illustrates the agonistic relation between the memory of trauma and the need to reconnect with the world and establish intimacy through language.

This dialectic between language as fulfillment and language as a blank or, to put it differently, between expression and silence finds its apogee in the last Grandma chapter. Her traumatic experience prompts her to dream of time doubling back upon itself so that history swerves away from its destined end: "In my dream, all of the collapsed ceilings reformed above us.   The fire went back into the bombs, which rose up and into the bellies of planes whose propellers turned backwards" (306–7). She acts out a fantasy, which, according to Sandra M. Gilbert, is found frequently among trauma victims or witnesses: the belief that "if it were only possible to run the film backward . . . , the inexorable plot of what-has-been might magically modulate into what-didn't-happen" ("Writing Wrong," 262).[9] Given that Grandma's world was wiped out, her wish to go back to her previous innocence is understandable. Yet Grandma takes this regression to its ultimate consequence. She dreams of reversing the book of Genesis and undoing the very creation:

> God brought together the land and the water, the sky and the water, the water and the water, evening and morning, something and nothing.
> He said, Let there be light.
> And there was darkness.   (313)

The attempt to radically revise history (in an effort to escape it) ends in a return to undifferentiated nothingness. In allowing language to propel her backward in time, Grandma discovers the limits of the compensatory imagination. To prefer dreaming and wish fulfillment over engagement with the world *as is* leads to eternal darkness. Her fantasy is an example of what the psychoanalyst Adrienne Harris calls "melancholic imagining"

("Relational Mourning," 149): her wish-dreams testify to an unassimilated past and are part of nonadaptive post-traumatic behavior. Over and against this, language can point in the other direction. It can signal an escape from trauma that is not illusory but grounded in restored trust and togetherness. Grandma ends her letter to Oskar by articulating what ultimately gives meaning to her life and, in this sense, truly counteracts the devastations of history:

> Here is the point of everything I have been trying to tell you, Oskar. . . .
> I love you,
> Grandma (314)

In these simple sentences (the last ones by Grandma in the novel), Grandma mentions herself and her grandson by name. Thus she establishes the articulation of mutual affection as the enabling condition for a renewed assertion of the self in relationship to the other. In this affirmation of a close family bond, she takes possession of her own being and her own present. In communicating to her grandson the lesson that life has taught her (the point of everything she has been trying to tell him), she demonstrates the undoing of the Dresden experience. Dresden is not annulled through daydreaming about the reversal of time. It is annulled in real time through the strengthening of intimate emotional attachments. As Judith Herman writes about trauma victims: "Their sense of self has been shattered. That sense can be rebuilt only as it was built initially, in connection with others" (*Trauma and Recovery*, 61).

Quest

When Oskar loses his father in the World Trade Center attacks, he looks for ways to recoup his loss. His effort is complicated by the fact that he did not just lose his father; he also failed him. When Oskar gets home from school ahead of his mother on September 11, he finds five messages from his father on the answering machine. From these increasingly fragmentary messages, it appears that Thomas Schell Jr. is trapped in the burning tower above the impact zone and is desperately trying to establish contact with his family. After listening to these messages, Oskar decides to hide them from his mother and grandmother in order to spare their feelings. While he carries this secret knowledge around as a burden, there is something else and even more serious that fuels his shame and guilt: after he gets home, the phone rings yet another time. He knows it is his father calling in distress and yet he is unable to answer: "He needed me, and I couldn't pick up. I just couldn't pick up. I just couldn't" (301). At the time of the terrorist attacks, little Oskar was a precocious and, in many respects, weird nine-year-old. But in many other respects, he was also an all-American kid, involved in run-of-the-mill American activities: collecting all sorts of stuff, listening to the tales of his father, participating in the daily drama of school and hobbies. September 11 puts an abrupt end to all of that. He now has to struggle with the trauma of losing his father, plus the secret of the phone messages and the feeling of having abandoned his father in his hour of need. What also weighs on him is the fact that in the final phone messages his father took his leave without once saying "I love you" (207).

As a result, he is at a loss, adrift: "A lot of the time I'd get that feeling like I was in the middle of a huge black ocean, or in deep space, but not in the fascinating way" (36). The whole task of Foer's novel is to describe a normalcy that has been brutally interrupted. The novel is the materialization of the condition of abnormality as a result of a devastating loss, projected against the family's larger losses and further abnormalities. Again, as with Grandpa and Grandma, this abnormality declares itself as a linguistic condition. Trauma reveals itself as a series of symptoms and coping mechanisms that are deeply inscribed into language.

The peculiar property of this novel is that, through indirection, the voice of the young protagonist is identified with trauma. His linguistic behavior is permeated by pain and sorrow. Some reviewers have missed out on that. The accusation of cuteness that has been leveled against the book is totally beside the point once one realizes that Oskar's quirky sayings are dodges and evasions, inspired by his simultaneous need to face up to his situation and to repress it. He uses euphemisms to refer to his condition: September 11 becomes "the worst day"; when he feels depressed, he is wearing "heavy boots"; when he feels the sting of guilt, "he gives himself a bruise." As deflective linguistic mechanisms, these coinages are on a par with the inappropriate and silly jokes he makes during his father's funeral. Most of all, his desperation shines through as he incessantly comes up with weird fantasies and inventions. These inventions come across as an obsessive linguistic tic. Oskar starts inventing things after 9/11 at a feverish pace, and then he cannot stop (36). This compulsive indulgence in excess compensatory imagination is so intrusive and the inventions themselves often so weird and off-the-wall that they color the whole novel. In fact, the narrative opens with one such madcap series of inventions, which deserves to be quoted at length:

> What about a teakettle? What if the spout opened and closed when the steam came out, so it would become a mouth, and it could whistle pretty melodies, or do Shakespeare, or just crack up with me? I could invent a teakettle that reads in Dad's voice, so I could fall asleep, or maybe a set of kettles that sings the chorus of "Yellow Submarine," which is a song by the Beatles, who I love, because entomology is one of my *raisons d'être*, which is a French expression that I know. Another good thing is that I could train my anus to talk when I farted. If I wanted to be extremely hilarious, I'd train it to say, "Wasn't me!" every time I made an incredibly bad fart. And if I ever made an incredibly bad fart in the Hall of Mirrors, which is in Versailles, which is outside of Paris, which is in France, obviously, my anus would say, "*Ce n'étais* [*sic*] *pas moi!*"　　　　　　　　　　(1)

As the opening of a 9/11 novel, such a passage obviously holds major risks. Foer has opted to present trauma in a goofy fashion. The contrast with Grandpa's morbid lucubrations or Grandma's belabored efforts at expressiveness could not be greater. Yet the playfulness—recurring as mood and tone throughout Oskar's chapters, skirting gimmickry and superficiality—acquires a tart edge and slowly reveals itself as a pathological condition. The inventions are an oblique way to refer to the loss of his father and an index to the young boy's extreme distress.

From the very first, Oskar's inventions speak to his intent to reinvent the world, to live in a world that has remained free from trauma, in which the unthinkable has not yet happened. He wants to make reality malleable so that it conforms to his desires. In particular, he wants his father to come back to life. Apart from a kettle that speaks in his dad's voice, he also "invents" microphones that register heartbeats (1), a birdseed shirt that would keep the wearer aloft (2), and "air bags for skyscrapers" (160). Among many other things, he "designs" "a Nature Hike Anklet, which leaves a trail of bright yellow dye when you walk, so in case you get lost, you can find your way back" (106). His inventions concern love and death and the need for transparency in a world that has gone suddenly murky. They are all about connectedness and the need to stay in touch. Many of these inventions are whimsical, but most are related, in one way or the other, to his fears and his grief. The death of his father permeates his every thought, and the inventions are proof of a morbid obsession. Oskar's smart-aleck demeanor—flaunting his knowledge of French and the arcana of entomology—is but a front. His showing off is a way to impress his deceased father. The inventions, in other words, are a posthumous dialogue, as intransitive as Grandpa's letters or Grandma's autobiography. They form the symptoms of a repetition compulsion, appropriately cast in an infantile key.

Elaborate as they are, Oskar's inventions are part of his problem or a symptom of his condition. In itself, the quirky syntax in which they are rendered in the opening passage quoted above shows a mind out of whack, tottering on the verge of insanity. If, nonetheless, Oskar's reaction to trauma turns out to be more salutary than that of his Grandma and especially his Grandpa, it is because, inspired by the words of his father, he sets out on a quest. "No type of story is more instantly recognisable to us than a Quest," writes Christopher Booker (*Seven Basic Plots*, 69). In depicting the coping mechanisms that Oskar marshals to counteract trauma, Foer uses all the traditional elements of the quest: the call to action, the dangers incurred, the helpers who assist in the effort but may also hinder it, and finally the last ordeal that leads the quester to his goal. In the Oskar chapters, the delivery plot of the 9/11 novel is reminiscent of children's stories but at the same time also resonates with overtones from the most canonical world literature. In both plot and tone, Foer manages to present serious grief in a frivolous guise.

A quest almost always begins with "a call": "The Quest usually begins on a note of the most urgent compulsion. For the hero to remain quietly 'at home' . . . has become impossible. Some fearful threat has risen. . . .

Something has gone seriously and terrifyingly wrong" (Booker, *Seven Basic Plots*, 70). The immediate reason for Oskar's quest is that in the aftermath of 9/11 he finds a mysterious key in an envelope marked "Black." He interprets this as a message from his father because on previous occasions his father had sent him off on "Reconnaissance Expeditions" (8), sometimes without providing him with a proper clue. In other words, the father has made a quester of Oskar. He has instilled in him an inquisitive spirit that seeks adventure for the sake of adventure. He has explained to his ever-curious son, who, in his precocious way, bothers him with questions about the ultimate meaning of the universe: "We exist because we exist" (13). On another occasion, he tells his son that making one's mark in life is not a question of "painting the *Mona Lisa* or curing cancer" (86), but simply of "moving... one grain of sand one millimeter" (86). It is in this can-do spirit that Oskar decides to venture forth and pay a visit to all the persons named Black in the five boroughs of New York, in an effort to find the lock that fits the mysterious key.

The search is not only a tribute to the father or an attempt to come closer to the father. (Oskar is aware of the Oedipal overtones; he realizes the search, while drawing him closer to his father, also estranges him from his mother [52].) More profoundly, the quest is a sort of secular theodicy and a test of the paternal law. Staunchly refusing the comforts of religion, Thomas Schell Jr. has urged on Oskar an acceptance of life as it is. He has stated that one's existence is unfathomable and inexplicable. But that does not signify that it is meaningless (13). When, as part of a Sunday game, he sends his son off on a Reconnaissance Expedition to Central Park without a single clue, except the injunction not to "stop looking" (10), he clearly wants to impress upon his son the tenets of a personal philosophy according to which the ultimate aim of the quest is the quest itself. That the instruction not to stop looking is part of a newspaper article that concerns a girl who is missing and who will later be found dead indicates the risk one runs when sticking strictly to a this-worldly perspective. The devastations of total loss are pitted against the exhilaration of a freewheeling existence—without the possibility of religious solace or comfort.

The bedtime story about the Sixth Borough—a fairy tale Dad tells Oskar the night before "the worst day"—can be seen as a further instruction that will be put to the test (or be put to use) during the young Schell's extensive quest. The story is a cautionary tale that warns against the dangers of solipsism and isolation. It is within this context that Oskar's father proclaims himself an optimist (221) who calculates life's chances as a toss-up between a love-driven dynamism (represented by New York) and the sterility that comes from the refusal to change (represented by the inhabitants of New York's lost Sixth Borough). In promoting a sense of wonder and confronting his son with the dire consequences of psychic fixity and stagnation, Schell formulates a counterideology to Grandma's and especially Grandpa's defeatism. In setting out on a quest rather than staying in a blue funk at home, Oskar proves himself to be his father's son (rather than his grandfather's grandson).

Within this self-made mythology, Central Park plays a special role as a place of enchantment and a testing ground. Oskar's father defines it as a place where "it's hard for anyone, even the most pessimistic of pessimists, to spend more than a few minutes . . . without feeling that he or she is experiencing some tense in addition to the present" (222). According to the fairy tale, Central Park originally belonged to the Sixth Borough but as the latter drifted off into isolation Central Park was dragged into Manhattan. In other words, it is a magical place saved from stasis and despondency. No wonder Dad sends his son on a Reconnaissance Expedition in the Park. Oskar is frustrated that without precise indications he does not even know what he is looking for. Exasperated, he asks his father: "But if you don't tell me anything, how can I ever be right?" (9). His dad's answer encapsulates the essential paternal advice: "Another way of looking at it would be, how could you ever be wrong?" (9).

Trying to implement his father's teachings, Oskar sets out to visit all the Blacks he finds in the New York telephone directory. Like the traditional quester, he encounters a great many dangers during his expeditions. These dangers are not physical, and some reviewers, not comprehending the metalinguistic cast of the tale, have expressed their disbelief that a nine-year-old could walk the streets of New York unharmed or that his mother would allow such unhampered roaming in the first place (Updike, "Mixed Messages"; Kakutani, "A Boy's Epic Quest"). Such objections overlook the allegorical sheen that covers the incidents in the novel and ignore the magic-realist styling that informs the story. Oskar's greatest enemies are within. His quest is but the externalization of an internal struggle. The overriding question is whether, in dramatically changed circumstances, he will be able to hold on to his father's stoic optimism once the originator of that optimism has died a violent, senseless and untimely death.

Not surprisingly, after the loss of his premier guide and instructor, Oskar suffers from all the symptoms that pertain to trauma. He has trouble sleeping (10, 36, 41, 74). He gives himself bruises, and even though this expression has to be taken mostly as a metaphor, it points to the use of self-mutilation as a "pathological soothing mechanism" (Herman, *Trauma and Recovery*, 109). He suffers from hyperarousal; that is, he cannot relax, tirelessly inventing things and sending off-beat letters to total strangers. He is hypervigilant, afraid of taking the subway, the ferry, the elevator (all possible terrorist targets) and shying away from people with mustaches or turbans (36). He is also subject to extreme mood swings (170–73). At times, he withdraws into himself (6, 37). At other times, he is seething with anger. And, though he suppresses that feeling most of the time, there is one moment when he gives in to spite and despair—a moment of total negative epiphany, in which nothing makes sense anymore (145–46).[10]

It is no coincidence that Oskar goes through this dark night of the soul when in the class play he is given the role in *Hamlet* of Yorick, the deceased court jester, whose skull Hamlet contemplates: "Alas, poor Yorick! I knew him, Horatio; a fellow of infinite jest, of most excellent fancy.... Here hung those lips that I have kissed I know not how oft. Where be your gibes now? your gambols? your songs? your flashes of merriment, that were wont to set the table on a roar?" (*Hamlet*, 5.1). All of Yorick's efforts have come to naught; this relativism inspires Oskar to brooding. Playing the wordless role of Yorick and hiding behind a papier-mâché skull, he embodies death and feels its attraction:

> I felt, that night, on that stage, under that skull, incredibly close to everything in the universe, but also extremely alone. I wondered, for the first time in my life, if life was worth all the work it took to live. What *exactly* made it worth it? What's so horrible about being dead forever, and not feeling anything, and not even dreaming? What's so great about feeling and dreaming? (145)

As a result of his father's death, Oskar is on the verge of forgetting his father's teachings. The melancholy Hamlet, insisting on the futility of man's actions, goes against Dad's idea that everything one does—no matter how small or insignificant—is worth doing. The central issue at stake in Oskar's quest is, in the terms of the Shakespeare play, which of the two will prevail: Oskar's father's "native hue of resolution" or Hamlet's "pale cast of thought" (*Hamlet*, 3.1).

There are episodes in the book in which Oskar comes across as desensitized and emotionally numb to the point of autism. When he gives a class presentation on the bombing of Hiroshima (downloaded verbatim from the Internet but without acknowledgment), he is totally unmoved by the extreme suffering that is described. Instead, he zooms in on some scientific epiphenomena, demonstrating astounding recall without the least affect. Similarly, he casually mentions that a few weeks earlier he had brought his beloved cat to school and by way of scientific experiment "dropped him from the roof to show how cats reach terminal velocity by making themselves into little parachutes" (190). Oskar seems to have no notion of cruelty and no sense of sympathy. His astonishing cerebrality is a screen that hides deadened emotions or that hides a surfeit of emotions. As he recognizes himself: "I'm having an impossible time with my life. . . . My insides don't match up with my outsides" (200–201). The reason for all of this is that humans, unlike cats, do not survive falls from high buildings. His insensitivity is one more sign of his enduring preoccupation with his father's death.

Shortly after 9/11, his confusion also shows when he starts sadistically taunting his grandmother. He pretends to have run away from her, knowing how solicitous she is about him and how losing him would be the realization of her worst fears (101). More drastically, the loss of the father estranges Oskar from his mother. She seems to have gotten over the trauma faster than he has. Because she has a friend (Ron), with whom she plays board games and listens to music, Oskar thinks, "She wasn't missing Dad" (36). The tragedy drives a wedge between them. The alienation from the mother demonstrates the extent to which the family has become unhinged, and it deprives Oskar from the loving presence that would have made his quest easier or perhaps completely unnecessary. He suspects that his mother would have preferred that he die rather than his father (6). And in a moment of extreme irritation, he tells his mother that he, in his turn, would have preferred that she die rather than his dad: "If I could have chosen, I would have chosen you" (171).

One of the things Oskar finds out during his quest is that, unbeknownst to him, the search for the father is at the same time the search for the mother. The family idyll belies Freudian schemes. The unbreakableness of the family unit—across the limits of death—adds a sentimental note to the story. But it also pinpoints the true sources of comfort in case of a disaster. As the psychoanalysts Peter Fonagy and Mary Target put it, a "child's attachment relationships function as the decisive buffer to trauma in childhood" ("Evolution," 99). A child as bereaved as Oskar can only be set right once he discovers that, in spite of death, mom and dad have stayed together and he is still the son of both. Moreover, it is not so much that Oskar has come to hate his mother. The events of September 11 seem to have blocked off his means of expressing his love for her. During the ride to the cemetery, he has an inkling of the mute suffering his mother is undergoing and he remarks, "Even though it was an incredibly sad day, she looked so, so beautiful. I kept trying to figure out a way to tell her that, but all of the ways I thought of were weird and wrong" (7). Again, trauma reveals itself as a form of aphasia or muteness. The catastrophe has damaged the ability to utter oneself in the most significant ways.

Within the allegorical scheme of the novel, however, Oskar has to do more than just wrestle with the specified symptoms of trauma and family tension (a formidable ordeal in its own right). The quest also takes within its purview a much larger aspect of the human condition and, apart from highlighting a psychological situation, it also addresses more general philosophical questions. In particular, in his search to live up to his father's example, Oskar has to overcome the depressing sense of anomie that results from living in a big city. The German sociologist Georg Simmel noted more than a hundred years ago, in a seminal essay, that the number and variety of stimuli that bombard the mind in an urban environment can lead to the kind of "unimaginable psychic state" ("The Metropolis," 53) that Oskar finds himself in. Moreover, apart from coming across the anomie of modernity, Oskar also has to confront the dispersion of meaning that is associated with postmodernity. During his Reconnaissance Expedition in Central Park, he discovers, by means of a metal detector, a great variety of objects hidden underground. There is no discernible meaningful link between the things he digs up: "a hair clip, and a roll of pennies, and a thumbtack, and a coat hanger, and a 9V battery, and a Swiss Army knife, and a tiny picture frame, and a tag for a dog named Turbo, and a square of aluminum foil, and a ring, and a razor, and an extremely old pocket watch that was stopped at 5:37" (10). The monotonously repeated "and" does not express plenitude but irritation and confusion at so many things aggregated without visible congruence. No matter how scrupulously Oskar examines the evidence under his microscope and no matter how diligently he observes exactly what kind of battery he has found or what kind of knife, scientific scrutiny does not allow him to raise the status of these objects or integrate them into a semblance of order. He is faced with the detritus of civilization and, by extension, with a sense of civilization as detritus. This feeling of disorientation (there is just too much stuff around) is heightened when he indicates the exact places where he found these things on a map and the dots "looked like the stars in the universe." Connecting the dots yields the word "fragile." But looked at differently, the lines between the dots constitute the word "door" or *"porte,"* while "cyborg," "platypus," "boobs," and even "Oskar" are also possibilities (10).

This is the first of a series of occasions on which Oskar discovers the multitude and uncontrollable polyinterpretability of things. "The more I found, the less I understood," he observes (10). Similarly, when he looks up the possible meanings of "black" on Google, he discovers that the Internet provides an enormous amount of information but no relevant clues (41–42). Major events of the twentieth century are meaningless to him (154), which proves the ephemeral nature of things: what is important to one generation is negligible for the next. In a scrapbook, which he entitles *Stuff That Happened to Me,* he assembles newspaper photographs that struck him. That random collection quickly becomes a metaphor for the haphazard impressions and sensations the mass media bombard us with. Oskar has the collector's instinct, but the mere paratactic juxtaposition of things gives rise to the "depthlessness" that Fredric Jameson associated with the condition of postmodernity (Jameson, *Postmodernism,* 9). In Oskar's observant but untrained mind, the world threatens to turn into pure semiosis run riot.

When Oskar applies his uncanny mathematical skills to the immediate problem at hand—finding the lock that fits the key—he once again runs up against a reality that turns out to be untraceable: "I timed myself and it took me 3 seconds to open a lock. Then I figured out that if a baby is born in New York every 50 seconds, and each person has 18 locks, a new lock is created in New York every 2.777 seconds. So even if all I did was open locks, I'd still be falling behind by .333 locks every second" (41). Mathematics does not provide a sure grip on reality. On the contrary, it points out how one cannot possibly keep up with changing circumstances. Through Oskar's calculations, anomie is joined by entropy. He discovers that there is a googolplex of everything. A googol is "one with one hundred zeroes after it," he explains, and a googolplex is "a googol to the googol power" (40). The task Oskar is facing is not simply to impose order on this chaos. According to his father's instructions, order should be without order. Even though clueless, he has to remain determined. The quest, which clearly has no finite destination, has to be undertaken with Nietzschean *"griechische Heiterkeit"* (the cheerfulness of the ancient Greeks) (*Die Geburt*, 130), or in the spirit of Albert Camus: *"Il faut imaginer Sisyphe heureux* [One must think of Sisyphus as a happy man]" (*Le mythe*, 168). It is the effort more than the outcome that determines the failure or success of the quest. Or to put it more epigrammatically, the effort is the outcome.

The pattern of the traditional quest is further completed by the many helpers Oskar comes across in his peregrinations. Thanks to these adult helpers, Oskar gains insights that will contribute to his fast maturation. Surprisingly, one of these advisers is the severely handicapped British astrophysicist Stephen Hawking. In an attempt to find a substitute authority figure after his father's death, Oskar has been sending off letters to people such as Ringo Starr, Jane Goodall, and Stephen Hawking. After some form letters, Hawking finally sends him a highly personal response in which he expresses his determination to make the most of his life, in spite of his debilitating physical difficulties. Hawking not only fulfills the role of substitute father but also reiterates and reinforces Oskar's father's upbeat teachings, writing: *"I've spent the past few days here, recovering from some medical treatment that has left me physically and emotionally depleted. As I moped about this morning, feeling sorry for myself, it occurred to me, like a simple solution to an impossible problem: today is the day I've been waiting for*" (304). This is a variant of Schell's "We exist because we exist." As an authority figure and substitute father Hawking advises Oskar to blithely acquiesce in life's offerings and to accept every day as a gift. His letter formulates what Oskar (but also Grandma [281]) gradually becomes aware of: since the future is uncertain (240, 286), it is important to fully appreciate the present. The trauma of the past follows from an unwarranted trust in the future and the subsequent undervaluation of the here and now.

A helper with a significantly larger role in the narrative is A. R. Black, one of the Blacks Oskar comes across in his quest. A. R. Black happens to live in the apartment right above Oskar's own, and he happens to be 103 years old. Born on January 1, 1900, he incorporates the whole of the twentieth century. He turns out to be "a benevolent, . . . wise old man," like Teiresias in *The Odyssey* or Anchises in *The Aeneid* (Booker, *Seven Basic Plots*, 77). But Foer problematizes the figure of the helper as he introduces it. While Black agrees to accompany Oskar on his quest and while he is instrumental in helping Oskar overcome some of his phobias, he is a helper who also needs help. If Oskar makes progress in shedding his obsessions and regaining a lost balance, it is in part thanks to the advice he gets from this mentor, but it is just as much because, in return, he learns to care for the old man and to cater to his wishes.

Given the preoccupations of this novel, it is no surprise that Oskar's doings with Black concern language, communication, violence, and love. The old man is a guide into the darker aspects of recent history. As a war correspondent, he visited 112 countries, witnessing "almost every war of the twentieth century" (154). He regrets he spent so much time on his travels and realized only belatedly that he sacrificed domestic bliss for the sake of professional ambition. His wife died twenty-four years ago, and since that day he has never left the apartment. His obsession with his loss also shows in that every day he drives a nail into his bed (made out of a Central Park tree over which his wife once tripped), thus making the bed so heavy that it threatens to collapse the floor. The literalization of his grief and his subsequent isolation is also manifest in the fact that for years he has turned off his hearing aids. In getting him out of the apartment and into the world and returning him to the world of sound by switching on the hearing aids, Oskar, in the spirit of his father's optimism, redeems the twentieth century, as it were. According to Christopher Booker, the chief companion in a quest story sometimes "embodies compensatory qualities missing in the hero" (*Seven Basic Plots*, 72). The extreme youth of Oskar is offset by the extreme age of Mr. Black. The former's innocence is wedded to the latter's experience so that both are invigorated (196).

The character of A. R. Black not only incorporates the twentieth century but also tries to give it shape in language. In this, he joins Grandpa's and Grandma's efforts to hold on to the past by writing it down, and, like them, he meets with only partial success. His life's experience—rich and variegated as it is—has found its way into his apartment as a collection of objects that, in the aggregate, summarize the century he is identified with. He tries to order this chaotic jumble by applying language to it. He has, for instance, a large biographical index with tens of thousands of entries—one one-word entry for every person he deemed "biographically significant" (157). This index is obviously an attempt to make information overload manageable, but since every person's life story is condensed into one word (mostly "war" and "money" [159]), these biographies are so reductionist in their logic that the manageability of the information has been acquired at the expense of meaningfulness and relevance. When Black changes his own designation from "war" to "husband," the shorthand is sufficient to indicate a major turnaround in his life and points to the opposition of violence and love, which is central to the novel. But when Oskar finds out that his father's name is missing in the index, it is obvious that the objectifying logic that decides who rates a mention in the catalogue and who does not has little to do with the subjective appreciation of history, that is, with the way lives are actually being led.

As memorabilia from his travels, Mr. Black also possesses "a bunch of rocks" displayed on the mantelpiece: "each rock had a little piece of paper next to it that said where the rock came from, and when it came from, like 'Normandy, 6/19/44,' 'Hwach'on Dam, 4/09/51,' and 'Dallas, 11/22/63'" (156). Black hopes to bring time to a standstill by the Adamic gesture of naming the rocks. He gives shape to the iconic moments of the century through language. He also has a collection of bullets on display.

But they remain unidentified because "a bullet's a bullet's a bullet" (156). Violence is always the same and needs no finer distinction or discrimination. But when Oskar asks: "Is a rose a rose?" Black answers, "No! A rose is not a rose is not a rose!" (156). In thus parodying Gertrude Stein and Ernest Hemingway, Foer points to an intricate nexus between the more elevating experiences in life (the living flower as against the death-dealing bullet), on the one hand, and the discerning use of language, on the other. Generic names do not do justice to the uniqueness of historical fact and the particularity of the creation's richness.

After accompanying Oskar for six and a half months, A. R. Black suddenly gives up on the quest. The reasons for this abrupt desertion are intricate. In part it is because, unbeknownst to Oskar, a new helper has appeared on the scene. In part it is because Black has developed a romantic interest in Ruth Black, a woman just as despondent and isolated as he is. The novel also leaves open the possibility that old Mr. Black has died. Whatever the case, it is obvious that, as a helper, Black proves that personal and historical trauma (as well as the infirmities of extreme age) can be vanquished by love and a cheerful engagement in the world. In addition, linguistically, Black's attempt to master history through the word points out the pitfalls of reductionism but also the opportunities language offers to suggest the singularity of every separate phenomenon. Language can be complicitous in flattening experience, and the need to catalogue—as a means of coping with postmodern anomie—can thin out life until nothing is left but an irrelevant designation. But language also possesses the potential to give every single rose its irreplaceable due and every single event its distinctive shape.

When Black gives up on the quest, Oskar has not yet achieved anything. He is just about to quit when the plot accelerates, and, like the quester in traditional tales, he is faced with a series of final ordeals. First of all, he meets Grandma's "renter," a man who for some months has been hiding in a room in Grandma's apartment. Second, he finds out that the mysterious key belongs to a certain William Black, a total stranger, and that it opens a safe-deposit box containing legal documents that have nothing to do with his father. The whole quest turns out to have been an exercise in futility, and Oskar fears that he "will wear heavy boots for the rest of ... [his] life" (302).

However, in ways that are not so obvious, the postmodernist model of a randomized search, in which the hero is sent off on a wild goose chase, is counteracted by more traditional echoes of the quest as a learning process and its outcome as a catharsis. For one thing, Oskar learns to persevere. His first encounter with a person named Black is so disappointing that he sinks down to the floor and starts to cry in despair (88). In what follows he discovers the value of endurance and insistence: "I was willing to be annoying if that's what was necessary" (90). He also conquers his fears and prejudices. When he first sets out, he is panicky walking over bridges and afraid of people who remind him of terrorists. But he remembers that "Dad used to say that sometimes you have to put your fears in order" (87), and from the quest's beginning, he resolves that he "wouldn't be sexist again, or racist, or ageist, or homophobic, or overly wimpy, or discriminatory to handicapped people or mental retards" (87). During the course of his trek around the city, he pretty much sticks to this resolution. At first, he flees when he meets a severely handicapped person (90), but the second time around he is unfazed and barely pays attention to the fact that the person he is talking to is in a wheelchair (194–96).

While Oskar crisscrosses the city and visits places he has never been before, there is redemptive value in the fact that his life touches those of other New Yorkers, however briefly. He meets Abe Black, with whom he rides the Cyclone on Coney Island. Ada Black is a millionaire who owns two Picasso paintings. In Harlem, he meets Peter Black and holds his newborn son in his arms. Alice Black is squatting in an industrial building; Albert Black's ambition is to be an actor; Ruth Black is unable to get over her husband's death. Fo Black is a Chinese immigrant, while Georgia Black and her husband idolize each other so much that they have made museums for each other. Some of these Blacks only get a line or two in the book; others occupy significant parts of one of Oskar's chapters. Some of the encounters are memorable, others less so. Yet in the aggregate, the diversity of the city, while adding to the questioning mood of the novel (what do all these lives amount to?) provides a counterbalance to personal devastation. The variety of the city itself produces epic momentum and psychic uplift. The confrontation with all these different people—all marching to their own drum beats—is a perfect foil for

Oskar's own expedition. His personal search is part and parcel of a rich and complicated collective destiny.

The linearity of the quest also counters the circularity of traumatic obsession. If trauma brings time to a standstill, the quest reintroduces development and movement. The sequentiality of looking up all the Blacks one by one and the physical and mental mobility that such a search requires offset the lethargy and melancholy that typify traumatic suffering. Thus Oskar's travels over the five boroughs of New York are redemptive. They signify, if not a resacralization of the territory, at least its reoccupation, after it has been usurped by the 9/11 terrorists. In the upbeat spirit of his dead father, Oskar's exploration of his native ground is an act of reconquest and reaffirmation: firsthand proof that the terrorists have failed to break the city's stride.

In addition, the ending of the quest—in spite of its disappointing outcome—gestures toward a resolution of trauma rather than to its unresolvable suspension. First of all, it is no coincidence that the solution to the riddle of the key lies in a house in Greenwich Village that has a sign above the door—Oskar provides us with a photograph to prove it—that says that "the poet Edna Saint Vincent Millay once lived in the house, and that it was the narrowest house in New York" (90). In a city that prizes bigness, the smallness of the house isomorphically gestures back to Oskar's father's belief that life's task consists not of performing world-shattering deeds, but simply of "moving . . . one grain of sand one millimeter" (86). That the house was once inhabited by a poet of note points to the power of language and the liberating possibility of articulating grief and life's secrets. That the poet is a woman anticipates Oskar's discovery of the importance of the matrilinear succession. Coming to terms with his father will turn out to be coterminous with coming to terms with his mother and grandmother.

Significantly, Abby Black, the woman who now lives in the narrow house and who is instrumental in solving the mystery of the key, is said to have a welcoming "face like Mom's" (91). Physically, she resembles Oskar's mother, and it becomes obvious from Oskar's ingratiating ways that he sees her as a substitute for his mother. With Abby he enacts the rite of reconciliation that he will be able to carry out with his real mother only much later. He tells Abby that she is "incredibly beautiful" (91)—the exact compliment he does not manage to formulate with regard to his own mother on the occasion of his father's funeral (7). Inappropriately, he also asks Abby if they could "kiss for a little bit" (99). It is a trenchant comment on our times that the nine-year-old Oskar expresses his affection for a forty-eight-year-old woman in sexual terms, even though he has no sexual feelings as yet. The sexual terminology has become so pervasive in the culture that it is used even by those who have no true understanding of the meaning of the terms. Also, in describing Abby, Oskar— in his smart-alecky way—adopts the sexual lingo of the day. We are told that Abby is "incredibly beautiful, with a face like Mom's, which seemed like it was smiling even when she wasn't smiling, and huge boobs" (91). However, when Oskar takes her picture, the photograph does not reveal any of these enticing features. Instead, it shows the back of her head with a shock of black hair chastely tied up in a pony tail (98). In order for the photograph to be more "truthful" (99), Abby is desexualized. As such, her qualities as substitute mother are emphasized. That we do not see her up front points to the fact, that, though she stands in for the mother, she is not Oskar's mother. Oskar still has a ways to go before he is able to look his own mother in the face. His spontaneous affection for Abby is but a way station in his further quest, a first awakening of his sympathetic imagination.

The one who proves to be in possession of the lock that fits the key is William Black, Abby's estranged husband. He is a total stranger to Oskar, and the safe-deposit box that the key opens contains nothing of any relevance to Oskar's quest. Yet the meeting with William Black is one more important milestone on the road to a final resolution. Like old A. R. Black, William is a helper also in need of help. Divorced from Abby, it is obvious he still loves her. And just like Oskar, he is immensely saddened by the fact that his recently deceased father took his leave without once saying "I love you" (297). Moreover, he physically resembles Oskar's father (292, 298). When Oskar takes a picture of him, it shows the back of his head. Just as in the case of Abby, this backward view underscores William's role as a mentor and father substitute. William, to whom Oskar immediately draws very close, not only solves the mystery of the key but is also the person to whom Oskar finally confesses the fact that he failed to pick up the phone on his father's last call.

Grandma's "renter" is the last helper, and he assists Oskar in finally coming to terms with his loss. Unbeknownst to Oskar, this "renter," whom he encounters in Grandma's apartment, is Grandpa, returned from Dresden after having heard that his son died on September 11. The patrilinear succession is reestablished when Oskar plays his father's recorded messages to the "renter" and arranges for the "renter" to assist him when he goes to the cemetery to dig up and rebury his father's empty coffin on the second anniversary of the latter's death. Though this ritual is not fully redemptive for Grandpa (who ultimately longs to go back to Dresden again), it is for Oskar. As a consequence, the second ride to the cemetery is very different from the first one. Instead of making feeble jokes to hide his emotions (5–6), Oskar now shows a genuine interest in the family life of the limousine driver (316–17). He sticks his arm out of the window of the car and curves his hand "like an airplane wing." "If my hand had been big enough," he thinks, "I could've made the limousine fly" (316). While this "invention" is again an expression of his childish wish to see things aloft (rather than collapsing to the ground like the Twin Towers), it also conveys a sense that his depressed mood is lifting. When he looks up at the night sky, he sees the stars and remarks: "in my head I connected them to make words, whatever words I wanted" (317). In looking at the night sky, he finds a semiotic license that is liberating rather than bewildering, in contrast to a much earlier episode in which connecting the dots on the Central Park map drives him to distraction.

Digging up the empty coffin is, in the words of Stephen Hawking's letter, a "simple solution to an impossible problem" (321). It is a symbolic act that signifies the son's reconciliation with the death of his father. He first thinks of filling the empty coffin with memorabilia, like Georgia Black and her husband, "who made museums of each other" (321). But he realizes that memorializing things is a way of fixating them and thus, in a way, comprises a sort of forgetting. He then contemplates filling the grave with the paraphernalia that are the symbols of his neediness and unresolved trauma: the "things I'm ashamed of" (322). But the "renter" reminds him that physically burying things does not really "*bury*" them (322). That he finally allows the coffin to be filled with the "renter's" unsent letters, even though he realizes the grave properly belongs to him and not to a stranger, shows that he has learned to reach out and accommodate another's wishes.

The four helpers whom Oskar meets in the course of his quest and who assist him in getting through his final ordeals have two things in common. All four of them—Stephen Hawking, old A. R. Black, William Black, and the "renter"—are male, and their assistance is conditioned by the fact that they are in need of help themselves. Grandpa obviously has to cope with the issue of the unassimilated past, while William Black is distraught and feels guilty after the death of his estranged father. Hawking combines a brilliant mind with a disintegrating body, while A. R. Black is burdened by the full weight of a tragic century. These helpers are not simply listeners to Oskar's story. They are truly interlocutors, in that their sympathy for Oskar originates in the personal experience of suffering and deprivation.

And yet the final reconciliation is between Oskar and the women in the book. Grandma ends her long letter to him by expressing her devotion in the most simple words: "I love you" (314). And after the reburial, when Oskar comes home, there is an emotional reunion with his mother, in which family relations are repaired and the blocked utterance of affection is lifted. The boy's frustration over his father's unceremonious farewell and lack of affectionate parting words is finally undone when his mother, just like his grandmother, tells him unequivocally: "I love you" (325). Thus life is reduced to its essential features: "In my only life, she was my mom, and I was her son" (324). It is this knowledge that restores broken connections and heralds a return to true normalcy. "Traumatic events," writes Herman, "destroy the victim's fundamental assumptions about the safety of the world, the positive value of the self, and the meaningful order of creation" (*Trauma and Recovery*, 51). The novel holds out the possibility—maybe too optimistically—that, in an act of love, all that violence destroyed can be mended; that the lost sense of security can be recovered. Most essentially, it becomes possible again to speak. Through the act of speaking, love conquers the suffering of generations.

This reintegration of the ruptured nuclear family is backed up by a final act of imaginative recovery. Oskar adopts his grandmother's dream logic, by which the order of events is reversed and history goes back upon itself so that "the worst day" never happens, his father is restored to him, and the family "would have been safe" (326). Thus trauma is resolved by the creation of an alternative world. He makes a flip book of pictures of a man falling from one of the WTC towers. By placing the pictures in reverse order, he makes the effect of a man not going down but "floating up through the sky" (325). Through the exercise of the compensatory imagination, Oskar, like his grandmother, wants to impose a happy ending on the events. "Sometimes people reenact the traumatic moment with a fantasy of changing the outcome of the dangerous encounter," writes Herman (*Trauma and Recovery*, 39). On the one hand, this wish to undo history is one more invention, showing the depth of his grief. On the other, it takes place in a changed context that suggests that Oskar has learned to cope with trauma and his quest has come to some kind of closure. To quote Herman one more time: "Not all reenactments are dangerous. Some, in fact, are adaptive. Survivors may find a way to integrate reliving experiences into their lives in a contained, even socially useful manner" (40). Whereas Grandma's imagining, ending in everlasting darkness is melancholic (in the clinical sense of the word), Oskar's is restorative. As Adrienne Harris puts it: "In the process of mourning, there is (perhaps always to some degree) the simultaneous need for acceptance and creative denial" ("Relational Mourning," 158).[11]

Oskar's final wish to see the effects of 9/11 annulled could be read as a facile way to undo the consequences of trauma. But since the dream sequence is couched in conditionals and thus indicates an awareness of the dream as mere wish fulfillment, it is also possible to interpret Oskar's imagined historical reversal as a productive way of coping with the past. Ripping the pages with the falling body out of his scrap book and reversing the order "so that the last one was first, and the first was last" (325) constitutes, if not an active intervention in the historical process, then at least the symbolic representation of his fears and desires. As such, it is of a piece with Oskar's peregrination through the city in search of the missing lock and with the reburial of his father, in that all these manifestations of agency are efforts to counter traumatic numbness. After the horror of bereavement, Oskar succeeds in making reality fluid again. He prevents traumatic shock from rigidifying into a chronic condition.

4

EXORCISING THE GHOST

IRONY AND SPECTRALIZATION IN FRÉDÉRIC BEIGBEDER'S *WINDOWS ON THE WORLD*

WINDOWS ON THE WORLD, by the French writer and enfant terrible Frédéric Beigbeder, is a book uncertain of its tone, uncertain of its message.[1] In many ways, it is a shallow book. As its two protagonists are forever sounding off and as their thoughts often lack perspicacity, the novel demonstrates that great events do not necessarily produce great thoughts. There is no automatic sublation to a higher level. The commonplace reigns. The cliché wins out.

And yet, though the novel was certainly written in great haste (there are some glaring inconsistencies),[2] it deserves in-depth consideration because it adds an international dimension to this discussion. In France it became a best-seller and won the prestigious Prix Interallié, while in the United Kingdom its translation into English was awarded the Independent Foreign Fiction Prize. The honors bestowed upon it prove that the novel must have struck a chord with its readership. Its very quirkiness catches the uncertain mood of the time, so much so that the reviewer for the *New York Times* called it a "funny and moving... book" (Metcalf). It communicates a definitive reading of 9/11, but this interpretation is cast in a form that defies easy comprehension. In particular, one is at a loss to know whether this novel announces the death of irony or whether it is an enactment of a sort of postapocalyptic irony. It is partly a conversion story, but partly, too, it spoofs the possibility of conversion. It denounces the whole postmodern mentality, yet it is also a shameless exponent of it.

The novel is an oddly bifurcated tale that refuses to conform to the conventions of doppelganger or alter ego. It has two narrator-protagonists. One is a middle-aged, well-heeled, and worldly Texas realtor by the name of Carthew Yorston, who finds himself trapped in the Windows on the World restaurant atop World Trade Center One on the fateful morning of September 11. He is a divorced man on a trip to New York to see his mistress (a fashion model, who "makes J-Lo look like a bag lady" [4]), but also to show the sights to his two young sons, Jerry, aged nine, and David, aged seven. The two youngsters are with him having breakfast in the restaurant when the first plane hits Tower One at 8.46 A.M. The other protagonist is called "Beigbeder" and is presented as a writer, who, in an effort to re-create the conditions his characters experience, goes off every morning to write in Le Ciel de Paris, the restaurant at the top of the Tour Montparnasse, the highest skyscraper in Paris.[3] The duality of main character and location is compounded by the fact that time is also duplicated and even multiplied. The novel presents itself as a semiotic hall of mirrors in which shards of knowledge and snippets of experience bounce off one another. All in all, there are a hundred and twenty short and sometimes extremely short chapters, in which Yorston (or occasionally one of his sons) and "Beigbeder" alternate as narrating voices. They mainly indulge in philosophizing and speculation; the novel has hardly any narrative.

(Hyper)realism

The confusion begins with the genre. The extremely self-conscious writer-narrator "Beigbeder" wavers between registers and styles and is undecided about which genre conventions will do justice to his topic. In a set of introductory mottoes he quotes Tom Wolfe: "A novelist who does not write realistic novels understands nothing of the world in which we live." Similarly, he refers to the singer Marilyn Manson, who stated, "The function of the artist is to plunge into the depths of hell." That these mottoes are called "lightning rods" ("*paratonnerres*" in the French original) points to the writer's awareness that 9/11 is a delicate topic, and he uses the mottoes to ward off criticism ahead of time. Whoever aestheticizes a disaster such a short time after the disaster (without sufficient time having elapsed to gain contemplative distance) is in danger of being accused of opportunism. In a grand gesture, the writer takes himself to task for indulging in "esthetics without ethics" (210). Elsewhere in the novel he admits he has the nagging sense that he is doing something illegitimate, that there is something shameful about being "so fascinated by destruction" (129). His excuse is the urge and indeed the artistic obligation "to plunge into the depths of hell." The means to carry out such a task are no longer the lyricism and allegory of Virgil or Dante but down-to-earth, honest-to-goodness realism.

"When one cannot answer the question 'Why?' one must at least attempt to answer the question 'How?'" "Beigbeder" writes (241). If 9/11 remains a "mystery" (like the Shoa, 268), of which the deeper reasons cannot be fathomed, the task of the novelist concerns the detailed circumstances (i.e., the imaginative reconstruction) of what actually took place. In this attempt to render through the imagination the horrors that no camera recorded and no firsthand witness survived, the author engages all the traditional markers of realism. The major locations (the Windows on the World restaurant and its "sister site" [37] Le Ciel de Paris) have more than an individual existence. Their specificity (their real-life quality) is emphasized by the fact that their addresses and phone numbers are given. We also get the full vital statistics of the two high-rises in which the restaurants are located: height, square footage, weight, cost, etc. The buildings are presented in their full and massive materiality—including, in the case of the Twin Towers, a report on the innovative building techniques, which, in part, were responsible for their collapsing (52).

If there is an exact indication of place, there is an equally exact temporal reckoning. The novel insists on the inexorable linearity of time: time is imaged as a vector that cleaves through all discourse and rhetoric and, in the case of 9/11, has an inevitable teleology. The tale proceeds minute by minute, each of the 120 short chapters carrying as title a time indication, starting at 8:30 (sixteen minutes before the first attack) and proceeding minute by minute to end at 10:29 (one minute after the collapse of the second tower). Beigbeder borrowed the device from a newspaper story he relied on for some of the context and some of the details (Dwyer et al., "102 Minutes"). But he exploits it to full effect, indicating the irreversibility of doom and emphasizing the impotence of human agency vis-à-vis fate. The tale of 9/11 is what Frank Kermode calls an "end-determined fiction," which gives "each moment its fullness" (*The Sense of an Ending*, 6).

Within the exact context of specified place and time, the characters—in order to obtain verisimilitude—are equally set forth as fully particularized individuals. We are told what Carthew Yorston looks like, how he made his fortune. We learn his exact age and the names of his wife, mistress and children. The children, Jerry and David, in their turn, are given distinctive psychological profiles, one gullible, the other less easily impressed. Similarly, "Beigbeder" derives a lifelike quality from his very name. He shares age, appearance, profession, and present and past circumstances with the real-life author, so that this book has repeatedly been characterized by some reviewers (Bee, "The Center"; Derbyshire, "Towering Voices") and by Beigbeder himself (Géniès, "September 11, the Novel") as part novel, part memoir or autobiography. Even the acknowledgments are actively brought to bear on giving fiction the semblance of reality. In the novel we are told that after a falling-out "Beigbeder" is going to propose marriage to his fiancée, "Amélie." In the acknowledgments we learn that the proposal has been successful, as Amélie Labrande receives thanks "for becoming Amélie Beigbeder."

By the use of individualized characters, a specific locale, and a meticulously observed chronology, the novel presents itself explicitly as an attempt to render the events of 9/11 in their stark historical materiality. At the same time, the novelist acknowledges that "since September 11, 2001, reality has not only outstripped fiction, it's destroying it" (8). Hence, in one of the many inconsistencies in the book, Beigbeder betrays the motto from Tom Wolfe, which as "lightning rod" not only provided the justification for his attempt to render the horrors of 9/11 but also enjoined upon him the obligation to write in a realistic vein. In order to define his rhetorical strategy, Beigbeder invents the label "hyperrealist" (8). It is by writing a "hyperrealist" novel that he intends to circumvent the unrepresentability of the events. Obviously, if September 11 has destroyed fiction, that is, has changed the parameters within which fiction is normally held to be capable of creating possible worlds and producing the effect of verisimilitude, the rules of the game have to be changed. Not realism but a newly invented novelistic form is called upon to do the job of relating the unrelatable.

The first thing that has to be said about the "hyperrealist" novel, as we find it in *Windows on the World*, is that it has nothing to do with Jean Baudrillard's notion of the hyperreal. For someone who in a previous novel wrote a scathing attack on advertising, it is strange that Beigbeder hardly talks about the mediatization that has so deeply affected the representation of 9/11. In fact, the novelist believes that he operates in a realm that is outside mediatized reality. "The role of books," he writes, "is to record what cannot be seen on television" (86). In that sense, literature provides a way out of the Baudrillardian hyperreal. At another spot in the novel, he affirms his romantic belief in the role of the imagination even more forcefully: "We must write what is forbidden," he asserts (301). In a few explicatory sentences he makes clear that his hyperrealist effort has television as its great opponent: "Nowadays, books must go where television does not. Show the invisible, speak the unspeakable. It may be impossible, but that is its raison d'être. Literature is a 'mission impossible'" (301).

The second thing that has to be said about Beigbeder's concept of hyperrealism is that in no way does the term imply an exaggerated attention to the minute details of reality. On the contrary, "hyperrealism," as Beigbeder uses the term, denotes a departure from the strictures of conventional realism. The text creates realistic expectations then goes on to mock and subvert them. It stages the realistic gesture in highly unlikely circumstances and thus destroys the reality effect that in other places is cultivated with great care. To give just one example: a mere three minutes after the impact of the plane Yorston and his sons try to escape through a smoke-filled, burning stairwell. Rather than exploring the horrors inherent to the enterprise, the text short-circuits itself. It cancels the reality effect for no obvious reason and with confusing results. Yorston interrupts his harrowing tale to present a gloss on his own performance as narrator: "I realize I've forgotten to describe myself" (66). The self-portrait that follows concerns the details of his outward appearance and the character traits of his children and it cannot possibly be construed as the reflections of the character in a time of crisis. Rather it issues from an unlocatable and extradiegetic voice. It comprises the thoughts of a self-conscious narrator, playacting in front of his putative readers. Since Yorston, however, does not survive the day and thus cannot possibly edit his own tale ex post facto, his comments introduce an undetermined, narratively unsettling vantage point. From a realist point of view, this speaking from an undefined center is certainly a weakness. From a "hyperrealist" point of view, it can be looked upon as an experiment dictated by the exigencies of a liminal topic. Is such a rupture of the realist frame the result of haste and clumsiness? Or is it part of a sophisticated attempt to ironize one's own "impossible" telling and put it *sous rature*? To put it more contentiously: Is *Windows on the World* a genuine attempt to come to terms with 9/11, or is it 9/11 kitsch?

One thing is obvious: in sending off fiction on its impossible mission of revealing the truth (over and against the deceptions of the mass media), Beigbeder heavily relies on various postmodernist literary experiments. He freely avails himself of the devices that have been developed in the last forty years to set the novel free from the conventions of realism. It is here that the question of irony comes in and the essential ambiguity of the novel manifests itself most strongly. If irony, in its wider sense, points to the questioning of conventional reality or conventional representations of reality, this novel enacts a postmodern and even postapocalyptic irony. It sabotages its own plot development because it consists of 120 short (sometimes excessively short) chapters. It comments on the conditions of its own being and self-reflexively mocks its own legitimacy. But the ironic spin, though it sweeps up the narrative material and sends it for a loop, peters out, and ultimately the self-parodying devices make way for a concluding and conclusive message. In plain English, the novel argues for a moral. In that sense, it sets out to prove that 9/11 meant the end of irony. In the light of mass death, a new seriousness installs itself. The cycle of irony ironizing itself comes to a grinding halt.

(Spectral) Time

Within the parameters of hyperrealism, time is the first realist convention that the text sets out to redefine. The very first sentence of the novel contains a surprising prolepsis. "You know how it ends: everybody dies" (1). The rectilinearity of time, so dramatically underscored by the chapter headings, is counteracted by the difference between narrated time and time of narration. The tale is set on September 11, 2001, and it proceeds minute by doom-laden minute. But the writer indicates that he starts writing the tale about a year later. Such a setup opposes in stark and unmitigated contrast, on the one hand, a vectorial sense of time, in which everything speeds towards a foreordained end, and, on the other, a more elastic notion of temporal crisscrossing. That "Beigbeder" fully profits from this time gap is well within the realistic horizon of expectation. Writing after the events, he is acquainted with the full arc of their unfolding. The hyperrealistic touch comes in when Yorston, who does not survive the day, is also allowed to move back and forth in time, making both analepses and prolepses. This means that at one point he is wondering whether he will be able to escape from the inferno, while, at another point of the narrative and within a different time dimension, he knows exactly that he will die and even when. It also allows him to continue his narrative even after he and his sons have jumped from the tower to escape the raging fire. Some of his comments come from within the strict confines of the top floors of World Trade Center One at a precise moment on the morning of September 11, 2001, and thus are subject to a realist time regime; others come drifting in from beyond the grave and thus defy realist assumptions.

September 11 is an extremely punctual event and does not allow the slightest deviation from a strict timeline. Every minute counts, and every minute brings the protagonist closer to his unavoidable death. Simultaneously, 9/11 also resonates far beyond its affixed date. The text drives this point home not simply by allowing the writer to intrude into the temporal dimension of his character (the normal situation) but also by enabling the character to catapult himself into the time frame of the writer, thus not only introducing a new sense of time but especially insisting on the after-existence of the building and its doomed residents. September 11 has an afterlife. Merely experiential, historical time does not tell the full story. Time acquires a spectral dimension. The collapse of the towers is not their true ending. Using a device that also appears in Art Spiegelman's In the Shadow of No Towers and in a short story collection edited by Ulrich Baer, Beigbeder wills the towers back into existence. The entry for 10:28, the exact minute the North Tower buckled, is given the graphic form of the two towers. The exact time of their disappearance is also the exact time of their imaginative resurrection.

Similarly, the protagonists are not truly dead. In one of the last entries Yorston writes about himself and his sons:

> We are not dead: we are prisoners of the sun or of the snow. Broken rays of sunlight dart between the snowflakes which fall in slow motion like a rain of confetti. Shards of glass apparently migrate beneath the skin. Put some glass in your veins. Do this in memory of me. I died for you and you and you and you and you and you and you and you. (299–300)

This little prose poem remains cryptic enough to avoid a maudlin tone. The mixture of blood and glass, a gruesome consequence of the compacting action of the falling towers, is heightened into a symbol of togetherness: not facile solidarity but implication. September 11 is featured as an occasion of universal and lasting pain and thus as an event that, transgressing its own time frame, leaves behind ghostly presences and spectral after-imaginings.

(Spectral) Space

The description of the towers is grounded in physical realities even as the towers themselves were grounded in Manhattan bedrock. But space in *Windows on the World*—like time—expands and then spills over the boundaries of conventional realism. In particular, space is first symbolized and then doubled—suggesting that 9/11 was a truly international event with ramifications far beyond the few acres of Ground Zero.

The amplification of space is a direct result of the fact that the Twin Towers are denoted as "the top of the world, . . . the center of the universe" (3), "the acme of Western achievement" (12). More than massive constructions in steel and glass, they embody a phantasmagoric, dominant space, symbolic of Western capitalism. Such is their symbolic relevance that their disappearance will ultimately be imaged as an epistemic shift, an apocalyptic refashioning of the reigning moral order.

The symbolic expansion of the towers involves the view from above, from below, and from inside, and it starts with the very first contribution by Yorston, who writes at 8:31 A.M.: "That morning, we were at the top of the world, and I was the center of the universe" (3). These words are repeated verbatim at the end of the book, after Yorston's demise (303). Yorston's interpretation of the significance of the towers is indistinguishable from the reading "Beigbeder" offers. Their physical height is an indication of their centrality and dominance. In his seminal essay "Walking in the City," the French philosopher Michel de Certeau writes about the South Tower of the World Trade Center: "The 1370 foot high tower that serves as a prow for Manhattan continues to construct the fiction that creates readers, makes the complexity of the city readable, and immobilizes its opaque mobility in a transparent text" (92). Similarly, Yorston looking out from Windows on the World a few minutes before the attacks, remarks: "the city stretches out like a huge checkerboard, all the right angles, the perpendicular cubes, the adjoining squares, the intersecting rectangles, the parallel lines, the network of ridges, a whole artificial geometry in gray, black, and white" (14). To look down on the city from on high is to revel in what de Certeau calls the "erotics of knowledge." "Seeing the whole" creates a "voluptuous pleasure" ("Walking in the City," 92), because such overview makes the city legible. Overflowing street life swallows up the individual and submerges her in a chaotic wash of sensations and impressions. In contrast, the observer at the top of the tower becomes the center around which the city revolves. From above, one has a sense of mastery. The confusing hustle and bustle at street level dissolves into an orderly geometry. It is that sense of order that will crumble after the terrorist attacks. As Una Chauduri wrote: "The Twin Towers include in their tragedy the arrogant illusion of abstract, distant, visual mastery. In their violent absenting we may discern the twin principles of classical tragedy: *hubris*; and *de casibus*, the fall of great ones"(Román et al., "A Forum," 97).

The view from above finds its counterpart (and thus the symbolic resonance of the towers is further expanded) in a virtuoso set piece in which "Beigbeder" as a ten-year-old boy is taken to visit the World Trade Center by his father. With a Super-8 camera, he begins to film the towers from below. "It was the first time," writes "Beigbeder," "I realized that being on the ground looking up was as frightening as being high up looking down" (247). He feels dwarfed by the towers—"*physically dominated*" (247; italics in the original)—but, in a typical upsurge of emotion closely related to the sense of the sublime, he also feels uplifted and inspired: "The crushing size of these colossuses was my first contact with the metaphysical—catechism lessons at the Ecole Bossuet were less exotic" (247). If looking down on the city from above induces "imaginary totalizations produced by the eye" (de Certeau, "Walking in the City," 93), the low-angle shot from below leads to a sense of being in the presence of the divine. The perspective is steeply perpendicular and seems like "a highway to heaven" (246). While the bird's eye view produces legibility and clarity, the worm's eye view results in notions of transcendence. In both cases, the sheer size of the buildings is responsible for the effect. To be at the top of the World Trade Center is to have visual and mental mastery over the city. To stand at the base of the towers is to receive an impression of the technological sublime and, if one follows the upward sweep of the columns reaching into the sky, even of a world beyond the merely physical.

If the views from above and from below expand the presence of the towers, the novel also provides an interior view of the towers and in this way complements the panoptic and transcendental readings with a third, purely materialistic one. As Roland Barthes remarks in "The Eiffel Tower," "architecture is always dream and function, expression of a utopia and instrument of a convenience" (6). That is to say, a building has a practical as well as a symbolic function. In this context Mark Wigley reminds us: "The key symbolic role of the World Trade Center, the rationale for both its design and is [sic] destruction, was to represent the global marketplace." And more clearly: "The corporate building provides a fixed, visible face for an unfixed, invisible and carnivorous organization" ("Insecurity by Design," 74, 75).

Yorston is made aware of this functionality of the tower when he remarks that through the telescopes on the top floor of the WTC one can see the secretaries arrive in the adjacent buildings: "cell phones glued to their ears, dressed in pale gray figure-hugging pantsuits, coiffured hair, expensive sneakers, pumps stuffed into their fake Prada handbags" (4). The secretaries are deindividualized, homogenized by late capitalism. They have become identified with their functions and associated with their (fake) fashion accessories, or, like the restaurant hostesses, made recognizable only by their "lapel badge[s]" (4). Similarly, the customers in the restaurant behave like anonymous monads, avoiding one another's glances. All they have in common is "their paunches" (31). They come from all over the world, and they all embody the caricature of the fat, gluttonous capitalist. To complete the cliché, a Brazilian businessman even lights a cigar (22). Sitting in the restaurant, Yorston overhears two stockbrokers (a man and a woman) mix adulterous talk with jargony comments on the rise and fall of stocks and bonds. Their banter stands for two forms of characteristically postmodern shallowness—marital faithlessness and financial greed—both of which are instances of unbridled desire. The stockbrokers are identified only by their designer clothes: "the guy in Kenneth Cole," "the blonde in Ralph Lauren." They exist by virtue of the commodity label.

The towers of the World Trade Center, as represented in *Windows on the World*, are productive of a mixed symbolism. Architecturally, they are minimalist boxes. Their identical form—one mirroring the other—and the identical plan of each floor replicate the replaceability and reproductivity of the economic system they are an important part of (Sorkin, *Starting from Zero*, 10). Their exterior simplicity, however, allows readings in many directions, of which the novel activates three, corresponding with the physical orientations of top-bottom, bottom-top, and level. The text presents these three cultural-semantic positions but also allows them to whirl through one another, collide, and remain in unresolved suspension. This becomes obvious in a prose poem in which "Beigbeder" evokes the towers in their full polysemy (238). He assigns them a quasi-religious role: "New Yorkers turned towards the World Trade Center as though toward Mecca" (238). And he asks himself whether the towers "fulfill[ed] some spiritual emptiness." Simultaneously, they are imaged as "the legs which supported the American dream." Throughout, the towers have a material and a metaphysical relevance. At dusk they stand out as "two columns of light," but from close up one can see "thousands of tiny yellow squares, the lighted windows of little offices, . . . in which thousands of marionettes answered their phones" (238). In all their magnificence, the towers boost morale. They form "the indomitable lighthouse of the world" to which New Yorkers turn as to a beacon. At the same time, they destroy morale. They are a "luminous anthill," in which the worker ants perform their endless and senseless routines. The towers embody the phantasmagoric bind, as Walter Benjamin described it: they represent simultaneously all that is enticing about the city and all that is mind-deadening and rebarbative (Leslie, *Benjamin*, 194).

If the materialist and the transcendental readings of the skyscrapers demonstrate unresolved tensions within the text, there is also a spatial-temporal conflict that is resolved only by the events of 9/11 themselves. The prose poem, in which the mixed meanings of the towers clash, is retrospective by necessity. The view of the towers is posthumous and a posteriori: the towers are no more. In other words, in a gesture that characterizes the novel as a whole, space rubs against time. Here space, like time, first turns spectral. The text shapes a chronotope, which consists not of the welding of space and time but the welding of time and nonspace. All one can say about the World Trade Center is inevitably colored by the tragic knowledge of its disappearance. This negative chronotope pervades the whole novel and appears with special sharpness in a number of individual scenes. When "Beigbeder" calls the telephone number of Windows on the World, he ironically reaches the answering machine of a "company specializing in event management" (8). When he looks up restaurant reviews in some old guidebooks (35–38), he finds that the fantastic views and the haute cuisine in Windows on the World receive equal praise. But this sense of the phantasmagoric has been pierced by time. The splendor that once was has been reduced to naught, and the old guidebook descriptions have become memento mori. The text rephrases the paradox of the empty chronotope: "The past is now the only place where you can find Windows on the World" (37).

Space also turns spectral in a second manner. Though the World Trade Center disappeared from the face of the earth and therefore is to be found nowhere (except in the past), by the same token it is now to be found everywhere. September 11, as an apocalyptic event, has seeped into the collective unconscious, and the absent towers are present everywhere as symptoms of a half-buried trauma. This awareness crops up even in unlikely places. Thus when "Beigbeder" visits the Empire State Building in the spring of 2003, he visits a World Trade Center analogue (203–5). To put it differently, the Empire State Building is haunted by its disappeared other. A visit to its observation deck can no longer be innocent. For one thing, the snow that is falling during his visit reminds "Beigbeder" of the "white powder" that fell from the heavens on 9/11 (203). For another, the Empire State Building's rediscovered prominence as the "pinnacle of the city" (205) is the result of the transformation of the skyline by terrorist violence. The absence of the Twin Towers is a ghostly presence. When one visits one building, the others necessarily shape the parameters within which the visit takes place.

More than the Empire State Building, however, it is the Tour Montparnasse in Paris that figures as the World Trade Center's *"endroit jumeau"* (French original, 51) or "sister site" (37). Imaginatively, the space of the World Trade Center is doubled. Even though "Beigbeder," the narrator-protagonist, realizes that "the Tour Montparnasse isn't the third World Trade Center tower" (155), and though he realizes that it is much smaller, he mentions a series of similarities, starting with the fact that in Paris the original idea was to build two identical towers one next to the other (70). The restaurants at the top of World Trade Center One and the Montparnasse building command magnificent views (7 and 115, 21). In both restaurants the protagonists overhear the "brainless conversations" (7) of stockbrokers and moneymakers, who speak a jargony lingo, full of barracks terms. Most of all, both buildings embody a utopian vision, the "age-old fantasy of man . . . to build his own mountains" (15). Both represent the euphoria and optimism of the 1970s, to which 9/11 put an abrupt stop.

Physically, the Parisian skyscraper is the survivor building: "Le Ciel de Paris is all that remains of the Windows on the World: an idea" (29). But the doom of the New York towers also foreshadows the fate of their Parisian counterpart. "Beigbeder's" whole approach to the Tour Montparnasse speaks to the globalization of gloom and fear. He sees the Parisian tower "as the last pin standing in a bowling alley" (70), about to be knocked down by the same violent forces that knocked down the World Trade Center, possibly some ten years later (76). His fears come to a head when, imitating the exodus from the New York buildings on September 11, he decides to go down the stairs from the top of the Tour Montparnasse all the way to street level. The Paris skyscraper becomes a spectral building, permeated by echoes of its doomed twin. "Since September 11," notes "Beigbeder," "I see the Tour Montparnasse differently" (70).

On February 15, 2003, he pays a visit to the rooftop of the Parisian building. Spatially and temporally removed from the event—he is some

3,000 miles away from New York, nearly a year and a half after 9/11—the visit is yet marked by a lingering 9/11 presence. In a way, his behavior in the Montparnasse tower testifies to the existence of a quiet apocalypse. September 11 is an enduring situation that "contaminates" spaces geographically far removed. Everything is laden with a new significance. He notices, for instance, how the fire regulations and emergency measures at the Tour Montparnasse are woefully inadequate. He notices, too, how planes take off from the nearby airport in Orly. Such views have no longer the neutrality they once had, and the ominous note that creeps into the text is spun off from 9/11, expressive of a general unrest—a world nervous and on edge.

Protagonists

One of the most puzzling features of *Windows on the World* is that the novel has two narrator-protagonists, from whose perspectives the story is told in short, alternating chapters that average only two pages in length. One protagonist is the writer himself, or rather "Beigbeder," his novelized self; the other is Carthew Yorston, his main character. "Beigbeder" is portrayed as a writer and journalist, enjoying modest fame in Paris; Yorston as an anonymous real estate agent from Texas, finding himself, in the company of his two young sons, in the wrong place at the wrong time. The troubling thing about this binary setup is that the two main characters are each other's doubles without being each other's alter egos. They resemble each other so much as to be virtually indistinguishable. Between the protagonists and within the economy of the novel there is not the division of labor one would expect. Given the different locations and circumstances of the two narrators, one would think that one narrative would by nature be experiential (Yorston's), the other reflective ("Beigbeder's"), that one would be characterized by participation, the other by contemplation, one by action and the other by thought, that one would represent the viewpoint of the traumatized firsthand victim, the other that of the sympathetic but ultimately uncomprehending bystander.

Instead, Yorston and "Beigbeder" resemble each other to a fault. They both complain about a boring childhood. They each have divorced the mother of their child ("Beigbeder") or children (Yorston), for which both feel guilty. The children themselves are spoiled and hard to handle, even though they are dearly loved. The protagonists both have a difficult relationship with a new girlfriend. In a phone message, Yorston promises his newfound love to marry her if he gets out of the tower, while "Beigbeder," after a falling-out, rushes back from New York to Paris to propose marriage to his fiancée. At one point it is suggested that the protagonists may be relatives, but that is later denied (361, 365). At any rate, both have a genealogy that goes back to the earliest days of the American Republic. At many removes, Yorston is related to John Adams, while "Beigbeder" has a distant ancestor who was mortally wounded in the Battle of Bunker Hill.

Most confusingly, the two protagonists speak with the same voice and share the same psychological outline. They are joyless hedonists. They experience the hunt for pleasure as a heavy burden imposed upon them by the zeitgeist, and they are disgusted by their own philandering. They present themselves as pathetic losers: "Beigbeder" thinks of himself as an "emotional cripple" (180), while Yorston compares himself to Lester Burnham (39–40), the beaten-down middle-class antihero of the suburban movie *American Beauty*. So closely related are their perspectives that it is sometimes hard to figure out whether Yorston or "Beigbeder" is speaking.

Such doubleness without difference has a number of drawbacks. Since the feelings, ideas, and existential situations of each protagonist echo the other's, the binary expectations of the reader are frustrated.[4] No dialectical tension develops, and the novel remains strangely monotonous or univocal. One wanders from one short chapter to the next without sense of a caesura. It should make a huge difference whether a fictionalized character sits cozily in the corner of a Parisian restaurant working away on a novel or is desperately fighting for air in a building where a fire rages. The main weakness of this novel is that it does not. Essential distinctions remain underarticulated. Obvious contrasts go unexplored.

This is related to yet another, even more crippling deficiency. Yorston—as the indistinguishable counterpart to the novelized author—has no existence of his own. His voice has no urgency. Just like "Beigbeder," he breaks out in miniessays that, given the precarious situation he finds himself in, lack all sense of verisimilitude. Yorston shares with "Beigbeder" indirectness and long-windedness. His contemplative intermezzos, in which the Texas real estate agent is supposed to be conversant with the writings of Kafka, the music of John Cage, and the intricacies of French history (e.g., the Saint Bartholomew's Day Massacre [231]), make the tale completely unrealistic. Even his description of the impact of the plane on the building has something distanced and measured to it, as if this were a tract more than a live report: "When a [*sic*] American Airlines Boeing 767 slams into a building below your feet, there are two immediate consequences. Firstly.... Secondly..." (59). Such discursive lassitude, wherein no subjective reality is tested by dramatic situation, eviscerates person and experience. An abstract vocabulary does little justice to the true horror of the situation. In all circumstances, Yorston's voice remains staid and reflective because the author is too obviously ventriloquizing through him. Since Yorston is nothing but a voice, and since he does not develop a voice of his own, Yorston does not exist except as the author-ventriloquist's puppet. This is a true shortcoming in the novel, and it cannot be glossed over by applying to it the label of hyperrealism. Beigbeder is good at flashy witticisms and sardonic comments, often at his own expense, and this sort of mundane *savoir-dire* serves him well in the portrayal of his fictional namesake. But his smart-aleck style misses a whole register. In depicting pain, suffering, and panic, he is simply hopeless. As Caroline Bee puts it, "[Beigbeder's] attempt to penetrate into the secrets of horror, panic and the pain of charred corpses plummeting to the sidewalks of New York is a total failure" ("The Center"). The scenes in the burning tower are woefully underimagined. As a result, the book is more an essay than a novel, in that lived experience is substituted by unsystematic and searching rumination.

The New International Novel

The undifferentiated treatment of the protagonists in *Windows on the World* makes for a thinness of texture and a psychological poverty. But at the level of ideas, the parallelism proves that, for better or worse, the condition of postmodernity is shared by Europe and the United States.

Yorston and "Beigbeder" are almost indistinguishable American and French incarnations of postmodernity; they share a common lifestyle and are immersed in the same semiotic codes. In the aggregate, they form a composite portrait of the postmodern Everyman, prosperous but adrift, enjoying "a hollow freedom" (169) within an apocalyptic scheme. They both undergo 9/11 as the occasion for a personal stock-taking. September 11 is an epochal event equally for the Texan real estate agent within the tower as for the Parisian writer far removed from it.

In other words, as an international novel, the book depicts September 11 as a historical episode that reestablishes the category of the transatlantic West. It does so militantly and unapologetically. Given the rift that opened between the United States and France as a result of the Iraq war, this assertion of a fundamental cultural unity is also a taboo-breaking challenge to the assumptions of the left-leaning French intelligentsia, whose anti-Americanism is inbred, automatic, and often hysterical.

The category of the West is reconstructed first of all *ex negativo*; that is to say, it is stridently anti-Muslim and anti-Arab. Yorston, in particular, rails at the "hairy, bearded sand eaters, crouching round in sandals with a machine gun in one hand, shouting slogans that are as hateful as they are incomprehensible" (292). He suggests somewhat contradictorily that the Judeo-Christian democracies have grown weak through compassion (288) and that the Arab countries lack culture and civilization because they do not have pity or mercy (293). He pokes fun at the "tender, charitable, liberal Judeo-Christians" (288), who turn the other cheek instead of meeting violence with violence.

His sentiments are shared by "Beigbeder," who calls the Islamic fundamentalists "bearded hypocrites" (289) and who reports the following incident when he takes his girlfriend to a nightclub in the basement of the Tour Montparnasse: "I hugged my darling to me and kissed her at the French equivalent of Ground Zero. I'd quite happily have had her in the restroom, but she refused. 'Sorry, tonight my pussy is observing Ramadan!'" (28). This tasteless remark is followed by a comment meant to add insult to injury:

> I'd like to apologize to the Muslim authorities in advance for the preceding joke. I know perfectly well that it is permitted to eat at night during

the Ramadan. Be magnanimous. There's no need for a fatwa: I'm famous enough already.... Apparently, the Tour Montparnasse is in no danger of an attack by Islamic fundamentalists because it houses the French offices of al-Jazeera. (28)

In this outrageous paragraph, the Muslim faith is equated with Islamic fundamentalism and both the fatwa against Salman Rushdie and the attacks of 9/11 are invoked as representative acts of Islam. Most aggressively, religious rituals are used metaphorically to refer to the protagonist's sexual predilections. As elsewhere in the novel (188), Western hedonism is contrasted with Islamic self-righteousness. According to this view, Muslims are hate-mongering spoilsports whose sexual frustrations result in death-dealing fanaticism.

However, the picture is more complicated. The West is not solely constructed by othering Islam. Yorston has no good word to say about the American born-again Christians among whom he grew up and whom he accuses of arrogance and indifference vis-à-vis the rest of the world (112). He calls the preponderant religion in America "a sister-enemy of fundamentalist Islam" (231), and he complains bitterly: "I am going to die because of an incestuous quarrel between billionaire sects" (231). Similarly, "Beigbeder" is aware of the fact that fundamentalism has its origins in the growing gap between rich and poor (115), and he pleads for the establishment of a world government, adding that the multicultural society in New York can serve as a model and example (251). What all of this amounts to is that the West is equated with a rationalist program that is threatened by intolerance and religious extremism both from within and without. The anti-Arab feeling is just one element in this complex mix. The outbreaks of anti-Muslim sentiment in the attitudes of both Yorston and "Beigbeder" must be understood as a knee-jerk reaction to the violence of 9/11. The novel illustrates how under extreme circumstances it is difficult to keep one's fair-mindedness and sense of nuance.

The attempt to picture a joint Western episteme gains further force through "Beigbeder's" unambiguous Americanophilia. Repeatedly, he points out how culturally, historically and linguistically, the United States and France are linked by an umbilical cord. For one thing, he mentions how the "United States was born" at 56 Rue Jacob, because it was there that the Treaty of Paris, putting an end to the War of Independence with the British, was signed (15). He points out how American culture has undergone several French influences and, more provocatively, how France has been permeated by things American. "I am writing this book," he remarks, "because I'm sick of bigoted anti-Americanism" (16–17). He follows this statement with a veritable love song to America, in which he enumerates all his favorite American writers, musicians, and film directors (17). He praises American artists for the quality of their work, their artistic courage, and their self-critical stance.

In the process, the novel also cheekily puts down French cultural and historical pretensions. Yorston's children, for instance, have never heard of France, which their father defines for them as a "small European country" (13). He explains that France "helped America to free itself from the yoke of English oppression between 1776 and 1783 and that, to show our appreciation, our soldiers liberated them from the Nazis in 1944" (13). Such a cameo history of French-U.S. relations does much to illustrate how, in the course of the centuries, the tables have been turned and how the historical advantage is now on the Western side of the Atlantic. When looking at the "glorious, ancient monuments" of Paris, "Beigbeder" exclaims: "the only thing Uncle Sam left us is our seniority" (114). The twentieth-century technological achievements of France are negligible when compared to those of the United States: the ill-fated French-British Concorde supersonic plane (taken out of service after a fatal crash) was born out of frustration with the American conquest of the moon (158). The Tour Montparnasse, not even half the height of the Twin Towers, is introduced as their "miniature replica" (136).

More devastatingly, France has also lost its cultural edge. The much-vaunted French "cultural exception" is defined self-disparagingly as the practice of "churning out exceptionally tedious movies, exceptionally slapdash books and, all in all, works of art which are exceptionally pedantic and self-satisfied" (19). Even the roots of May '68, an iconic French event, lie in the United States, according to "Beigbeder" (76), while the sexual revolution was also an American product invented and promoted by Hugh Hefner in particular, who created "the man without seriousness," the man "who must have pleasure at any price" (142). Yet "Beigbeder" also identifies America with "cultural xenophobia, corporate contempt, and advertising overkill" (19), and elsewhere he points out that France can still be useful to the United States (194). His pro-Americanism is not without reservations, and the sense predominates that the two societies are interdependent. September 11 has intensified this feeling of essential unity: "We are the same: even if we are not all Americans, our problems are theirs, and theirs ours" (305). The new international novel does not play off American innocence against European corruption but emphasizes the connections between the continents, which are the cultural product of globalization, the universal media, and frequent and cheap travel. Most of all, the newfound unity is the product of shared trauma: 9/11 is not an exclusively American tragedy but a condition shared by all of the advanced nations.

Babel

In describing the shared post-9/11 condition, Beigbeder quotes repeatedly from one of Western culture's oldest disaster narratives, involving the building and the ruin of a tower. As a running comment, which oddly stands outside the narrative's alternating between Yorston and "Beigbeder" and which appears for the first time in the chapter describing the impact of the plane, the author recounts the story of the tower of Babel: how by constructing a high edifice the human race grew proud, defied God, and was punished by having its unified language scattered and "the link between word and object" destroyed (121).

The reference to Babel reinforces the reading of 9/11 as an apocalyptic event. More particularly, it stresses how 9/11, as an "unrelatable" occurrence, involves the disintegration of language and thus has to be staged as a discursive dispersal, a linguistic brokenness. In one of his first entries "Beigbeder" notes: "It's impossible to write about this subject, and yet impossible to write about anything else. Nothing else touches us" (8); a page later: "This thing happened, and it is impossible to relate" (9). The novel explicitly and implicitly spells out the conditions of this impossibility, and, emphatically, 9/11 is imaged as the shattering of language. Its effects can only be evoked in fits and starts and not through systematic recall or an integrated "working through." That is why the novel gives the impression of stylistic brinkmanship (which sometimes spills over into kitschy trickiness).

Here are some of the devices Beigbeder uses:

1. The 120 short chapters read like diary jottings or journal entries. Self-mockingly, "Beigbeder" calls them "ITNNOTs (Instant Though Not Necessarily Original Theories)" (280). Ideas are caught on the wing. There is a footlooseness and lack of rigor within those hastily scribbled notes, which, within the same entry, send the reader from the horrors in the offices of Cantor Fitzgerald in the burning tower to a lame description of "Beigbeder's" visit to the observation deck of the Empire State Building. Logical connections are cut. The intent behind many of the entries is to link "Beigbeder's" experience to that of the people in the towers. The disparateness of the comments suggests that such links are far-fetched and hard to come by. The events of 9/11 stay outside the reach of ordinary parlance and there is no adequate equivalent in normal experience. Thus the novel—in a sort of self-destructive move—attacks its own premises and questions the transferability of the trauma it is describing.

2. Goofiness, inappropriateness, thumbing one's nose at seriousness, madcap meditations: these suggest that the only adequate discursive reaction to 9/11 is to transgress. What should the reader make, for instance, of the following passage?

> Who is mad? Who is sacred? Our God is crucified. We worship a bearded man in a loincloth tortured on a cross. It is time to found a new religion whose symbol would be two towers ablaze. Let us build churches of parallel parallelepipeds in which, at the moment of communion, two remote-controlled scale models of planes would be crashed. At the moment when the planes pierce the towers, the congregation would be asked to kneel.
>
> (280)

An entry like this shows a typical mixture of blasphemous arrogance, discursive desperation, and seriousness. The text indicates that 9/11 was a sacred moment, a moment of transubstantiation. Such serious thought can only be relayed, though, if accompanied by a large dose of subversive humor. It is in passages like these that one feels that Beigbeder's concept of hyperrealism involves a recoding of reality: the events are rewritten in a different key and, in fact, are purposely and ironically off-key.

3. "Beigbeder" demonstrates how a 9/11 consciousness has seeped into the language and poses "a serious semantic problem" (93) asking himself, "What verb should one use for parking a plane in a building?" (93). The passage that follows consists of one more bewildering gimmick, but it reveals that language (as the repository of common knowledge) is not prepared to deal with this unprecedented event. Language has to be stretched to accommodate a new reality; neologisms have to be coined to reflect a totally unexpected situation. The linguistic difficulty that is presented by 9/11 is further stressed by the fact that the ultimate pun the author comes up with (*"attourrissage,"* French original, 120) proves to be untranslatable in English.

4. Some of the concluding chapters are exceedingly short, as the result of what the author announces to be deliberate cuts. He writes: "Please excuse our misuse of ellipses. I have cut out the awful descriptions. I have not done so out of propriety, nor out of respect for the victims because I believe that describing their slow agonies, their ordeal, is also a mark of respect. I cut them because, in my opinion, it is more appalling still to allow you to imagine what became of them" (276). Whether such reticence is a gimmick or a sign that "Beigbeder," for all his volubility, recognizes the functionality of silence, remains a moot point.

5. The characters undertake desperate attempts to recode the event in order to grasp and control the situation. Often popular culture serves as a frame of reference, often, not surprisingly, movies, especially disaster and action movies (148), which seem to be the only analogues to 9/11 the culture has to offer. Along the same lines, Yorston tries to becalm his children by pretending the attack is part of a theme-park ride, and his youngest son keeps believing that his father will turn into Ultra-Dude and is only waiting for an opportune moment to come to the rescue by unleashing his "googolplex superpowers" (139) or "trajectoral hyperpowers" (213). While this recourse to commercially marketed game scenarios may be interpreted as a particularly painful illustration of the commodification of the hitherto uncommodified and the colonization of the unconscious, one can also see it as the stubborn refusal of the young

child to let the events slip out of the bounds of familiarity. Discursively, David fights the indefinable with the few linguistic tools that are available to him.

6. Other discursive devices that, in their hour of need, the characters resort to are prayer (127), song (Irving Berlin's "God Bless America," 239), popular quiz games, a government questionnaire, and, more surprisingly but emphatically, poetry. One of the epigraphs of the book is a long extract from Walt Whitman's *Leaves of Grass*, while the American poet's "Salut au Monde" also figures largely (16). One of "Beigbeder's" sections is taken up by a prose poem of Baudelaire's from the 1865 *Paris Spleen* series, which a parenthetical note tells us "should be retitled *New York Spleen*" (294). Finally, Yorston himself (half an hour into the disaster) composes a prose poem. Again, this must be accounted for as a hyperreality rather than a reality effect. And it represents one more recoding of the event, one more effort to master it discursively. Yorston mainly enumerates what he sees around him in the abandoned offices of the burning tower. But the layout of the page, and in particular the broad white margin and the double spaces between the lines, turn observation into poetry, which in this way gets a privileged position as an expressive means to go beyond mere description and to introduce a note of stillness and meditation. In this effort the whiteness of the page is all-important, as it surrounds the objects with an air of eternity and gives them depth:

An abandoned wheelchair

Brokers' offices but no brokers

A stapler forgotten on a photocopier

Filling [*sic*] cabinets overturned with the files still filed

(149)

This is a Whitmanesque catalogue, but the shortness of the phrases (as opposed to Whitman's winding periods) and the whiteness surrounding the lines introduce a Baudelairean note of spleen. Mentioning the objects evokes their absence. Simple names are loaded with the forebodings of doom.

7. At some crucial points in the text, it is no longer possible to figure out which voice one is hearing. To quote one example among many: the section at 9:31 is written from David's perspective, but the final paragraph (in which the empty Command Center on the twenty-second floor of the North Tower is imagined as a symbol of a universe without a God [197]), could not possibly reflect the thoughts of a seven-year-old and therefore must be interpreted as a sudden intrusion by the author. Thus not only is the neat alternation between chapters featuring "Beigbeder's" voice and Yorston's interrupted by a few sections written from the viewpoints of the children, Jerry or David, but within the sections themselves there are strange *obiter dicta* and *membra disjecta* that do not seem to belong anywhere. The straightjacket that the author has imposed upon himself to present the material is not tenable; the form will not hold. Comments, sneers, and ironic interjections cannot be postponed. The formal rigidity cracks under the weight of the egregious circumstances.

8. All in all, the dodges and stratagems indicate that 9/11 is an untranslatable and unnarratable event: all the discursive strategies fail. There is no narrative ploy strong enough to deflect the event, no trope or stylistic device capable of stopping the irreversible progress of time. Several discourses (religious, poetic, demotic) are pitted against the event. But it does not budge. There is no way around it. The "inexplicable" disaster is bound to happen. The ineluctable is ineluctable. Discourse ultimately proves to be useless and empty.

Babylon or the End of Irony

"The moments we call crises are ends and beginnings," writes Frank Kermode in his seminal study on apocalyptic literature (*The Sense of an Ending*, 96). The apocalypse is literally an un-veiling, a revelation of hidden truth. More specifically, "what was *chronos* becomes *kairos*" (46), *chronos* being mere "'passing time' or 'waiting time'" (46), while "*kairos* is the season, a point in time filled with significance, charged with a meaning derived from its relation to the end" (46). The difference between *chronos* and *kairos* is that between mere "chronicity and times which are concordant and full" (49–50).

For all the disparateness of its stylistic means and the postmodernity of its protagonists, *Windows on the World* inscribes itself perfectly into an apocalyptic scheme that envisages the end of one world as the birth of a new one. September 11 is presented as an epoch-making event, demarcating a before and an after—a historical caesura that ushers in a new and better order. Apocalyptic events, writes James Berger, "function as definitive historical divides, as ruptures, pivots, fulcrums separating what came before from what came after.... Previous historical narratives are shattered; new understandings of the world are generated. Apocalypse thus, finally, has an interpretive, explanatory function, which is, of course, its etymological sense: as revelation, unveiling, uncovering" (*After the End*, 5).

Windows on the World is ripped apart and acquires an air of bewilderment and oddity by the disparateness of its stylistic means, on the one hand, and the weightiness of the apocalyptic moral it urges, on the other. The bad jokes, the offhand remarks, and the zigzagging lucubrations all tend to ironize content. Yet underneath the mundane polish there is a thesis that begs to be taken seriously. The fall of the towers betokens the fall of an era. The scheme enacted is one of shattering, but in true apocalyptic fashion, it also involves repentance and restoration, public and personal, historical and private. That is to say, the unified West that the novel evokes is not only an analogue to the biblical Babel. It is also a new version of Babylon, the city of moral decadence and turpitude that is destroyed in the Book of the Apocalypse only to be replaced by the New Jerusalem, an ideal city of harmony and love. "Hedonism is at its peak," "Beigbeder" concludes. "Babylon lives again!"(189).

Two of the people dying in Tower One are the adulterous stockbrokers identified only as "the guy in Kenneth Cole" and "the blonde in Ralph Lauren." What happens between them is a typical vignette of decadence, reflecting the degraded mores of the early twenty-first century. Their interests are purely materialistic to the point where "the guy in Kenneth Cole" regrets most of all that, in case they die, his lover will "never get to see [his] home cinema system ... plasma screen the size

of Lake Superior" (159; ellipsis in the original). Even though she is offered the opportunity and even though she realizes that it may be her
last chance, the "blonde in Ralph Lauren" refuses to call her mother
because she has nothing to say, illustrating the demise of the family as a
structuring agent. As their last living deed, the two lovers clamber onto
a large conference table and, knowing they will perish, proceed to have
uninhibited sex. The scene—which for some reason has been bowdler-
ized in the English translation—is essential to the novel. Even though it
is highly unrealistic, it carries an important allegorical charge. The unre-
strained, bawdy talk and the unashamed corporeal abandon of the commercial class dying in the World Trade Center—the financial heart of the
financial capital of the world—stands for a lifestyle in which the pursuit
of happiness has been degraded into a pursuit of sex and money.

In the novel nobody escapes this condition of moral decrepitude.
Apart from the two traders, the two protagonists also provide portraits
of preapocalyptic decadence. Yorston left his wife and led the life of
the philandering socialite because, after making a small fortune in real
estate, he asked himself: "What was the point of earning all that money
if I was going to be stuck with the same woman every night?" (48). He
is aware that, in abandoning his family, he acted like "a bastard" (106).
But he blames society in general for his lack of responsibility. The role
of pater familias is no longer sustained by the culture, which promotes
pleasure at all costs: "How could anyone want to be like Lester Burnham
when society idolizes Jim Morrison?" (106).

Similarly, "Beigbeder," amateur of nightclubs and connoisseur of the
delights of lap dances, feels guilty for having divorced the mother of his
little daughter. In a series of savage satirical rants, he accuses himself of
emotional instability but blames "the consumer society for making me
what I am: insatiable" (182). And he reproaches his parents (divorced,
too) for making him "vague" (182; "déstructuré," French original, 223).
He mentions how Hugh Hefner, the founder of *Playboy*, has destroyed
the old morality and introduced the "INTERNATIONAL PLAYBOY,"
"the man without seriousness," "who never looks for love, only for pleasure" (142). "Freedom had killed off marriage and the family, couples,
and children. Faithfulness had become a concept that was reactionary,
impossible, inhuman" (142). Since he lives "in no man's land: neither an

INTERNATIONAL PLAYBOY or MARRIED AND PROUD OF IT" (180), he is full of self-disgust. He has the feeling that he is "squatting [his] own life" (183), and his motto is: "become what you despise"(220). September 11 puts an end to this empty frivolity. It is the apocalyptic turning point that erases the past and ushers in a new future. "There is a communist utopia," writes "Beigbeder"; "that utopia died in 1989. There is a capitalist utopia; that died in 2001" (164). The downfall of the towers is embedded in a historical scheme and comes to signify "the breakdown of the designer-label society" (284), "the collapse of a house of credit cards" (9). September 11 is a moment of enlightenment. In extremis, Yorston realizes that his betrayal of the family was wrong and his libertinism a fraud: "I realized I'd been wrong about everything" (202). Taking stock of his life the moment he is about to lose it, he becomes aware that his hedonistic wishes are beside the point and that it would have been more fulfilling simply to have been a "better man" (218).

For "Beigbeder," too, the events of September 11 are an ethical turning point. He indicates that "like all the writers of my generation, I was forever marked by the eighties religion of money, hypnotized by the glamor, the arrogance of yuppies, synthesizer music and designer furniture, fashion shows and the democratization of porn, the taste for discotheques and the poetry of airports" (284). In the penultimate chapter, faced with Ground Zero ("the largest crematorium in the world" [308]), he renounces his material and carnal interests. He decides to propose marriage to his fiancée, because "love alone gives . . . the right to hope" (308).

Thus the time before 9/11 is denoted as *chronos*, mere waiting or passing time. The personal pasts of the two protagonists—wanton dissoluteness and sexual license—are projected upon the pre-9/11 era as a whole. "Beigbeder" evokes the razzle-dazzle quality of the sexual free-for-all in the 1970s and 1980s. At the same time, he indicates the fatigue, the saturation, and the lassitude: "There are no winners, only losers like me" (189). "We laugh ourselves silly one minute, next minute we're miserable" (190).

Within this context of "chronic irresponsibility" and "ontological cowardice" (211), the collapse of the World Trade Center ushers in a transfigurative experience: "the immovable is movable. What we thought was fixed is shifting. What we thought solid is liquid" (8). The old contours melt. Out of the crucible of fire comes a new era: that of *kairos*, the fullness of time, when the shallowness of postmodern liberty and irony gives way to a new seriousness, sensual indulgence is replaced by spousal steadfastness and parental responsibility, and the brokenness of language is restored and words regain their true meaning.

It adds to the quirkiness of this novel that these claims for a moral reawakening in the face of tragedy are made with the greatest seriousness. That times of crisis lead to hopes of a better world is a historical constant (see L. Kaplan, "American Idle") as well as an intrinsic feature of the apocalyptic as literary genre. But in this case, there is so much that works against the object lessons voiced explicitly and repeatedly that it becomes difficult to take so much seriousness seriously. The definitive reading of 9/11 clashes with the self-reflexivity and the spatiotemporal games in the novel. And the rollicking pleasure that is evident in describing the delights of decadence contradicts the final moral note. The message—for all its fervor—seems tacked on and only half sincere. But it is in this ambiguity that the novel's saving grace rests. *Windows on the World* may fail as a novel of conversion, but it provides arresting testimony to the mental crisis 9/11 provoked and to the moral confusion left in its wake.

5

SEPTEMBER 11 AND THE OTHER

FOR SOME DECADES NOW the concept of the Other (most often capitalized) has become a mainstay of cultural and literary studies. The concept was pioneered by the French philosopher Emmanuel Levinas, who substituted ethics for ontology as first philosophy. In the words of Sean Hand: "whereas Heidegger locates signification in existence as a project, Levinas locates it in responsibility for the Other" (in Levinas, *Reader*, 4). According to Levinas, everyone is essentially and before anything else interpellated by the face of the Other. He calls this interpellation, substitution, or passivity. By this he means that our intuition is ethical in that, before we come to self-awareness, we are preordained to be touched by what happens to the Other, in particular the suffering Other. In the words of Robert Eaglestone, according to Levinas, our "unconditional responsibility [for the Other] is not something we take on or a rule by which we agree to be bound: instead, it exists before us and we are 'thrown' into it, without any choice" (Eaglestone, *Ethical Criticism*, 138). In Levinas's own words, "Substitution frees the subject from ennui, that is, from the enchainment to itself, where the ego suffocates in itself due to the tautological way of identity, and ceaselessly seeks after the distraction of games and sleep in a movement that never wears out" (*Otherwise*, 124). For Levinas, the self finds itself by losing itself. True contentment (as opposed to ennui, enchainment, suffocation, or distraction) is the result of self-distancing. Ethical dedication to the Other amounts to self-fulfillment. Subjectivity is inextricably intertwined with and a function of substitution, taking the Other's place.

The concept of alterity has a related yet somewhat different meaning in postcolonial studies. Most influentially, Edward Said has pointed out that Western views of the East are tainted by Orientalism; that is, the "foreign" presence is not recognized in its own right but looked upon through the distorting lens of Eurocentric opinions. In this context, disrespect for the Other has come to be known (somewhat confusingly) as "othering" (lower-case), which means to treat somebody as an alien. The Other (upper-case) as a concept involves the recognition of the singular and self-generated identity of someone else, in particular someone belonging to a different ethnicity or culture. By contrast, "othering" is an act of exclusion, whereby, through prejudice, ignorance, or both, one refuses to treat someone else fully as an individual.

These multiple resonances of the complex concept of alterity come into play when one considers that, in the immediate aftermath of 9/11, the spontaneous expressions of sympathy with the victims and the tendency to side with the United States as the aggrieved nation almost inevitably entailed the practice of pinpointing and then accusing the enemy. In times of extreme stress, othering seems a normal reflex. Events as traumatic as the destruction of the Twin Towers are read as apocalyptic: there is a before and after, and that sharp demarcation also involves separating those who are "with us" from those who are "against us." In that process of othering, the Levinasian appeal of the Other's face tends to disappear in a tide of revanchist emotion and clannish togetherness. As the critic David Simpson writes: "war cannot easily survive the capacity to imagine oneself in the body of the other" (9/11, 99). In times of war, "othering" easily takes precedence over the recognition of the Other.

Such a tendency to make nonnegotiable, polarizing distinctions characterized the reaction of the Bush administration to 9/11 from the beginning. "The initial response of President Bush," writes Richard Kearney, "was to divide the world into good and evil" (*Strangers*, 111). While this political Manichaeism has been the subject of extensive commentary, it has largely escaped the attention of observers that, in the immediate aftermath of the events, when the opinions of American novelists were eagerly solicited by newspapers and magazines, they, too, struggled to find an appropriate tone to speak about the terrorist attacks. The creative imagination is usually associated with a certain power of explanation, a kind of affective or empathic understanding. Writers are supposed to practice imaginative identification, that is, the ability to get into someone else's skin, to feel, as Keats did, at one even with a sparrow in the gravel. In other words, novelists are supposed to have a special affinity with the Other. Even so, the immediate reaction of as savvy a novelist as Don DeLillo in his early essay in *Harper's Magazine* reveals how difficult it was at the time even for writers not to dichotomize the events, that is, not to fixate understandable anger on a well-defined enemy (see chapter 1). When the images of people jumping from the towers and of the towers themselves collapsing are still fresh on the retina and when an act of utter barbarity screams for revenge, it is difficult to maintain the empathic imagination. Novelists recoiled in horror and, in dealing with 9/11, in the mature manner of their craft—that is to say, staying away from the simplifications bandied around by most media and politicians at the time—they were confronted with a difficult question: how to exercise one's freedom of the imagination when faced with those who do not hesitate to use horrendous violence in order to abrogate that freedom and replace openness of thinking by prescription and religious dictate? How to practice the essential virtues of the West vis-à-vis those who hate the West and consider its regime too liberal and "too lax" (Updike, "Tuesday, and After," 28)? How to react humanely to inhuman violence? More pressingly even, does the interpellation of the Other, the exercise of imaginative identification and the practice of viewing a situation in its full complexity also entail the obligation to encompass the viewpoint of the terrorist? How, without for a moment condoning violence or implying moral equivalency, can one explore the roots of terrorism and explain the grounds of its existence?

As the psychoanalyst Ruth Stein puts it,

> Thinking about evil requires a tremendous effort of the imagination and a willingness to encompass mentally a totally threatening phenomenon. It is no easy task to enter deeply into a superhumanly entitled yet utterly despairing, radically contemptuous yet self-hating, ecstatically numbed state of mind.... Such a state of mind may feel alien and disturbing to one's usual self-states; pursued deeply, it becomes frightening. The shocking absence of compassion in evildoing is jarringly discordant with our Western ideals and humanistic values.   ("Evil as Love," 396)

Intrinsically, it is hard to imagine what drives a person to be the agent and principal in an intentional act of mass killing. In order not to "other" the terrorist, the effort required is "to understand something that is meant precisely to annihilate any understanding as well as any physical (or normal) existence" (Stein, "Evil as Love," 396).

The Writer's Dilemma

In immediate responses to what happened on that bright Tuesday morning, both John Updike and Paul Auster implicitly contrast the pluralism and multivocality of New York as a city to the single-minded bigotry of the terrorists. As such, they plunge into the heart of the writer's dilemma. They make respect for and tolerance of the Other the lynchpin of their defense of Western values. As a result, they necessarily and unavoidably "other" those who attack those values. September 11 shows the limits of tolerance and posits the problem of how to behave toward those who are intolerant of one's tolerance.

In notes jotted down on the day itself, Auster ruefully (and presciently) observes, "The consequences of this assault will no doubt be terrible. More violence, more death, more pain for everyone" ("Random Notes," 35). To counterpoise this dreadful prospect, he depicts a scene in the New York subway. He strangely calls his little tableau "Underground" (using the English rather than the American term for the metro), no doubt in order to suggest the Dantesque overtones the subway often carries. Traditionally, the subway, as a literary motif, figures as "a place of alienation, 'infelicitous space,' ... 'the space of hatred and combat'" (Versluys, "Voyages Into the Dark," 330). Its typical poets are T. S. Eliot, Hart Crane, and Allen Tate, who introduce the motif to disparage modernity as "a principle of disorder" ("Voyages into the Dark," 338). In contradistinction, Auster uses this most unprepossessing of places to project a Whitmanesque scene and adopts Whitmanesque rhythms in order to evoke the true spirit of New York. Without any form of introduction, as a self-evident counterexample to the mayhem caused by the terrorists—at the same time as nothing less than a love song to the city—he asyndetically describes the passengers in the train: "The thin men with their briefcases, the voluminous women with their Bibles and devotional pamphlets, the high school kids with their forty-pound textbooks. Trashy novels, comic books, Melville and Tolstoy, *How to Attain Inner Peace*" (36). Borrowing a page from Whitman, Auster uses the momentum built up in the paragraph by sheer juxtaposition to describe what he calls the "delicate, altogether civilized art of minding one's own business" (36). Implicitly, while praising the inclusiveness that marks the cosmopolitan habitus and habitat, he condemns those who put that consensus at risk. This is most obvious when he stages a mini-crisis and demonstrates the exemplary behavior of the true New Yorker: "And then, never for any apparent reason, the lights go out, the fans stop whirring and everyone sits in silence, waiting for the train to start moving again. Never a word from anyone. Rarely even a sigh. My fellow New Yorkers sit in the dark, waiting with the patience of angels" (36). This is how the little vignette ends. The German sociologist Georg Simmel has famously associated urbanity with "reserve" and the practice of aloofness ("The Metropolis," 53). In bringing his impressions of 9/11 to a close, Auster refutes this whole dialectic of modernity and alienation to replace it with images implying fellowship, stoicism, and endurance. The message is clear: the patience of the "angels" sitting quietly in the subway is a response to the terrorists, whose impetuousness and intolerance brands them as devils.

By coincidence, John Updike, like Auster, found himself in Brooklyn that fateful morning. He watched the events unfold from a tenth-floor apartment across the East River. With the surefootedness that characterizes the veteran novelist, he immediately, in the opening sentence of his short contribution to *The New Yorker* of September 24, pinpoints the essential artistic challenge: "Suddenly summoned to witness something great and horrendous, we keep fighting not to reduce it to our own smallness" ("Tuesday, and After," 28). Updike instinctively understood that coping with the unprecedented brutality on display involved a measure of self-distancing and self-effacement. The method chosen to achieve this involves, in his case, the practice of aesthetic *Aufhebung*, or sublation. For him no Whitmanesque dithyrambs or breathless enumerations. It is not so much the vivacity of the city that commands his respect as its shimmering beauty. The sinuousness of his sentences—clause gliding into subclause, phrases surprising not just by the felicity of their diction but equally by their virtuoso syntactical arrangement—forms the linguistic equivalent of the complex texture of urban existence, which the terrorists, in their single-minded bigotry, want to destroy. Updike's very prose demonstrates freedom in action. Aesthetics is turned into a form of ethics, in that the subtlety of his observations and the felicity of formulation counter the fierce literalness of terrorist violence and vouchsafe a sensibility utterly alien to the vehemence of blind ideological alliance.

Yet even in this most delicately handled witness account of 9/11, it is not possible to avoid the conundrum of the Other and othering. At one point Updike writes, "War is conducted with a fury that requires abstraction—that turns a planeful of peaceful passengers, children included, into a missile the faceless enemy deserves. The other side has the abstractions" (28). This observation tallies with a remark Don De-Lillo would make a few weeks later in his essay in *Harper's*. Concerning the mindset of the terrorist, DeLillo writes, "Does the sight of a woman pushing a stroller soften the man to her humanity and vulnerability, and her child's as well, and all the people he is here to kill? . . . [T]here is no defenseless human at the end of his gaze" ("In the Ruins" 34).

Both Updike and DeLillo indicate that an elaborate system of "othering" and dehumanizing, in the name of abstract ideology, makes it possible for the terrorist to kill innocent people, including even children. Needless to say, in order to make this observation one has no choice but to "other" the terrorist oneself. From the terrorist's viewpoint, no doubt, homicidal attacks are justified not by mechanisms of dehumanization but by notions of self-sacrifice and holy struggle. Moreover, the assertion of freedom—as made manifest in the intricacies of Updike's syntax and the nuance of his assertions—is defenseless against abstractions that kill. In order to defend oneself, in order to claim one's right to survive (which is the very premise on which freedom is built), one has no choice but to hit back. Updike, aware that sensibility in itself is no shield again premeditated malice, writes, "walking around Brooklyn Heights that afternoon, as ash drifted in the air and cars were few and open-air lunches continued as usual on Montague Street, renewed the impression that, with all its failings, this is a country worth fighting for" (29). The built-in self-contradiction, as the political and military sequel would prove all too tragically, is that all wars are indeed fueled by abstractions, including the war waged to ward off the killer-abstractions of the other side. The sensitivity Updike displays and the cosmopolitan diversity he celebrates can only be maintained if protected by a military apparatus that is capacitated by the single-minded proclamation of one's own righteousness and thus by the very denial of diversity.

Triangulation

How to avoid, then, the knotty problem of "us" versus "them"? Obviously, when faced with an intransigent enemy, it is impossible to deny that there are insurmountable differences. In some cases, the Other insists on an otherness so complete that it refuses to be addressed and excludes all common ground. For radical Islamists, the West consists of infidel dogs. Against such unilateral rejection of communality there is no defense, except (armed) self-defense. And yet the efforts of many authors to deal with 9/11 (that most palpable symbol of enemy intractability) consists of an attempt to triangulate the situation, to find a way to avoid a stark binary split or dichotomy between one side that is totally right and the other side that is totally wrong.

A case in point is Nicholas Rinaldi's *Between Two Rivers*. In this underrated novel, Rinaldi succeeds in altering the one-sided, cliché perspective from which 9/11 is usually seen. He does so without stridency. There is no explicit repudiation of the political exploitation of the tragedy. The standard patriotic take on the events is in no way undermined or subverted. Yet in configuring the narrative in such a way that an uncanny isomorphism comes into existence between the celebration of Independence Day on July 4 and the downfall of the WTC towers on September 11, Rinaldi suggests that the city is subject to a rhythm in which urban eroticism and urban Gothicism alternate over time. The parallelism between the flaunting of patriotism and its humiliation points to an intricate sense of the city as a web of interwoven purposes—a mesh of actions and motivations. Moreover, just as he looks at World War II in a number of flashbacks through the eyes of a former Luftwaffe pilot, Rinaldi delivers a minutely detailed account of the circumstances in the towers that fatal morning from the vantage point of an Arab. Abdul Saad, son of Iraqi expatriates, makes his way down the stairs of the South

Tower, uncertain of the fate of his father, whose office is located in the North Tower. The point is never made explicitly, but the implication is obvious: since the protagonist of the hair-raising account of the escape from the inferno is an Iraqi, the reader is led to identify with the Other. The heteropathic imagination individualizes the victim. Making this victim synonymous with the alleged and officially appointed aggressor (the Arabs, the Iraqis) effectively blocks off the reductionist logic that would simplify a complex event into a ready-made rationale for action and revenge.

The Terrorist as Ultimate Other

More thorough and risky than Rinaldi's method of triangulation are the efforts of those authors who have ventured to deal with 9/11 not by looking at the events from the viewpoint of the victims but by concentrating on the minds of the perpetrators. As a legal concept, terrorism is necessarily boxed in into the dialectic of crime and punishment. Since literature creates possible worlds (and therefore is free from the strictures of the real world), there is room in novels and short stories for a more varied gamut of reactions besides (though not excluding) outright condemnation. In trying to meet the Other, including the ultimate Other, the terrorist—the person whose mindset is completely "discordant with our Western ideals and humanistic values of morality and compassion," to quote Stein again ("Evil as Love," 396)—authors explore the tension between the terrorist as a legal concept and the terrorist as a linguistic, imaginative construct. In doing so, they respond, on the one hand, simply to the exigencies of narrative. That a terrorist commits acts of horrendous, unjustifiable aggression is a statement. Triangulation is a method to turn this statement into a significant story. On the other hand, if, as Levinas argues, "ethics is precisely a struggle to keep fear and anxiety from turning into murderous action" (Butler, *Precarious Life*, xviii), the effort to describe terrorism from within contains an ethical dimension: the effort to escape binary thinking is the opposite of both the terrorist mindset (with its notions of jihadistic violence) and the counterterrorist reaction (with its notions of justified revenge).

In his response to September 11 a mere week after the events, the British writer Martin Amis realized immediately that what had happened in New York and Washington was a watershed.[1] He identifies the impact of the second plane as "the defining moment" ("Fear and Loathing"). Its glint, he writes, "was the worldflash of a coming future." Amis was aware right away that everything had changed and nothing would be the same again. America had lost its innocence, and the whole Western world from now on would be governed by fear. Parents were robbed of the illusion that they could protect their children. And Western technology proved to be vulnerable; all safety procedures failed as the terrorists found the chink in the armor through which to wedge their box cutters. The technology of transportation carries with it the utopian potential of globalization, as the world becomes one great village. "An American passenger jet is . . . a symbol," Amis writes, "—of indigenous mobility and zest, and of the galaxy of glittering destinations." If, with the simplest of means, a mere handful of determined zealots can destroy one of the most powerful symbols of the West, the feeling of safety becomes a thing of the past, and hundreds of millions are terrified.

As to the wider implications of 9/11, Amis writes, "All over again the west confronts an irrationalist, agonistic, theocratic/ideocratic system which is essentially and unappeasably opposed to its existence." Amis's viewpoint is that of the Western citizen (and father), who feels threatened by the prospect of a world that has lost its sense of safety and in which essential freedoms are curbed for fear they will be abused. In addition, as a Western secularist, he is full of loathing for a theocratic order that wants to impose its will by means of violence. However, his viewpoint should not be mistaken for an unconditional endorsement of the West. For one thing, he accuses Americans of a lack of empathy ("How many of them know, for example, that their government has destroyed at least 5% of the Iraqi population?" he writes long before the invasion of Iraq). For another, he sees American self-glorification and "insidious geographical incuriosity" as problems as grave as Muslim fundamentalism. What this balanced view ultimately amounts to is a position "over and above nationalisms, blocs, religions, ethnicities." Just one week after the destruction of the towers, Amis was able to distance himself from feelings of unqualified wrath, pleading for what he calls "species consciousness." "During this week of incredulous misery," he writes, "I have been trying to apply such a consciousness, and such a sensibility. Thinking of the victims, the perpetrators, and the near future, I felt species grief, then species shame, then species fear."

In subsequent magazine articles and public statements, Amis's attitude hardened, as "species consciousness" gives way to shrill polemics. The initially balanced reaction changes into an apocalyptic interpretation of world events. In a piece that was published in the *Guardian* on June 1, 2002, he calls September 11 "a day of de-Enlightenment":

> Politics stood revealed as a veritable Walpurgis Night of the irrational. And such old, old stuff. The conflicts we now face or fear involve opposed geographical arenas, but also opposed centuries or millennia. It is a landscape of ferocious anachronisms: nuclear jihad in the Indian subcontinent; the medieval agonism of Islam; the Bronze Age blunderings of the Middle East.   ("The Voice of the Lonely Crowd")

Increasingly, he comes to see the current conflict as one between the West, the locus of rationalism and good government, over and against the East, which is associated with an unenlightened theocratic polity. "To be clear," he writes, "a religion is a belief system with no basis in reality whatever. Religious belief is without reason and without dignity, and its record is near-universally dreadful. . . . if God existed, and if He cared for humankind, He would never have given us religion."

This antipathy to any creed forms the background to Amis's all-out attack on Islamic fundamentalism (Islamism) in a long and controversial article that appeared on the occasion of the fifth anniversary of 9/11 ("The Age of Horrorism"). He posits that moderate Islam has caved in to radicalism, and he describes at length the career of Sayyid Qutb, the putative "father of Islamism," whose hatred of the West is represented as the result of pathological misogynism and sexual panic. In Amis's ever more strident opinion, the penchant in Islamist circles to practice and glorify suicide and mass murder is "a pathological cult," "a cult of death," which is so alien to Western thought as to be inexplicable. By trying to ground it in a rationale and finding objective underlying reasons for it (Third World poverty, hurt pride, the Palestinian question), Western intellectuals display weakness, not tolerance, let alone any deep understanding of history. "Suicide-mass murder," Amis writes, "is more than terrorism: it is horrorism." The only appropriate reaction to it should be "like an unvarying factory siren of unanimous disgust."

The Indian writer Pankaj Mishra has called Amis's magazine article "a bold and hectic display of prejudice and ignorance," and he pours scorn on what he terms "Amis's genitals-centric analysis (constipation and sexual frustration) of radical Islam" ("The Politics of Paranoia"). Mishra's reaction smacks of Third World snobbery—its main point being that Western intellectuals have no right to pontificate on anything outside the Western Hemisphere—and it certainly proves that polemics tend to be one-dimensional: one outspoken viewpoint clashes with another one just as outspoken and well argued. It is when Amis turns to fiction that the question of "othering" and the Other appears in a more interesting guise. His prose itself works against the tendentiousness of his message. It is in the self-undermining quality of the story (the magnanimity, as it were, of the words themselves) that the interpellation of the Other unintentionally and unexpectedly manifests itself.

In a sense, the short story "The Last Days of Muhammad Atta," published in April 2006, is as much a piercing screed as the magazine article. The portrait of the terrorist, which details his actions and whereabouts from the moment he wakes up on September 11 till the plane impacts on the North Tower, is an exercise not of the heteropathic but the idiopathic imagination. Scrupulously attentive to realistic minutiae and thus claiming veracity and verisimilitude, the story is yet a fictional portrait of the "horrorist," as described in the magazine piece. The thesis it carries is that Atta's outrage can only be understood as the action of an inveterate hater, suffering from a "detestation of everything" (153), a "pan-anathema" (161, 162). As depicted in the story, Atta is constitutionally unable to have any fun; he lacks all curiosity and zest. He detests music and laughter. Above all, he shows "extreme hostility" (154) toward women and heartily approves of the Koranic sanctions: "Adultery punished by whipping, sodomy by burial alive" (155). He kills because he hates life, including his own.

Thus Atta is depicted as the embodiment of an attitude described in the magazine article as "astonishingly alien, so alien, in fact, that Western opinion has been unable to formulate a rational response to it" ("The Age of Horrorism"). As a pure projection of Amis's own viewpoint, Atta is utterly "othered." Having no access to the private thoughts of the historical Muhammad Atta, Amis has created a character that is the incarnation of his idiosyncratic take on Islamic terrorism. What complicates the fictional construct, however, is that, even though the story is full of reality effects, it exposes its own bias and thus contains an element of relativism that is completely absent in the earlier magazine article. Muhammad Atta is dehumanized and shown to be a soulless creature. Yet by the momentum of storytelling itself, he is partly rehumanized in surprising ways. Even in this highly prejudicial fiction, there is a glimmer of "species consciousness" left.

The story begins as follows:

On 11 September 2001, he opened his eyes at 4am, in Portland, Maine; and Muhammad Atta's last day began.

What was the scene of this awakening? A room in a hotel, of the type designated as 'budget' in his guidebook—one up from 'basic'.   (153)

This opening has the marks of traditional realism: individuality of a named character, accuracy of place and time. And yet from the outset the story is unmoored, taken from its realist anchorage by the interposition of a distancing question. In asking what the scene of Atta's awakening might be, the author at the same time indicates his factual ignorance and claims the free run of his imagination. In thus infusing the tale with a modicum of reserve and skepticism, the author shows his hand, and the story exposes its own fictionality. At a crucial juncture, the text reveals its own limitations as an imaginative construct.

While this happens at the beginning of the story and thus sets the tone, the same self-reflexive note creeps in at the end, when the author describes Atta's death. At the moment of impact, when the plane explodes against the New York skyscraper, Atta's body dies instantaneously. But, in Amis's telling of this cataclysmic ending, Atta's mind flickers on and it becomes obvious that, though an incorrigible killer who hates life (including his own), Atta has badly underestimated his will to live. This belated insight is a redemption of sorts and its highly staged character (the result of the author's intervention) is evident. It is at its margins that Amis's prose spills over the narrow confines of its frame. By setting out with a question and ending with an improbable flourish (beyond the reach of pure realistic observation), the story points to something incommensurate, outside the author's grasp. In no way is this an exculpatory gesture for Atta. He stands firmly condemned (and—one could safely add—rightly so). But by indirectly indicating that the act of othering Atta is the empowering condition for this portrait, the author also indicates that his appropriation of his subject is not complete and that there is more to the terrorist than his narrative lets on.

Further evidence of the narrative's self-transcendence comes from the fact that the story ends with the same sentence with which it begins: "On 11 September 2001, he opened his eyes at 4am, in Portland, Maine; and Muhammad Atta's last day began" (163). This curious doubling back suggests a kind of narrative perpetual motion. The narrative has gone one round. It could easily go another one (and after that, another one, and so on, ad infinitum). Oddly, the story is entitled "The Last *Days* of Muhammad Atta," even though it describes only one day, the last. The plural in the title and the recapitulation of the first sentence as the last sentence point to the impossibility of coming to a closure. The author has presented a "slice of life"—the attendant suggestion being that Atta's life can be sliced in any number of different ways and alternative renderings of the events are not only possible but required. This may look like a marginal concession to doubt and contingency. But the psychologist Robert Karen has pointed out the importance of imaginatively sidestepping the wholesale condemnation of one's enemies:

> *Just knowing this*—that we are capable of ... demonizing our enemies, but that there is at least a jot of contingency to it, and that it is within us to retract that demonization—represents both a preservation of complexity as well as a shift towards the forgiving end of the spectrum. It softens our tendency to view the world in good-versus-evil terms and moves us, however slightly, toward recognition of the humanity in those we fight, even if it is a humanity that at that moment we would prefer to ignore.
>
> ("Terror and Forgiveness," 536–37)

To a large extent, the persona of Atta—as evoked in the story—is modeled on the dour figure of Sayyid Qutb, and in this sense, too, the story is but the fictionalized version of the ideas set out in the magazine article on horrorism. The radicalism of both Atta (as imagined by Amis) and that of Sayyid Qutb are the outcome of wide-ranging frustration (sexual and otherwise) and the utter inability to find any delight in the ordinary things of life. Two further elements, though, qualify Amis's condemnation of Islamic fundamentalism. First of all, the short story is told from Atta's perspective. The narrative is in the third person with Atta as sole focalizer. Thus identification with the main character—an almost automatic reflex in reading—clashes with condemnation. The result is an odd mixture of narrative nearness and distance. If Amis looks for an explanation of Atta's murderous thrust in his estrangement from common humanity, the focalization of the story suggests that Atta is a kind of Everyman, the embodiment of common humanity. By its content, the story proclaims: nobody is like Muhammad Atta; his malignity is absolute and beyond explanation. By its construction, the story countermands this imperative and suggests: *In potentia* we are all like Muhammad Atta. His disgust is a feature shared by all; his murderous tendencies are lodged in all of our psyches.

If the invented Atta resembles the historic Sayyid Qutb (at least as Amis distills him from his erudite reading on the subject), there is yet one big difference. Qutb is a religious fanatic. Islam is his end-all and be-all. By contrast, in Amis's imagining and against the historical record, Atta considers religion a sham. He is a terrorist for "the core reason" (154, 159, 162, 163): a hunger to kill that is the result of an "all-inclusive detestation" (161) of life in all its aspects. Unlike the other 9/11 terrorists, he is free from all religious ardor. This total candor about his motives (and thus the complete absence of self-delusion) is why his body rebels against his murderous intentions and why he suffers from "perpetrator trauma"[2] in the form of extreme constipation and crippling headaches. Atta's loathing of religious claptrap and the fiendish glee he takes in besetting the other hijackers with religious conundrums and thus introducing religious doubt, make him not only utterly different from the religious fanatic Sayyid Qutb and from the historical Atta, who, in his suicide letter "frequently mentions love of God and God's satisfaction with the act to be accomplished" (Stein, "Evil as Love," 397). More strangely, it makes Atta resemble no one more than Amis himself. It is obvious that Atta's impatience with religion is directly borrowed from Amis's own strong opinions on the topic. In other words, Atta as Amis's projection is in part also Amis's self-projection. In lending the figure of Atta his own antireligious bias, Amis indicates the inextricable implication of the self with the Other. Even a strenuous exercise in absolute "othering" bears the marks of ineluctable reciprocity and human interdependence.

Saintliness

The call of the Other is also at the center of Michael Cunningham's long short story "The Children's Crusade," a narrative in which the author gauges the viability of Walt Whitman's utopian message in the post 9/11 present.[3] In extreme circumstances, Cat Martin, a thirty-eight-year-old black forensic psychologist working in the deterrence unit of the NYPD, makes the ultimate sacrifice. In order to save a misshapen and abused young child, she extricates herself from the thick skein of social and legal obligations in which she is enmeshed but that also provide her with a sense of security and belonging. The result is not so much a deliberate act of self-oblivion as one of self-obliteration.

In *Alterity and Transcendence* Levinas writes:

> Man is the being who recognizes saintliness and the forgetting of self. . . . We live in a state in which the idea of justice is superimposed on that initial charity, but it is in that initial charity that the human resides; justice itself can be traced back to it. Man is not only the being who understands what being means, as Heidegger would have it, but the being who has already heard and understood the commandment of saintliness in the face of the other man. (180)

More than any text by Walt Whitman this passage provides a clue to Cunningham's story, in which the formative tension is precisely that between justice and charity. In order to shape his theme, Cunningham introduces the guilty innocent, the child terrorist. The essential choice Cat has to make is between regarding, from the strict viewpoint of justice, the child terrorist as a potential killer or, from the viewpoint of charity, as an aggrieved and abused individual. Foregoing her own right to normalcy and happiness, she opts for the latter. In doing so, she practices self-forgetting to her own detriment and answers "the commandment of saintliness" in the most radical of ways.

Cat's act of self-abnegation has long been in the making. Her task at the NYPD is to field phone calls from the "citizens of the Bizarro Dimension" (153, 190), lunatics who utter bomb threats and live within their own macabre apocalyptic fantasies. When she is called up by a young boy, who announces that he will "blow somebody up" (101), she does not realize the seriousness of the threat until the act of terrorism is carried out. When a second boy blows himself up, taking with him an innocent bystander, it becomes obvious that a gang of child terrorists is at work and that they justify their murderous doings by quoting lines from Walt Whitman. The plot comes to a head when a third boy from the gang shows up on Cat's doorstep—a pipe bomb, ready to explode, strapped to his chest.

In this emergency, Cat is unable to act properly as an officer of justice. In Levinas's terms, she is held hostage by her obligation to recognize the absolute moral claims of the Other. At her own peril and against her better judgment, she takes up her responsibility as a practitioner of charity. She succeeds in disarming the boy, but, rather than turning him in, she takes pity on him. She realizes that if left in the clutches of the law, he will be sent to an anonymous institution or handed over to uncaring foster parents. To avert such a fate, she runs off, taking the child with her. She realizes she will be caught eventually and that she will be severely punished. Yet it seems that she has no choice but to take this risk. Even when her womanly instinct and her training as a psychologist tell her that the kid is damaged beyond repair and that one day he will reveal himself as a pathological killer, an irresistible urge forces her to cut the threads with her former life and go AWOL from her duties (196). Levinas writes: "The self is through and through a hostage, older than the ego, prior to principles. What is at stake for the self, in its being, is not to be." (*Reader*, 107). By her act of self-sacrifice, Cat realizes her deepest potential, but she does it at the cost of her ego. Her "normal" existence, within a well-regulated routine and prescribed social boundaries, is relinquished, when, regardless of the consequences, she answers the call of the Other.

In the light of 9/11, this story of utter empathy with the child terrorist entails an implicit understanding of terrorism as an utter rejection of the status quo and a longing for a tabula rasa. As Jane Stevenson puts it in her review of the story, "By the end, the terrorists' view that the world has become so horrible it must be transformed by force becomes strangely appealing to [Cat]" ("Ghost Machines"). Cunningham walks a tightrope (and reformulates the writer's essential dilemma involving the Other and othering) when he situates the self-sacrificing nonviolence of Cat against the background of her growing disenchantment with life as it is led in the contemporary United States. Cat's frustrations, in other words, are not merely personal. The presentation of New York in the story (the office where Cat works, the place she lives, the shoddy goods that are hawked in the streets) is ubiquitously dystopian. Both her neighborhood and her own apartment show signs of neglect and demonstrate a downward slide. She moves in a society in which there is no room for a fully developed subjective presence. The city comes across as a corrosive social entity, threatening authentic personality. As a black woman, Cat is exposed to manifestations of both sexism and racism. Social rites are acts of dishonesty and impression management. This is true even of her relationship with her lover, Simon, who is rich and white and five years her junior. As a successful futures trader, he introduces glamour in her life: "He could have been fresh off the assembly line of whatever corporation produced the Great American Beauties" (111). He comes from Iowa and made it in the big city without losing his sense of purpose and drive: "Simon was so heedlessly alive, so unquestionably glad about it" (113). Yet even her attraction to this great American innocent is socially mediated and tainted (134). Cat and Simon are lovers, but it is not love that they share. His attraction for her is that he offers a luxurious lifestyle and careless prosperity, while he is attracted by the lure of her professional standing. Simon sees her as the police woman, as he knows the cliché from Hollywood movies. He is "turned on" when she acts the part (110). As soon as she shows personal emotion and thus fails to correspond to the stereotype of the hard-boiled detective (164–65), the affair begins to deteriorate. Cat realizes she has been involved in a proprietary relationship. To Simon she was nothing more than "a collector's item" (166).

At the moment of absolute choice, Cat walks out on her duties because she wants to protect an innocent and ill-used child against the rigors of the law. She also walks out because she seems "not to want this life or anything else that's readily available" (191). Paradoxically, in refusing to other the terrorist, Cat others the ambient world. She feels alienated from and by her daily routine. As a result of her unease, she is in a constant conversation with herself and scribbles down lists of items that, by means of free association, express her discontent. At moments of great tension, she reveals herself as someone who longs for an act of terrorism in the most secret recesses of her mind. About her callers, who threaten violence, she says: "You hoped none of them would follow through. You hoped, on your worst days (no one liked to talk about this), that one of them would" (112). When her frustration peaked, "she seemed to have wanted . . . to tear everything apart, to go down, to be as crazy and destructive and irresponsible as the people who called her" (118). In one sense, Cunningham's story is a trite variation on what has become a stereotype: the flawed cop. Softened up by personal setbacks and trauma (a failed private practice, divorce, and most poignantly the death of her three-year-old son), Cat hasn't got what it takes. But more profoundly, the story demonstrates a hidden side of Levinasian alterity: in the absoluteness of its claim, the embrace of the Other involves the rejection of the ego, and this rejection, when pushed to its extreme, entails the destruction (real or symbolic) of the ego's sustaining ambience.

As a 9/11 parable, "The Children's Crusade" goes a long way toward recognizing the Other, even in the terrorist. When Cat opts out of society, it is an inspired act of radical empathy. The detective is supposed to flush out the guilty, but instead she discovers her own essential and undeniable responsibility. The story implies that this responsibility is not only to a helpless, distraught boy, whose vulnerability is obvious, but also to a Whitmanesque vision of wholeness and sanity that the United States has utterly betrayed. The country's practice of justice is so far removed from a vision of charity that, by a strict application of Whitman's idealistic standards, there are only two options left. That neither option can produce lasting results exacerbates the crisis of American values: in no way can the use of terrorist violence alter the balance of power, but Cat's nonviolent opting out, while holding out the possibility of a temporary personal salvation, is a futile protest against the status quo. Her response to terrorism involves responsibility. But her responsible act finds no niche in a juridical universe that recognizes only the polarity of crime and punishment.

The Growth of the Mind

John Updike's is the most elaborate attempt to understand the mind of a terrorist. He touches upon the subject in a short story entitled "Varieties of Religious Experience." In that story, terrorism manifests itself immediately as a topic so adamant that it evades symbolic representation and so disruptive that it upsets Updike's customary narrative strategy. Typically, the hallmark of an Updike story is that, even in the small compass of a few thousand words, several narrative strands, separately spun out, are, in the end, felicitously intertwined and hold out the prospect of muted but sustainable happiness. In this case, however, the gravitational pull of the story fails to position terrorism within manageable reality. The far-flung narrative strands do not come together. No overarching image or metaphor can be found to tie up all loose ends.[4] The story is an example of the heteropathic imagination, but at the same time it announces its defeat. In its very structure, the story dramatizes terrorism as an impossible topic.

Updike looks at 9/11 from all possible sides. The story features an outside spectator, Dan Kellogg, who watches the events unfold from a top-floor terrace in Brooklyn. It also features Mohamed Atta, the terrorist (whose name is spelled differently in the different stories), getting drunk in a sleazy striptease joint in Florida. Next, the scene shifts to an office worker in the burning tower, who calls his wife just before jumping out of the building. In yet another unexpected lurch, the struggle aboard the Pennsylvania plane is rendered from the vantage point of an elderly female passenger until, finally, the narrative returns to Dan Kellogg, six months later. In his attempt to fully "inhabit the event"—the term is Marco Abel's ("DeLillo's," 1241)—Updike has covered all the angles: those of victims, perpetrator, and observer alike.

At one level, the short story illustrates Dan Kellogg's loss of faith when confronted with the mystery of iniquity. On existential grounds, he becomes an atheist. This is familiar Updike territory—the collapse of the WTC towers being merely one of the historical circumstances suggesting that no beneficent deity is watching over mankind. What Kellogg is facing, when he sees the South Tower come down, is an event that no religious metaphor can encompass. After "God had been purged from his brain" (94), he is awash in sensory impressions that do not cohere. What hurts in particular is the indifference of the universe, the realization that he does not find himself in the middle of it (94). September 11 has created metaphysical disarray. For Dan Kellogg, it has destabilized traditional master narratives. As a result, the world has become substantially less hospitable.

Six months later, however, he is still attending church. In part, he sticks to his congregation for reasons of bonhomie and good-fellowship; in part, he has recovered the awareness of a "shadowy God" (104). He harbors an adumbration that things—no matter how puzzling to the human mind—do add up in the end: "Human consciousness had curious properties. However big things were, it could encompass them, as if it were even bigger. And it kept insisting on making a narrative of his life, however nonsensically truncated the lives of others" (104). Such a return to the comprehensibility of existence—wrapping it up in a consistent narrative—can be read as the return of normalcy, the sign that a traumatic shake-up has run its course and things are again as they were before. Dan Kellogg has found his footing again—attending services on Sunday and caring for "his progeny, his tickets to genetic perpetuation" (104). After a momentary loss of equilibrium, Kellogg resumes his place in the forward march of the generations.

Or so it seems. In and of itself, Kellogg's religious crisis comes to a resolution. But its relation to the larger circumstances and the relation of Kellogg's individual fate to that of the other characters in the story remains oddly suspended. Kellogg's narrative, while enfolding the other three, does not succeed in integrating them. The four narrative strands never cohere or even touch. Why was it necessary, then, to insert the (imagined) experiences of Mohamed Atta, the office worker, and the elderly woman in the first place? The story dramatizes a particular dialectic of approximation and distantiation. It contains what is undoubtedly the most poetic description of the collapse of the South Tower:

> He [Kellogg] was still puzzling over the vast quantities of persistent oily smoke, and the nature of the myriad pieces of what seemed to be white cardboard fluttering within the smoke's dark column, and who and what the perpetrators and purpose of this event might have been, when, as abruptly as a girl letting fall her silken gown, the entire skyscraper dropped its sheath and vanished, with a silvery rippling noise. (93)

Kellogg's uncertainty about what is happening and the shock when the tower collapses give rise to an image that is as delicate as it is unexpected. Yet when the story talks about Kellogg's regained trust in the religious metaphor, it does so in the most contorted of ways: "The towers' distant absence seemed a light throwing a shadow behind him, a weak shadow, but inextricable from his presence—the price, it could be said, of his living presence" (104). The vivacity of the sensory description in the first passage contrasts with the confused troping in the second. Rhetorically, an interesting reversal takes place. The cause of the religious crisis is rendered in the most limpid of terms, but the restoration of trust and religious conviction is voiced in the murkiest and most contorted of expressions.

A panoramic rendering of 9/11 necessarily entails an attempt to meet the Other on his own ground. Updike has attempted to stage all the interpellations September 11 makes on the imagination. He recognizes the challenge the event represents and goes out of his way "not to reduce it to our own smallness" ("Tuesday, and After," 28). Kellogg succeeds in reintegrating the events into his private mythology. But the rhetoric suggests that the character is not wholly present to himself and that the reintegration, therefore, is tentative and precarious. Most importantly, contradicting the object lesson of Kellogg's regained equilibrium, the surrounding narratives continue to raise disquieting questions. In refusing "to other" even the terrorist, the story leaves the mystery of the Other intact. In that delicacy lies its mystery and its import.

On a larger scale and using a much expanded canvas, Updike tried to capture the phenomenon of jihad violence in the 2006 novel *Terrorist*. Whereas in the short story, terrorism defeats the integrative tendency typical of most Updike stories, reviewers generally accuse the novel of cozying up to terrorism, of not fully grasping its devastating impact and its complete otherness. "Varieties of Religious Experience" demonstrates how terrorism remains outside the grasp of the shaping imagination, defeating conventional narrative strategies. In contrast, the novel has been decried and derided as pure projection and as a self-serving exercise in the idiopathic imagination. While some critics have termed Updike's effort brave, most consider it to be presumptuous and ineffective.[5]

The protagonist of the novel, Ahmad Mulloy, is the son of an Irish American mother and an Egyptian scholarship student who disappears a couple of years after Ahmad's birth and is never heard from again. As an eleven-year-old, in an attempt to find "a trace of the handsome father who had receded at the moment his memories were beginning" (99), Ahmad starts visiting a small, run-down mosque in New Prospects, the depressed mill town in northern New Jersey in which he grows up. Taking religious instruction from Shaik Rashid, the imam of the mosque, he acquires a smattering of knowledge of the Qur'an in the original and also becomes more and more alienated from American society and disgusted by its gross materialism. Shortly after he graduates from high school, he is ripe to be recruited by Islamic fundamentalists. At the end of a rather feeble cloak-and-dagger intrigue, he is directed to drive a truck filled with explosives into the Lincoln Tunnel and detonate its load at the point where the tunnel is structurally weakest.

In a typical comment, Jonathan Raban contends that Updike fails "to imaginatively comprehend the roots and character of Islamist jihad against the West." According to Raban, Updike has not succeeded in presenting true Islamist rage. Ahmad is too nice a person; his ideology insufficiently inspired by blind hatred ("The Good Soldier"). Along the same lines, James Wood calls Ahmad "a solemn robot" ("Jihad and the Novel"), and Michiko Kakutani writes in the *New York Times*,

> Unfortunately, the would-be terrorist in this novel turns out to be a completely unbelievable individual: more robot than human being and such a

cliché that the reader cannot help suspecting that Mr. Updike found the idea of such a person so incomprehensible that he at some point abandoned any earnest attempt to depict his inner life and settled instead for giving us a static, one-dimensional stereotype.

("John Updike's 'Terrorist'")

Other critics have pointed out that while ostensibly breaking new ground, Updike recycles his familiar signature themes: religion, sex, adultery, high school rivalries. More specifically, both Jonathan Raban and James Wood regard *Terrorist* as "a sort of Islamicized re-writing of *Roger's Version*" (Wood, "Jihad and the Novel"), a novel that appeared twenty years earlier and that is deeply steeped in Christian polemics and theology. In short, Updike is faulted for confusing information with imagination (Shainin, "The Plot"). Reviewers accuse him of substituting sociological research for the depiction of lived experience. In Levinasian terms, he is suspected of rendering the Other as the same. James Wood is particularly trenchant in this respect: "It is the otherness of Islamicism that is missing in this book" ("Jihad and the Novel").

Interestingly, there are dissenting voices. In the *Boston Globe*, Gail Caldwell writes: "Updike's ability to get inside the mind of his Ahmad—to deliver the young man's devotion as well as his fear, uncertainty, and malleable innocence—is what renders the novel credible and sometimes wrenching in its authenticity" ("Gods and Monsters"). What can explain such a divergence of opinion? There can be no doubt that in many ways Ahmad is a projection, the sibling of the many troubled young men in Updike's short stories or novels who, beset by the too-much-ness of everything, long for purity. (David Kern in the short story "Pigeon Feathers" has been cited as another obvious precedent; see Shainin, "The Plot"; and Doody, "John Updike.") This resemblance of an Islamic convert to various other Christian Updike protagonists diminishes the mimetic impact of the novel and disqualifies it as an imaginative portrait of a Mohamed Atta–like protagonist. And Updike's knowledge of the Qur'an (displayed sometimes with the panache of a show-off) is the result of diligent research rather than of lived experience. Yet terming Ahmad "a static, one-dimensional stereotype" (Kakutani, "John Updike's 'Terrorist'") is to give short shrift to the finely filigreed portrait of the young protagonist.

Ahmad has to be looked at in his own right rather than judged by whether or not he is a plausible Atta look-alike. In that respect, it is important to note that Ahmad is not a foreign-born immigrant or visitor but an American-born youngster—a native-born American. While that loosens the parallel with the 9/11 hijackers and thus increases the imaginative leeway Updike created for himself, it is equally significant that, in their censoriousness and strictures, the critics lose sight of the fact that Updike's intention was not to portray a jihadist but rather the inner struggles of a boy adrift, who is attracted to the certainties of fundamentalist Islam but ultimately declines to pursue a life-denying ideology to its logical conclusion. In other words, if *Terrorist* does not make sense as the portrait of a terrorist, it does make sense as the portrait of a terrorist manqué. *Terrorist* is not so much a thriller as it is a bildungsroman, describing the growth of a young man's mind. His coming of age takes the form of the realization of what his Americanness and his Islamic identity truly add up to.

What is it that inspires Ahmad to drive his explosive-laden truck into the tunnel, ready to wipe out as many lives as possible? What is it that, in the last resort, makes it impossible for him to push the button on the detonator? This last gesture may be regarded as a sentimental cop-out. When one expects from the novel a strict imaginative accounting for the doings of the 9/11 terrorists (who, of course, did not show such last-minute qualms), Ahmad's final relenting undoubtedly comes across as a facile peripeteia. But Ahmad's ultimate compunction does square with Updike's avowed intention to draw a "sympathetic and, in a way, . . . loving portrait of a terrorist" (McGrath, "A Cautious Novelist"). The novel may not achieve "the examination of the psychological sources of resentment" produced by the classic fictional descriptions of terrorism in Dostoevsky or Conrad (Wood, "Black Noise," 50). But it does contain an imaginative assessment of what it is in American society that might inspire disgust (to the point of violent revolt) and what it is that inspires loyalty and admiration. It succeeds in making terrorism plausible as a form of societal commitment, and at the same time it condemns terrorism as a horror and an outrage. Most strikingly of all, if the imagined terrorist abandons his intentions out of respect for the Other, that gesture is reciprocated by the author, who makes good his self-avowed intention "to say [something] from the standpoint of a terrorist" (McGrath, "A Cautious Novelist").

In its attempt to highlight current events, *Terrorist* is basically three things: a scathing, unrelenting attack on U.S. inanity; a description of religion as a heuristic enterprise; and, most prominently, an imaginative construct with an exogenous dimension, so that meeting the Other becomes a function of the language. At first sight, the novel is an example of simple realism. It is a straightforward tale with a clunky plot (including a soppy happy ending), so riddled with improbabilities that it seems only a poor pretext for the deployment of Updike's well-known stylistic bravura. Moreover, as a would-be thriller, *Terrorist* gains momentum or suspense (to a moderate degree) only in the last forty pages. Yet, without the use of pyrotechnics and in a way only Updike, among major contemporary authors, could pull off, it is the details that are unsettling and the use of language that reaches out toward an unknown dimension.

A short-hand way of indicating what, at the deepest level of meaning, is going on in *Terrorist* is to say that everyday objects tend toward transcendence. The least observation is saturated with analogy—an analogy that has as its ultimate referent the sacredness of life. That is not to say that the novel is filled with sentimental claptrap. The social satire is hard-edged and unrelenting: America comes across as the land of the fat and fatuous. In any number of episodes and descriptions, Ahmad's disgust with his native country is substantiated and legitimized. The novel is characterized by an enormous amount of observed detail, which, in the aggregate, compresses the physical reality of the United States into a haunted, nightmarish landscape: the realm of the walking dead, the direct descendant of T. S. Eliot's descriptions of London in *The Waste Land* or Fitzgerald's "valley of ashes" (Stone, "Updike's Other"). It is obvious that Ahmad's alliance with the terrorists is also a function of America's failure to keep its promise—a failure that is encrypted in its decaying environment and its jaded inhabitants.

Yet when working as a delivery man for a furniture firm and driving his truck all around New Jersey, Ahmad comes to see American reality as "a sprawling ferment for which he feels the mild pity owed a failed experiment" (177). He is even more affirmative when the imam asks him about the world he has encountered during these trips around New Jersey:

"This isn't the fanciest part of the planet, I guess, and it has its share of losers, but I enjoyed being out in it, really. People are pretty nice, mostly" (233).When Ahmad looks around at his dreary surroundings, there is a glint of excitement that attaches even to the most derelict of objects and environments. The objects in their decay are off-putting. Ahmad sees in them daily proof of the necessary self-denial and disdain of materialism that his religion propagates. Yet at the same time, the physical world is endearing. In some cases it inspires "mild pity"; in others, awe and admiration. Ahmad's awareness of the presence of God, who, according to an oft-cited verse of the Qur'an, is as close to him as the vein in his neck (152, 188, 225, 233, 252, 274, 286), is mediated through everyday reality. Even the grimy loading platform and the parking lot for the truck are experienced as "a place God has breathed upon" (153).

There are several key scenes in which this tug-of-war between the directives of a strictly interpreted and death-driven Islam are opposed to the promptings of instinct and the joy-giving evidence of the senses (and thus to a different, more "liberal" interpretation of Islam). All of those scenes complicate Ahmad as a character and can be seen as proof of a worldly orientation that countervails the religious purity he longs for. He is daily instructed by his imam and by Charlie Chehab, the son of the owner of the furniture firm and another master plotter, to hate America, a subtle preparation for Ahmad's *istisshād* (act of martyrdom). In the novel, Ahmad's dim view of America gets corroboration from the sad lives of Jack Levy, his jaded and disappointed guidance counselor at high school, and Beth Fogel, Jack's grotesquely obese and daytime-soap-addicted wife. Yet, subtextually and gradually, Ahmad's *Bildung* goes in another direction. For all of its obvious flaws, the novel gains depth and narrative momentum from the fact that Ahmad's explicit religious instruction and his progress on the way to self-sacrifice is paralleled by his gradual discovery of a transcendence that is inherent in the meanest of objects—a transcendence that vouchsafes creation rather than destruction and elicits sympathy rather than condemnation. The critics hostile to the book see in this discovery an example of pure idiopathic projection (Updike endowing his protagonist with his own idiosyncratic sensibility). The story, however, is too complex and the narrative takes too many loops and bizarre twists for such an offhand (and ultimately unfair) assessment to carry conviction. It is more accurate to say that Updike's attempt to represent the Other (the terrorist, the Muslim) results in the Other discovering the Other (Ahmad's discovery of his own fealty to mundane American reality). As a literary achievement, this is very different from rendering the Other as the same.

The most obvious scene in which the double education of Ahmad is highlighted is the one in which he commits himself to die for the cause. It begins as follows:

> One July day, on the way back to the store, Charlie directs him [Ahmad] to swing into Jersey City, through a warehouse region rich in chain-link fences and glittering coils of razor wire and the rusting rails of abandoned freight-car spurs. They proceed past new glass-skinned tall apartment buildings being erected in place of old warehouses, to a park on a point from which the Statue of Liberty and lower Manhattan loom close. (186)

In this passage, characteristic of the novel because the theme is embedded in its linguistic expression, Updike takes his protagonist to an iconic site, laden with symbolic significance.

It is possible to read the protagonist's progress through the industrial wasteland of northern New Jersey in a Benjaminian way and consider the vantage point from which the beauty of lower Manhattan is in view as a phantasmagoric place. In this reading, the old warehouses and abandoned railroad spurs hint at the human effort and suffering that underlie capitalist euphoria, as they are gifted with a sort of after-life (*Nachleben* [Gilloch, *Myth*, 111]). As in an archeological display, the relics of a more flourishing industrial age illustrate the underside of decadence and decay, which is covered up by the splendor of lower Manhattan. That, at any rate, is the reading Charlie wants to enforce. When discussing the disappearance of the WTC towers, which are conspicuously absent from the riverside view, Charlie points out that the victims of the 9/11 attacks were people who "worked in finance, furthering the interests of the American empire" (187). Concurring with Charlie, Ahmad promises to give his life to the cause of jihad, "if God wills it" (189). Yet, at the same time, he expresses pity for the victims of 9/11 ("especially those that jumped" [187]).

More significantly even, he is enchanted by the beauty of the urban land-scape in front of him:

> The sky cloudless but for a puffy far scatter over Long Island, the ozone at the zenith so intense it seems a smooth-walled pit of blue fire, the accu-mulated towers of lower Manhattan a single gleaming mass, speedboats purring and sailboats tilting in the bay, the cries and conversations of the tourist crowd making a dapple of harmless sound around them.   (188)

Updike concludes this scene by having Ahmad ponder, "*This beauty . . . must mean something*—a hint from Allah, a foreshadow of Paradise" (188). Strictly speaking, such an explicit object lesson is redundant, as, in itself, the wording of the passage (the pure lyricism and the fluent cadences of the description) carries home the education of Ahmad's senses. In retro-spect, it also makes clear that the depiction of the industrial wasteland of New Jersey, as it leads to the splendors of the riverside view, can be read differently: rather than looking back at abandoned modes of production and exposing built-in obsolescence, the passage points up the chrysalis-like development from past to present, the surge forward, for which the common name is the American dream and of which the most visible signs were the now absent World Trade Center towers.

Two further scenes, which are part and parcel of Ahmad's informal education (counteracting the formal indoctrination by the imam), con-cern Joryleen Grant, a black classmate on whom he has a secret crush. Not surprisingly, given Updike's novelistic preoccupations, sex and religion are the leitmotifs that recur in these encounters. For Ahmad, Joryleen is the ultimate Other: female versus male, Christian versus Muslim, voluptuous and promiscuous versus prim, proper, and sup-pressed. Yet, in these two key scenes, Joryleen, surprisingly, lives up to the reverberations of her surname: in her unplumbable strangeness (which Updike charges to an extreme) she is a gift to Ahmad. She "grants" him access to realms of experience that lie outside the limited scope of his training in piety. As in Updike's hands both characters are sketched as complex individuals, they supersede racial or religious typecasting. In themselves, the encounters between the Muslim and the black youths contain all the promise and the richness of American multiculturalism.

First of all, Ahmad accepts Joryleen's invitation to come and hear her sing in the choir of her church. As it purports to describe a Christian ritual from a Muslim perspective, the description of the black church service is a risky exercise in imaginative identification—twice removed from Updike's own world as a white nonobservant Lutheran. In this set piece, which even hostile critics have recognized as a tour de force (Raban, "The Good Soldier"; Riemer, "Terrorist"), multiculturalism is imaged as culture shock (far different from the easy accommodations implied in the traditional and now discarded melting-pot analogy). Ahmad's consternation and ignorance lead to some dramatic irony and mild intercultural humor: when looking up in the church, the Muslim youngster stares uncomprehendingly at a "high, grimy triple window showing a pigeon about to alight on the head of a white-bearded man" (49). This failure to recognize and identify Christian symbols is only part of the unease he feels. He notices how, in contradistinction to the customs at the mosque, the congregants are arranged in "receding rows of seated and sexually mixed people" (49). This offhand remark is developed into an in-depth appreciation of how religion becomes the lived stuff of life, a matter not merely of conviction and faith, but also of tactile sensations and ingrained protocol, when Updike writes, "Accustomed to worshippers squatting and kneeling on a floor, emphasizing God's height above them, Ahmad feels, even seated, dizzily, blasphemously tall" (50). Religion and ritual turn into habitus, a series of reflexes that may be more decisive in anchoring identity than mere dogma or orthodoxy. It is through small details like these that Ahmad, as a Muslim, comes into his own and the discomfiting impact of his visit to the church is made palpable.

Ahmad had hoped to sneak into the church unobserved. But he is welcomed and "tenaciously greeted" (50) by an usher, who leads him to one of the front pews. There he is joined by a "large black family," of which the pater familias "reaches over the laps of several small daughters to offer Ahmad his broad brown hand and a smile of welcome in which a gold tooth gleams" (50). So much familiarity—"all this kafir friendliness" (51)—is disconcerting to Ahmad, especially when one of the little girls keeps looking at him during the service, curiously and entreatingly, with "bright dog-eyes" (63). Ahmad feels that Joryleen has lured him into a "sticky trap" (51) and that he is indulging in shamefaced voyeurism. When finally the little girl snuggles up against him (to fall asleep in his lap a little later), "he stiffly ignores her, looking straight ahead" (63).

Simultaneously, though, Ahmad finds it impossible to extricate himself completely from what is happening in the church. As soon as the sermon and the singing begin, willy-nilly, he begins to warm to the occasion. The sensation-laden ritual, the burning oratory of the black minister, the sweeping tones of the songs and incantations, and the instances of religious ecstasy stir even Ahmad, especially because the lesson of the day's sermon (the story of Moses and Aaron) is that, against all the odds and whisperings of common sense, one needs to have faith. The virtuoso rendition of the black preacher's sermon shows Updike to be a keen observer of Americana (and religious programs on television?), but, above all, it complicates the text with a dazzling mixture of perspectives. The white Anglo-Saxon author invents a scene in a black church, with which, reluctantly at first, the Muslim protagonist comes to identify. Ahmad becomes aware of the fact that leavening the privileged moments of ritual as well as the mundane details of everyday existence with an elevated sense of divine election is not the monopoly of Islam. The black preacher appeals to the "Lord of us all" (61). This wide-flung supplication introduces Ahmad to the notion of a shared, not strictly denominational religiosity, and, even though he tries to resist the implications of that appeal and though he finds the service, especially the singing, "very sensual" (68), he is reminded of the third sura of the Qur'an, in which the Prophet himself affirms the links of Islam to Judaism and Christianity (62). Most profoundly, maybe, the sermon in the black church alerts Ahmad to the fact that religion is handed down as a potent language construct. The parallels with the teaching sessions in which the imam tutors him in the finer points of the Qur'an are obvious. In both cases, religious instruction revolves around (and depends on) the explication of Holy Writ: how to apply old stories and timeworn texts to present-day situations. Thus Ahmad discovers that the past holds its grip on the present through the power of exegesis and heuristics. His most heartfelt convictions rely on analogy and metaphor rather than on some absolute and nonnegotiable relation with the truth.

The next time Ahmad meets Joryleen, it is in different circumstances. To please her unworthy boyfriend, she has turned to prostitution and, somewhat implausibly, she is hired by Charlie to "devirginate" Ahmad. Updike, who in previous novels has amply demonstrated his acquaintance with all the gradations of sexual enjoyment and who is without equal when it comes to expounding the moral intricacies involved, is even more sensitive than usual in this scene. The pages devoted to this tryst are riddled with unlikely plot elements and bizarre twists and turnings. But they contain a touching evocation of Ahmad's curiosity, lust, sweetness, and repulsion. The fact that, plot-wise, the meeting depends on a number of coincidences and that it therefore derives its effectiveness solely from its taking shape in language, marks it as a site of great symbolic import. It is the place where Ahmad's struggle with "the devils" of American decadence is at its most acute—his struggle to preserve purity in a world that is contaminated. He ends up compromised, or half-compromised. At any rate, he reaches a standoff with the world that does not leave him a small-minded bigot. Moreover, in treating Joryleen as someone far above the station associated with her profession, he acquires a sense of human complexity. As a strange conclusion to the encounter, he asks her to sing—a memento of her better self in church, a token, too, of his refusal to reduce her to commodified corporeality. Joryleen, who has turned prostitute out of selfless affection for her bullying boyfriend, initiates Ahmad not only into the secrets of sex, but, more significantly, also into the intricacies of human behavior. She loosens up his sense of moral rectitude in that she introduces him to a situation that cannot be judged by a simple binary logic of virtue versus vice or good versus evil.

The antithesis between a death-driven religion and a sense of inner goodness (or religiosity) comes to a head in the last and climactic scene of the novel. Ahmad spends the night before the terrorist assault in a safe room, which is "religiously clean" (268) and uncluttered. The room embodies the purity he longs for and stands in contrast to the accumulated bric-a-brac that characterizes American lives. His desire is to sweep his life history away in one apocalyptic moment. Instructed by the imam and feeling that he is hurrying toward a "great cleansing" (281), he is prepared to act "out of hatred of those who mock and ignore God" (270).

But there are complications. First of all, the sura he studies in the last hours before the attack stresses that Allah is the life giver (the principle of growth) and not the destroyer. The half-mile walk he has to undertake to meet Charlie is pervaded by the joy of being alive and partaking in the delight of movement and sensations. Most unexpectedly (and again as the result of a most unlikely plot development), he is joined in the explosive-laden truck by Jack Levy, the high school counselor. In the extraordinary final pages of the book, the two men, who are each other's opposites in all respects—young versus old, Arab versus Jew—assess their lives. In a great interethnic encounter (reminiscent of the interracial friends in classical American literature) and as a further confirmation of the potential of American multiculturalism, the trip to the Lincoln Tunnel is an act of taking stock for both characters. Surprisingly, it is not the older man who convinces the younger one to call off the suicide bombing. After some initial half-hearted attempts to convince Ahmad not to push the button, the older man, world-weary and disappointed in love, acquiesces and is quite content to die. His lassitude and his disgust with the way things are in the United States are such that they override his feeble will to live. At the last minute, it is not Jack's pleading but Ahmad's own inner guidance system that gets the better of him.

The first sentence of the novel reads: "*Devils*, Ahmad thinks. *These devils seek to take away my God*" (3). The last sentence is an echo of this: "*These devils*, Ahmad thinks, *have taken away my God*" (310). In both cases, Ahmad shows himself to be locked up in closed, binary thinking. America is demonized, and, as a result, it deserves to be punished. If ultimately Ahmad relents and desists, it is because, remembering sura 56, he realizes God "does not want to desecrate His creation by willing death. He wills life" (306). In addition, something else has interposed itself—not Jack's weak pleading but something truly transcendental. At the last moment, Ahmad is mollified by the face of the Other. In the family car that files into the tunnel just ahead of the doomed truck, a black boy and girl playfully try to draw his attention by waving their hands and making faces. Echoing his standoffish attitude toward the black child in church, Ahmad first ignores them. But finally he responds. He recognizes their irreducible uniqueness and their undeniable appeal as fellow human beings, which no ideology or religion can gainsay. The face of the Other implies the absolute injunction—stranger and stronger than any indoctrination—not to take the Other's life.

Ahmad's final decision follows from his discovery of the right relation between life and religion. Related to that is also the realization that he has taken nourishment from his caring mother more than from his absentee father (241). Ahmad's religion is an attempt to get in touch with the missing male parent (99). Allah is the substitute father, and, consequently, after his martyr's death, Ahmad expects to be greeted by God "as His son" (305). By postponing his longing "to see the face of God" (303)—giving preference instead to the recognition of the face of the children—he shows himself more the son of his mother than of his absent father. His mother is a nurse's aid and an amateur painter with a checkered and varied love life (Jack Levy being the most recent of her conquests). In her professional life, she is acquainted with human suffering and used to dealing with the most abject aspects of human corporeality. Yet, as a painter, she is fascinated by the creation of beauty, which she was denied in her strict, Catholic upbringing: "The nuns put such ridiculous stock in [religious rules and theological distinctions], and expected us children to, too, but all I saw was a beautiful world around me, for however briefly, and I wanted to make images of its beauty" (240). As a lover, she unabashedly indulges in the delights of the body (for instance, she wants Jack to sing the praises of her "cunt" [160]). Ahmad's religious inclinations are gendered as male. But it is his mother's joie de vivre that will prevent him from carrying out his errand of death. It is the female in him that allows him to escape the strict binary logic that the imam (not coincidentally the male proponent of a male-directed religion) propounds.

Saying

In trying to explain Levinas's complex notion of transcendental saying (le dire) as opposed to the immanent said (le dit), Robert Eaglestone writes, "The saying breaks up identity and opens to the other because it is in the saying that the finite and limiting structures of being, of essence, of identity standing alone are overcome.... The saying leads to the 'breaking up of inwardness and the abandon of all shelter'" (Ethical Criticism, 143). Amis, Cunningham, and Updike write realist texts. The precision of their expression seems to exclude the transcendent dimension of saying and to be immured in what Levinas calls *"le dit,"* the logos that thematizes reality and robs it of its essential strangeness. If, as Eaglestone further contends, the " 'saying' in literature is precisely that uncanny moment when we are made to feel not at home with the text or in ourselves," (175) it is mostly hermetic texts (scanned through deconstructionist readings) that are deemed to have the power to interrupt our routine relation with the Other, with the self, and with outside reality. The particular merit of the texts that have been looked at in this chapter is that, within the context of realist diction, by subtle shifts in perspectives, they yet succeed in conveying the way in which 9/11 has ruptured normalcy and created opportunities to come face to face with the Other. As Judith Butler writes, taking her cue from Levinas, "The very 'I' is called into question by its relation to the Other, a relation that does not precisely reduce me to speechlessness, but does nevertheless clutter my speech with signs of its undoing" (*Precarious Life*, 23). Such signs of a text questioning its own premises and thus breaking up the fixity of identity and facilitating the approach to the Other do not advertise themselves within a realist context. It is the quietness of these disturbances that point to 9/11 as a momentous occasion, in which binary schisms yield to the interpellation of the Other and the assumption of responsibility.

EPILOGUE

THE TEXTS THAT HAVE BEEN discussed in this study prove that, far from paralyzing the writerly imagination into silence, world historical events such as the terrorist attacks of September 11 continue to make demands on novelists as the chroniclers of their time. It is safe to assume that in the future new works will join the existing corpus of 9/11 fiction. At the same time, it is impossible to predict exactly what direction this new fiction will take or whether 9/11 will produce a novel of such stature that it will become the indexical landmark for all other 9/11 fiction (including the ones treated in this study). It is also a matter of mere conjecture whether the new 9/11 fiction will remain the preserve of male white writers or whether it will be marked by more gender and ethnic diversity or acquire a more outspoken international dimension.[1] Yet whatever form the new 9/11 fiction will take, one may venture the guess that, almost eight years after the events, the immediate shock has worn off and that, as a result, the concerns expressed will be less directly related to the experience of trauma. While much of the extant 9/11 fiction zooms in on the anamorphosic experience of pain and loss and the efforts to recover trust in the future, it is obvious already in the works of Cunningham and Updike, which deal with the aftermath (rather than the events themselves), that the focus is shifting away from the perpetrator-victim dichotomy, which the trauma paradigm implies, to a triangulating discourse in which the confrontation with the Other is the central concern. In other words, whereas in works such as *Falling Man*, *In the Shadow of No Towers*, *Extremely Loud and Incredibly Close*, and *Windows on the World*, the emphasis is on the mold-breaking impact of a liminal event, "The Children's Crusade" and *Terrorist* begin to explore how, in the words of Judith Butler, "the narcissistic preoccupation of melancholia can be moved into a consideration of the vulnerability of others" (*Precarious Life*, 30).

The events of that day are slowly receding into the past, and memories, no matter how sharp and pointed, are unavoidably beginning to fade. As I teach a class on September 11 in Fiction, it is sobering to realize that some of the students were a mere twelve years old when the planes hit the WTC Towers. If I were to teach the same course in another five years' time, some of the participants will only have vague childhood memories of the events; in ten years' time, few if any undergraduates will actively remember what happened that day. For them, 9/11 will truly have become a "historical" event, part of the handed-down record rather than a lived experience—on a par with the assassination of JFK, the Vietnam War, or the Watergate affair.

Shortly after September 11, the author Jane Smiley confessed that "her mind felt dissipated and shallow" and she found herself incapable of finishing the novel she was working on (4). That sense of overwhelming concern has slowly evaporated. September 11 has begun a sort of underground existence, no longer foremost in people's minds as other topical interests (many of them, though, indirectly related to 9/11) crowd the headlines of newspapers and cry for attention. Nonetheless, one can anticipate that somehow 9/11 will continue to crop up as a vestige, as a trace that marks the cultural landscape. This spectralization is noticeable already in some of the fiction that was discussed in the chapters of this book. It is also part and parcel of the several novels that deal with 9/11 tangentially or indirectly, as part of a larger plot.[2] By way of epilogue, I would like to look briefly at two such novels, as they illustrate several of the trends that might well characterize the 9/11 fiction to come.

Anita Shreve's *A Wedding in December* is a novel about personal relations. It tells the story of a number of high school classmates who reunite twenty-seven years after graduation to celebrate a marriage in a country inn in the Berkshires. As the date is December 2001, the events of a mere three months before drift in and out of the conversations. All in all, there are twelve mentions of September 11—short vignettes that are either part of the reacquainting rituals (where were you on the day?) or else brief philosophical speculations dealing with the existential conundrums provoked by such a wholesale disaster and touching upon the question of ownership (who can truly claim to be affected by 9/11?). As such, September 11 is of a piece with (and actually takes second place to) other pressing concerns of the characters, mainly love, aging, and disease. Without truly taking hold as a focal point, 9/11 is part of the tale's tapestry. In a novel that places itself solidly in a conventional narrative tradition, to the point even of occasional tackiness, 9/11 serves as part of the reality effect: without fully taking possession of the characters, it has to be there on the margins of their consciousness for the novel to claim authenticity and to occupy a recognizable position in time.

And yet obliquely, the novel is pervaded by the need to come to terms with September 11. Some of the liveliest writing in the book is devoted to the Halifax explosion of December 6, 1917, when after a collision in the harbor of the Canadian city Halifax, a munitions ship exploded, killing 2,000 people and wounding 9,000. In a particularly gruesome turn of events, the fire in the harbor, preceding the explosion, had attracted many people to watch from their windows. When the ship blew up, glass shards were lodged in their eyes, and 200 spectators were completely or partially blinded (*Wedding*, 22).

Two things stand out about the Halifax subplot. First of all, it is a story within a story. While it is lengthy and powerfully imagined in many of its details, it remains largely detached from the main story. As one of the characters is writing up the Halifax episode while she is attending the wedding, it interposes itself between the developments in the country inn without becoming truly integrated. Paradoxically, the relative isolation of the tale from the rest of the narrative proves the intrusiveness of 9/11. While the events of three months before are only slightly touched upon in the main narrative (almost as a grace note), the need to deal with them *in extenso* is subsumed by an analogue—a historical event (largely forgotten) that suddenly gathers new relevance.

Second, the retelling of the Halifax explosion necessarily provides a framework in which to interpret the more recent catastrophe. Within the context of the historical analogy, the difference between a cataclysmic accident and a deliberate act of terror is elided. Both are defined as primarily human tragedies. While such a leveling gives short shrift to actual geopolitical circumstances and thus renders the analogy invalid in part, it speaks to a willed effort to extricate 9/11 from an overly topical approach. The message is not only that catastrophes do happen and thus that, on a larger view, 9/11 is not without precedent or antecedent. The novel also insists on the blinding effect of collective trauma. The victims are literally made sightless. More symbolically, their suffering has no specific justification. It does not allow for a rational explanation and thus excludes an effective preventive or ex post facto action. If anything at all, it shows up the brutality and total absurdity of war.

Such an absolutizing of the event disqualifies revenge as an adequate or appropriate response, but it does not preclude agency. The focalizer of the Halifax episode is a young eye surgeon. In the stoic exercise of his professional duties, responsibility rather than revenge is the leitmotif. In so far as the Halifax explosion and thus, by analogy, September 11 are moments in which the general human condition manifests itself as one of universal vulnerability, the countervailing force at work in the text is that of sacrifice and compassion.

The special merit of *A Wedding in December* may well be that it shows how these forces also play themselves out in the everyday concerns of the characters. The high school reunion is overshadowed by the memory of a tragic drowning of one of the classmates. Apart from that, the several characters shoulder their own burdens (death and disease, marital unhappiness). In that respect, the events of 9/11 (directly and indirectly via the Halifax episode) step out of the background and fulfill a function that is more central than just grounding the novel's realism. The cataclysmic occurrences—now identified as recurrences by the historical narrative—are in extremis a continuation or, more exactly, an intensification of the everyday. There is no misleading confusion here between structural and historical trauma (as is the case, for instance, in DeLillo's *Falling Man*). Rather, the implication of the interweaving of the everyday and the exceptional seems to be that, at a level deeper than the social amenities prevailing among erstwhile best friends, existence is one protracted confrontation with the Lacanian Real, to which, haltingly, one makes adjustments and accommodations. The characters do not come across as "accomplished survivors" of universalized trauma (Wulf Kanterstein, as quoted in Luckhurst, *The Trauma Question*, 13) nor do they participate in a culture of complaint (Robert Hughes's term). In the face of disaster (public or personal), they muddle through, guided not by feelings of aggrievement or revenge but by a pragmatic sense of agency and commonsense morality.

The way the drowning of the classmate figures in the narrative is a case in point. Even though the episode took place twenty-seven years before, it is still on the minds of the participants of the reunion. It has kept festering as a wound. And the brashest and least sensitive person in the group causes great unease by bringing it up at the most inopportune moments. In its belatedness, the issue remains unresolved, until the former best friend of the drowning victim confesses the full circumstances in which the accident took place to the drowning victim's former girlfriend. While the shadow of Sigmund Freud looms large when this confession proves to entail a healing of the wound, its sequel signals a significant shift from the traumatic to the tragic. As the confession ushers in a sexual episode between the two interlocutors, the trauma gets absorbed, as it were, in a finely filigreed mesh of human relations and responsibilities. The moment of erotic excitement is fraught with feelings of guilt, as it is interwoven with the drowning death of, respectively, friend and boyfriend. At the same time, it is a recognition of a long slumbering attachment, which has survived twenty-seven years of separation and marriage to third parties. After their brief reunion, the two lovers, however, go back to their professional and familial responsibilities. The plot does not ripen to the level of the pathological, nor does it probe the recesses of the antisocial, the suicidal, or the truly traumatic. The tragic side of existence, while duly acknowledged and experienced, is integrated into an awareness of life as rich in content and opportunities, provided a sense of balance is maintained and an awareness of necessary limitations prevails.

As a tale within a tale, the Halifax episode demonstrates how, in this process of adjustment and accommodation, language also plays an important part. The author of the inner tale—herself a character in the main tale—self-consciously steers and even stage-manages the recounting of the Halifax disaster, so much so that the story of the young eye surgeon takes on the contours of her own life's trajectory. This points to the troping of reality. Equally, it reveals the role language and the imagination play in dealing with the Real. That role, while one of deflection and distortion, is yet one, if not of catharsis and therapy (which would again pertain to the experience of trauma), then at least of absorption and comforting (which belong to everyday ways of coping and getting by).

A similar emphasis on responsibility and the primacy of relationality is paramount in Ian McEwan's *Saturday*. This story also involves a doctor as, synecdochically, medical healers provide ready-made examples of the faculty of agency in times of distress. *Saturday* presents twenty-four hours in the life of Henry Perowne, a successful London neurosurgeon. The date is February 15, 2003, when hundreds of thousands of marchers in London and in cities all over the world gathered to demonstrate against the impending war in Iraq. Perowne's story starts from the premise that the times are "baffled and fearful" (4). As a result of 9/11, no life, no matter how secure at the surface, is safe anymore. Perowne's name contains a reference to possession and identity. The questions the novel poses are what, in the aftermath of September 11, one owns, how tight one's grip on life is, and how quickly one can lose it.

Perowne is so well established that he "owns" a roomy house on one of London's beautiful eighteenth-century squares in the posh Fitzrovia neighborhood—a neighborhood symbolic of a city that Henry thinks of as "a success, a brilliant invention, a biological masterpiece—millions teeming around the accumulated and layered achievements of the centuries . . . harmonious for the most part, nearly everyone wanting it to work" (5). The perfect symmetry of the square—"an eighteenth-century dream bathed and embraced by modernity" (5)—tallies with Henry's trust in the social contract undergirding the complex coexistence of millions of his fellow Londoners. Dominating the square is the Post Office Tower, built in the 1960s, "a valiant memorial to more optimistic days" (4). When for no reason Henry finds himself wide awake at 3:40 in the morning, feeling "unencumbered" and "elated" (3), he looks out at the square with obvious contentment. His posh surroundings mirror his own perfectly settled existence—his peaceful and productive bourgeois life, in which he dedicates himself to his wife and children and to his demanding but rewarding profession.

Yet even while contemplating this peaceful vignette from his bedroom window, Perowne undergoes the sense of "general unease" (39) that has established itself in the culture after 9/11. For one thing, towers in and of themselves carry ominous overtones. For another, Henry becomes aware of a tiny, bright spot in the dark sky, which he first identifies as a meteor until he realizes it is an airplane, making its run toward

Heathrow with one of its engines on fire. This is the first in a series of 9/11-like incidents, which are spread throughout the novel and constitute an intrusion of something horrible and incomprehensible into the banal and the everyday.[3] The neurosurgeon, who has acquired the skill to penetrate the human brain and undo the damage caused by accident or disease, comes up against forces of evil that are not susceptible to his rational calculus or to the intercession of even the most advanced technology. Such a run-in with inexplicable irrationalism is the new order of the day. Played off against Henry's domestic bliss, hints of the apocalyptic shape his existence.

There is no better day than February 15, 2003, to demonstrate how and to what extent Henry's private utopia is put under pressure by public events. The thousands of marchers are a reminder of the fact that outside forces partly determine one's personal well-being. Perowne, for all the satisfaction he derives from both his professional and family life, is so much attuned to the goings-on in the world that he suffers from media addiction: "His nerves, like tautened strings, vibrate obediently with each news 'release'" (181). He is so acutely aware of the general state of things that he (and thus McEwan) has the foresight to predict the London bombings of July 7, 2005, long before they actually happened. His strong sense of selfhood is wrapped up in the reciprocity of family affection and the fulfillment produced by a busy, productive professional life. Yet something tugs at him. The very London landscape through which he navigates is marked by a nondescript, pervasive sense of anxiety and dread, which not only undermines his sense of well-being but also informs his identifiable (and beautifully realized) subjectivity.

Educated in a rigorously scientific tradition, the doctor at first wistfully believes that the international crisis, following 9/11, will be resolved since "reason, being a powerful tool, was irresistible, the only way out" (32). This optimistic take on world affairs is not only of a piece with the triumphs of medical technology he performs daily in the operating theater—"three years' misery, of sharp, stabbing pain, ended" in the mere fifteen minutes it takes to relieve a patient of a painful facial tic (7)—but it also squares with his Darwinistic belief in never-ending progress. The events of September 11, however, are so shattering that he now realizes there is "no going back" (32). Everything has changed. The terrorist actions usher in a new era, and he tends to concur with the conclusions of the political scientist Fred Halliday, who stated that the attacks on the World Trade Center "precipitated a global crisis that would, if we were lucky, take a hundred years to resolve" (32–33). Such awareness, however, dawns slowly, and Henry has a vague feeling of unease or embarrassment as a result of "his readiness to be persuaded that the world has changed beyond recall" (76). Everyday reality reassures him: "the self-evident fact of the streets and people on them are their own justification, their own insurance" (76–77). The tangible nature of things gainsays doomsday scenarios and allays his fears. Yet, ultimately, pondering the news that assails him from all sides, he has no choice but to conclude: "The world probably has changed fundamentally" (80). When the doctor's day comes full circle and he finds himself, at the end of the tale, standing again at his bedroom window, looking out at the peaceful scene of a somnolent London, he is aware of the shadow 9/11 has thrown over the future. He imagines a doctor, middle-aged as he is, standing in front of that selfsame window a hundred years earlier, pondering the new century that had just begun:

> February 1903. You might envy this Edwardian gent all he didn't know. If he had young boys, he could lose them within a dozen years, at the Somme. And what was their body count, Hitler, Stalin, Mao? Fifty million, a hundred? If you described the hell that lay ahead, if you warned him, the good doctor—an affable product of prosperity and decades of peace—would not believe you. Beware the utopianists, zealous men certain of the path to the ideal social order. Here they are again, totalitarians in a different form, still scattered and weak, but growing, and angry, and thirsty for another mass killing. A hundred years to resolve.(276–77)

Henry ponders the possibility that, enjoying an idyllic existence, he finds himself in a fool's paradise, living on borrowed time. Yet, in its turn, this dark foreboding is again called into question as possibly nothing but "an indulgence, an idle, overblown fantasy, a night-thought about a passing disturbance that time and good sense will settle and rearrange" (277). Wavering between the hope that everything will pretty much remain the cozy way it is and the fear that the events of 9/11 are the prelude to a new and devastating Hundred Years' War, Henry's mind, brooding on the future, is torn between visions of the domestic and the apocalyptic. The hope that everything will turn out all right and good sense will prevail alternates with nightmarish visions of history repeating the worst horrors of the past century.

Ultimately, Henry's answer to the outside threats, of which in the post-9/11 climate he is acutely aware but about which he can do little or nothing, is to live a life marked by decency and a concern for the Other. The obvious fragility of his existence—in part dependent on external forces far beyond his control—is translated into a meticulous observation of duty and a respect for reciprocity. Part of this solicitude is turned inward, toward the gift of family life. As a uxorious husband, so much in love with his wife that when "he thinks of sex, he thinks of her" (39), he also invests time in the relationship with his demented mother and with his son and daughter. Part of Henry's commitment, however, goes significantly further. He is sensitive to "the expanding circle of moral sympathy" (127), so much so that, at the fish market, he turns his gaze away in shame from the crates with crabs and lobsters, realizing these sentient creatures are in agony. Similarly, when meeting a street sweeper and looking him in the eye, for "a vertiginous moment Henry feels himself bound to the other man, as though on a seesaw with him, pinned to an axis that could tip them into each other's life" (74). Henry, in other words, is susceptible to the interpellation of the Other. Even though his surname, Perowne, suggests introversion and self-preoccupation, he is aware of privilege and the injustice this entails. The hidden subtext in these encounters is the confrontation between the have and the have-not. This confrontation has overlays of the uncanny: the fear of the owner to be disowned. But it also introduces questions of accountability and moral obligation.

These questions come to a head when, en route to his weekly squash game, Perowne, as the result of a minor traffic accident, gets into a heated argument with an uncouth character and small-time hoodlum by the name of Baxter. Baxter plays the role of revenant, the ghost of irrationalism that haunts and threatens a perfectly ordered existence. In addition, within the larger political scheme of the novel, he can be seen as a substitute terrorist. Suffering from a debilitating genetic neurological disorder, subject to sudden mood swings and at times dangerously aggressive, he is, like the terrorist, the ultimate Other, who comes to disturb the bourgeois idyll and family quiet. In the end, when Baxter has penetrated the posh house in Fitzrovia (thus in miniature and symbolically gathering in his persona all the outside forces that 9/11 has unleashed and that threaten domestic peace and stability), Henry, with the help of his son, can overpower the intruder and avoid a major disaster. But even when the violent confrontation is in full progress, Henry is bothered by feelings of guilt and a sense of unfairness. He asks himself whether he handled the altercation after the traffic accident correctly and why it is that he, as a successful professional, has got everything, whereas fate has saddled Baxter with a defective gene and, in consequence, he has nothing. Even though at one point Baxter is on the verge of committing the ultimate outrage (raping Henry's pregnant daughter in full view of the other family members), responsibility carries the day over revenge, when, after throwing Baxter down the stairs and severely injuring his head, Henry hurries to the hospital and decides to take care of Baxter and perform a life-saving operation.

Part and parcel of this encounter with the Other is, in the terms of Emmanuel Levinas, the interruption of the said by the saying. This unexpected interposition of language as an agent of transcendent recognition takes place when Daisy, Henry's daughter, who is a published poet, is able to detract Baxter from his foul intentions by reciting Matthew Arnold's "Dover Beach." In and of itself, this is a most implausible scene: the hardened criminal is softened up by listening to a staid nineteenth-century poem about the decline of faith and the saving grace of love.[4] Yet the very egregiousness of the passage enforces its meaning. It fits a running argument between father and daughter about the importance of literature. As a scientist, Perowne is steeped in the said. The technical vocabulary he uses in his daily practice and that is faithfully mirrored in the novel both adds to the reality effect of the tale and demonstrates the grip of reality on language. In Perowne's mastery of the surgical jargon, there seems to be no crack or fissure between a phenomenon and its denomination. The object and the name of the object are so closely related as to be indistinguishable. This dedication to utmost precision may explain why Henry has little use for the products of the imagination.

In his judgment, realist masterpieces are but "the products of steady, workmanlike accumulation" (67), while magical realists indulge in "irksome confections" (67)—"the recourse of an insufficient imagination, a dereliction of duty, a childish evasion of the difficulties and wonders of the real" (67–68). Henry's strong positivistic attitude—his literalism—accounts for his reverence for the "demonstrably true" (56) (an expression that Daisy finds old-fashioned but that has deep meaning for her father). By the same token, it makes him ill-prepared for the run-in with the uncanny and even more so for the encounter with the magic of words, to which even Baxter is sensitive.

Poetry is interruption. In the novel, it interrupts the scene of horror literally. But its typical discourse is also an interruption of the everyday. In the terms of Levinas, dependent on the immanence of the said yet at the same time hinting at something that transcends the strictures of reality, poetry is the discourse par excellence where the doubleness, "the amphibology" of language is most constitutive.[5] It is the type of utterance that relies on meter, sound effect, and trope to interrupt the said by the saying. As such, poetry has an ethical appeal: in overcoming "the finite and limiting structures of being, of essence, of identity" (Eaglestone, *Ethical Criticism*, 143), it prepares the ground for the denucleation of the self and the priority of the Other (Hatley, *Suffering Witness*, 141). It may be this that Baxter understood and feels interpellated by. His response to the poetry makes him, as it were, amphibological himself. A hardened criminal yet sensitive to the reverberations of the transcendent, he represents the Other in his inalienable completeness—a fellow creature, whose very vulnerability comprises an appeal to closeness and solidarity.

NOTES

INTRODUCTION. 9/11: THE DISCURSIVE RESPONSES

1. Slavoj Žižek writes about Oliver Stone's movie: "in the case of WTC, one can easily imagine exactly the same film in which the twin towers would have collapsed as the result of an earthquake" (Žižek, "On 9/11"). Along similar lines, the *New York Times* critic Alessandra Stanley wrote, "For all its awe-inspiring special effects and operatic touches, *World Trade Center* is as focused on the effort to rescue two Port Authority officers as a made-for-television movie; it could almost as easily have been about trapped West Virginia miners or mountain climbers buried under an avalanche" (qtd. in Faludi, *The Terror Dream*, 3).

2. See Craps, "Conjuring Trauma."

3. All translations from Lang's book are mine.

4. For more on Lang's book, see Versluys, "9/11 as a European Event."

5. Simon Stow takes a much darker view of these "Portraits of Grief." For him, they add up to a "pornography of grief" ("Portraits 9/11/01"). David Simpson is also critical in his assessment. For him, the portraits betray "an interest in the projection of an all-American wholeness of spirit and a national state of health and happiness" (*9/11*, 46). As such, they are self-congratulatory instruments of patriotic propaganda. Along similar lines, Judith Butler points out that the obituary is "an act of nation-building." To her, it "is the means by which a life becomes, or fails to become, a publicly grievable life, an icon for national self-recognition, the means by which a life becomes noteworthy" (*Precarious Life*, 34).

6. "To write poetry after Auschwitz is barbaric" (Adorno, "Cultural Criticism," 34). "There is no possible way of responding to Belsen and Buchenwald. The activity of the mind fails before the incommunicability of man's suffering" (Trilling, *The Liberal Imagination*, 256).

7. Examples are the novels by Ken Kalfus, Nick McDonell, McInerney, Claire Messud, Joseph O'Neill, Reynolds Price, and Schwartz, and also those by Anita Shreve and Ian McEwan, about which more in the epilogue.

8. Examples are the novels by Charlotte Vale Allen, Rick Amburgey, Karen Kingsbury, and Kingsbury with Gary Smalley. Fetishistic 9/11 narratives mostly demonstrate a right-wing political bias, but not always. Pete Hamill's historical novel *Forever* is a left-liberal account of New York's past. When, however, in the immediate aftermath of the destruction of the Twin Towers, the protagonist's son is born, Hamill, in using such a transparent symbol of the city's resilience, is reaching for a solution that is too pat and an ending that is too facilely optimistic. Nor does the dividing line between fetishistic and nonfetishistic narratives coincide with a distinction between highbrow and lowbrow literature. Various nonfetishistic narratives that will be discussed in this study, such as Art Spiegelman's *In the Shadow of No Towers*, Jonathan Safran Foer's *Extremely Loud and Incredibly Close*, and Frédéric Beigbeder's *Windows on the World*, heavily rely on motifs and devices borrowed from popular culture.

1. AMERICAN MELANCHOLIA: DON DELILLO'S *FALLING MAN*

1. In an erudite but misconceived article, Marco Abel completely ignores the sharply divisive stance that structures "In the Ruins of the Future" to assert that the essay resists "the demand to speak with moral clarity and declare what the event means" ("Delillo's," 1236).

2. Keith Neudecker's name (*"neu"* is German for "new") provides an indication of his role as prototypical American, the successor (of German rather than of English stock) of Christopher Newman, the main character of Henry James's *The American*.

3. See the AP article from June 16, 2005, at http://www.foxnews.com/story/0,2933,159772,00.html.

4. For an enlightening discussion of the question of belief in DeLillo's novels, see Kavadlo, *Don DeLillo: Balance at the Edge of Belief*.

5. DeLillo makes the same point in "In the Ruins of the Future," 34.

6. Most reviewers have been unkind to the novel, precisely because its lopsided emphasis on passive submission seems to violate both the dynamics of human behavior and the reality of post-9/11 New York and America. "By focusing so single-mindedly on [the] anesthetized aftermath," writes Adam Kirsch, "Falling Man" ends up feeling willed and shrunken." For Laura Frost, the novel "is an act of art-terrorism inflicted upon a dazed audience," while James Wood states that the book is "all limbs" without a "living, pulsing center" (50). Most devastatingly, the novel has been characterized as a recherché exercise in negative feelings and a staged vehicle for self-indulgence. In

a particularly withering phrase, James Wood writes: "one feels it has been pumped with rarefied air, and is just floating away on its own pretentiousness" (49). In the same vein, Adam Kirsch remarks that "Mr. DeLillo's quietness even feels like a kind of showing off, an attitudinizing grief that is never wholly unaware of its own sleek profile."

2. ART SPIEGELMAN'S *IN THE SHADOW OF NO TOWERS*: THE POLITICS OF TRAUMA

1. See, for instance, Samuels, "Crossing Over," 91: "For the three months after the fall of the towers, I rode the subway anticipating a sarin gas attack or an abandoned knapsack containing a bomb." Also E. Kaplan, "A Camera," 97: "at any moment, it seemed, another attack could take place, the subway could blow up, gas might fill the tunnels." In more general terms, Derrida points out that "traumatism is produced by the *future*, by the *to come*, by the threat of the worst *to come*, rather than by an aggression that is 'over and done with'" (qtd. in Borradori, *Philosophy*, 97).

2. See Laub: "The fear that fate will strike again is crucial to the memory of trauma" (Felman and Laub, *Testimony*, 67).

3. See, e.g., Haspiel, "91101," 92; Roberta Allen, 26; Kingsbury and Smalley, *Remember*, 179.

4. Judging from the autobiographical evidence in *Maus*, Spiegelman is in this more the heir of his mother than his father. In the Holocaust narrative his father is pictured as an eminently resourceful survivor. The mother figure, on the contrary, while surviving Auschwitz, ultimately succumbs to her psychic wounds and commits suicide many years after the war. On Holocaust sensitivity and 9/11, see also Appelfeld, "Talk of the Town," 5: "I used to feel that those of us who had suffered in the Holocaust were immune to fear. I was wrong. We are more sensitive to danger. We can smell it."

5. Pinsker, *Schlemiel as Metaphor*, 4–22.

6. This stands in sharp contrast to Lee, Severin, and Bruzenak, whose revanchist cartoon strip "The Sleeping Giant: A Hitherto Undiscovered Aesop's Fable" features mice as terrorists. In this kind of comics the terrorists also often figure as rats.

7. In this also the self-identification shows traces of the figure of the schlemiel, who is a fool, but at the same time "the only morally sane man" (Wisse, *Schlemiel as Modern Hero*, 4).

8. This panel is clearly inspired by an episode from Winsor McCay's comic strip *Little Nemo in Slumberland*, which is reproduced as plate VI in the

illustrations that follow the Comic Supplement section of *In the Shadow of No Towers*.

9. See the introduction, note 6.

10. E. Kaplan and Wang, "Traumatic Paralysis," 8–9; LaCapra, *History* 110–13, 183; LaCapra, *Writing History* 21–22.

11. In the introduction Spiegelman writes: "The unstated epiphany that underlies all the pages is only implied: I made a vow that morning to return to making comix full-time."

12. Laub, "Truth," 70; Caruth, "Interview," 138; Douglass and Vogler, introduction, 41; and Hungerford, *Holocaust*, 94.

13. Spiegelman himself uses the word "sublime" to denote the impression the collapse of the North Tower made on him (*In the Shadow*, plate 4).

14. LaCapra, *History*, 154; Langer, *Preempting*, 126; Young, "Holocaust," 676; McGlothlin, "No Time," 177–98.

15. See Glejzer, "Witnessing 9/11," 100: "whereas *Maus* offered Spiegelman distance from the events he describes, *In the Shadow of No Towers* is about the failure to achieve such distance."

16. Cathy Caruth defines PTSD as "a response … to an overwhelming event or events, which takes the form of repeated, intrusive hallucinations, dreams, thoughts or behaviors stemming from the event" (*Trauma*, 4).

17. Also see Marianne Hirsch: "At the moment of trauma, time stands still, images are frozen, like the glowing tower that is repeated over and over in the pages of Spiegelman's work" ("Editor's Column," 1213).

18. On the importance of Union Square, see also DeLillo, "In the Ruins," 35, and E. Kaplan, "A Camera," 97.

19. Martha Wolfenstein's term as quoted in Erikson, "Notes on Trauma," 189.

20. Comix is Spiegelman's term for a mixture of pictures and words. Some critics who have discussed Spiegelman's coinage "comix" are LaCapra, *History* 145; Hutcheon, "Literature," 5; and Young, "Holocaust," 672.

3. A ROSE IS NOT A ROSE IS NOT A ROSE: HISTORY AND LANGUAGE IN JONATHAN SAFRAN FOER'S *EXTREMELY LOUD AND INCREDIBLY CLOSE*

1. Contributing to the historical extension of September 11 is also the fact that Oskar (spelled the German way), who goes around playing his tambourine, is intertextually connected to Oskar Matzerath, the protagonist of Günther Grass's *Tin Drum*, a novel about World War II.

2. In his hostile review Walter Kirn calls the novel a "triumph of human cuteness over human suffering."

3. In all fairness, one must add that the family, though German, is anti-Nazi.

4. Cf. LaCapra, *Writing History*: "To the extent someone is possessed by the past and acting out a repetition compulsion, he or she may be incapable of ethically responsible behavior" (70).

5. Thus Foer refutes Forster's statement to the effect that "flat people are not in themselves as big achievements as round ones, and that they are best when they are comic. A serious or tragic flat character is apt to be a bore" (*Aspects*, 70).

6. Cf. LaCapra, *Writing History*, who writes about Holocaust survivors: "In the United States, the survivors didn't have an audience in the general public either. To oversimplify, it was almost like going from Auschwitz to Disney World—and in Disney World, people don't want to hear about Auschwitz. It's a very different context" (158).

7. In the description of the Dresden bombings, Foer lifts scenes and phrases from at least two sources: the witness account of Lothar Metzger and an article by Edda West that appeared in 2003 in the journal *Current Concerns*, no. 2. Also, Foer takes the description of the Hiroshima bombing (by means of a class presentation by Oskar) in large part from the testimony of Kinue Tomoyasu. The name of this Japanese source is mentioned in the novel, but the extent of the borrowing remains unstated.

8. Dori Laub has pointed out that "the speakers about trauma on some level prefer silence so as to protect themselves from the fear of being listened to—and of listening to themselves. That while silence is defeat, it serves them both as sanctuary and as a place of bondage. Silence is for them a fated exile, yet also a home, a destination, and a binding oath" (Felman and Laub, *Testimony*, 58).

9. The device might also owe something to Kurt Vonnegut's *Slaughterhouse-Five*, in which Billy Pilgrim watches a movie of a World War II bombardment backward (73–75).

10. Oskar's symptoms correspond to the "possible reactions in children after trauma/disaster" as summed up in Gurwitch, Pfefferbaum, and Leftwich, "The Impact of Terrorism." They also fit Freud's description of melancholy. See Freud, *On Murder*, 206.

11. In the Freudian scheme, Oskar's reversal of the historical process, whereby a man is borne aloft instead of plunging down, is a symbol of the process of mourning or working through, whereas the countervailing image of the falling man in DeLillo's novel of that name illustrates the devastations of acting out or melancholy.

4. EXORCISING THE GHOST: IRONY AND SPECTRALIZATION IN FRÉDÉRIC BEIGBEDER'S *WINDOWS ON THE WORLD*

1. All references are to Frank Wynne's English translation unless otherwise indicated.

2. The character Jerry, for instance, is more doubtful than David when the disaster is presented as a theme-park ride (60), but on p. 78 Jerry is said to be taken in by the deception, while David remains skeptical. While the tower is burning the people trapped in it are said to suffer from a lack of water, but on p. 262 a water cooler is mentioned. The discussion of the novel is complicated by the fact that the English translation is of varying quality: sometimes it is brilliant, sometimes flat, sometimes sloppy, and sometimes dead wrong. Moreover, as the copyright page indicates, the "English language edition differs in part from the original French." A lot has been left out (especially in the more sexually explicit passages) and in at least one instance a sentence has been added.

3. The name "Beigbeder" will appear in inverted commas to distinguish the character in the novel from the real-life author.

4. On the bifurcated novel, see Burwick, "'Transcendental Buffoonery.'"

5. SEPTEMBER 11 AND THE OTHER

1. Amis's writings on 9/11 have been collected in *The Second Plane*. For a short review of the reactions that his controversial viewpoints evoked, see Donadio, "Amis and Islam."

2. The term is LaCapra's: *Writing History*, 79.

3. "The Children's Crusade" is the middle section of the three-part collection *Specimen Days*. In the other two stories the viability of Whitman's message is tested in the past (the industrial nineteenth century) and an unspecified postnuclear future.

4. On the typical configuration of an Updike story, see Versluys, "'Nakedness.'"

5. The novel's ranking at Metacritic.com is a meager 47 out of 100.

EPILOGUE

1. Female writers such as Claire Messud and Lynne Sharon Schwartz have written important novels in which 9/11 figures as a plot element, but no American female or minority author has yet treated 9/11 as a central theme. As major international contributions to 9/11 fiction, only the works by Lang, Beigbeder, and McEwan have come to my attention.

2. Examples are the novels by McInerney, Kalfus, Messud, Price, Schwartz, McDonell, and O'Neill.

3. Such an intrusion is the hallmark of McEwan's fiction. This justifies Lee Siegel's apt remark that in the wake of September 11, "public consciousness has finally caught up with Ian McEwan's vision of life" ("The Imagination of Disaster").

4. See Carpenter, "Girl Band": "The denouement of this climactic scene is so strikingly improbable that it stretches the limits of credulity, as several critics have remarked." Otherwise Carpenter's reading of this scene is different from mine. In her interpretation, "British tradition (as embodied by Matthew Arnold's poem "Dover Beach") saves the day, and thuggish terrorism is put down by the keepers of the British spirit of fair play" (154–55).

5. Cf. Eaglestone, *Ethical Criticism*: "The saying can never be totally engulfed in the said. The saying appears through its manifestation as a disruption of the said.... In the said 'the spirit hears the echo of the *otherwise.*'... This is the amphibology of language, which is made up of the saying and the said ... Language itself is an amphibology because it has one 'meaning' in the saying—a 'meaning' beyond meaning—and, at the same time, a different meaning in the said" (147).

BIBLIOGRAPHY

Abel, Marco. "Don DeLillo's 'In the Ruins of the Future': Literature, Images, and the Rhetoric of Seeing 9/11." *PMLA* 118 (2003): 1236–50.

Abell, Stephen. "Moments of Truth: Don DeLillo's Imaginative Testimony to a Disaster and Its Details." *Times Literary Supplement*, May 18, 2007, 21–22.

Adorno, Theodor. "Cultural Criticism and Society." In *Prisms*, trans. Samuel and Shierry Weber, 17–34. Cambridge, Mass.: MIT Press, 1981.

Agamben, Giorgio. *Homo Sacer: Sovereign Power and Bare Life*. Trans. Daniel Heller-Roazen. Stanford, Calif.: Stanford University Press, 1998.

Agosin, Marjorie, and Betty Jean Craige, eds. *To Mend the World: Women Reflect on 9/11*. Buffalo, N.Y.: White Pine Press, 2002.

Allen, Charlotte Vale. *Sudden Moves*. Don Mills, Ont.: Mira Books, 2004.

Allen, Roberta. "The Sky Was So Blue." In *110 Stories: New York Writes After September 11*, ed. Ulrich Baer, 26–27. New York: New York University Press, 2002.

Amburgey, Rick. *United We Stand*. Baltimore: PublishAmerica, 2003.

Amis, Martin. "The Age of Horrorism." *Observer*, September 10, 2006. http://observer.guardian.co.uk/review/story/0,,1868732,00.html. Accessed May 25, 2007.

——. "Fear and Loathing." *Guardian*, September 18, 2001. http://books.guardian.co.uk/departments/politicsphilosophyandsociety/story/0,,553923,00.html. Accessed September 10, 2005.

——. "The Last Days of Muhammad Atta." *New Yorker*, April 24, 2006, 152–63.

——. *The Second Plane: September 11, 2001–2007*. London: Jonathan Cape, 2008.

——. "The Voice of the Lonely Crowd." *Guardian*, June 1, 2002. http://books.guardian.co.uk/review/story/0,12084,725608,00.html. Accessed August 25, 2005.

Annesley, James. *Fictions of Globalization*. London: Continuum, 2006.

Appelfeld, Aharon. "Talk of the Town." *New Yorker*, September 24, 2001. http://www.newyorker.com/printable/?talk/010924ta_talk_wtc. Accessed October 29, 2004.

Auster, Paul. "Random Notes—September 11, 2001, 4:00 P.M.. Underground."
In *110 Stories: New York Writes After September 11*, ed. Ulrich Baer, 34–36. New
York: New York University Press, 2002.

Baer, Ulrich, ed. *110 Stories: New York Writes After September 11*. New York: New
York University Press, 2002.

——. "Introduction." In *110 Stories: New York Writes After September 11*, ed. Baer,
1–9. New York: New York University Press, 2002.

Barthes, Roland. "The Eiffel Tower." In *The Eiffel Tower and Other Mythologies*.
Trans. Richard Howard, 3–17. 1979. Berkeley: University of California Press,
1997.

Bassin, Donna. "A Not So Temporary Occupation." In *Trauma at Home: After 9/11*,
ed. Judith Greenberg, 195–203. Lincoln: University of Nebraska Press, 2003.

Baudrillard, Jean. *The Spirit of Terrorism*. Trans. Chris Turner. London Verso,
2002.

Bee, Caroline. "The Center of the Universe." Trans. Edward C. Hollo. Parutions.
com. August 29, 2003. http://www.parutions.com/index.php?pid=1&rid=89&
srid=438&ida=5954. Accessed March 29, 2005.

Begley, Adam. "Image of Twin Towers Ablaze Haunts Narcissistic Cartoonist."
Review of *In the Shadow of No Towers*, by Art Spiegelman. *New York Observer*,
September 13, 2004. http://www.observer.com/node/49724. Accessed Sep-
tember 23, 2004.

Beigbeder, Frédéric. *Windows on the World: A Novel*. Trans. Frank Wynne. London: Fourth Estate, 2004.

——. *Windows on the World. Roman*. Paris: Grasset, 2003.

Berger, Alan L. *Children of Job: American Second-Generation Witnesses to the Holocaust*. Albany: State University of New York Press, 1997

Berger, Alan L., and Naomi Berger, eds. *Second Generation Voices: Reflections by
Children of Holocaust Survivors and Perpetrators*. Syracuse, N.Y.: Syracuse University Press, 2001.

Berger, James. *After the End: Representations of Post-Apocalypse*. Minneapolis: University of Minnesota Press, 1999.

——. "'There's No Backhand to This.'" In *Trauma at Home: After 9/11*, ed. Judith
Greenberg, 52–59. Lincoln: University of Nebraska Press, 2003.

Berman, Marshall. "When Bad Buildings Happen to Good People." In *After the
World Trade Center: Rethinking New York City*, ed. Michael Sorkin and Sharon
Zukin, 1–12. New York: Routledge, 2002.

Black, Star. "Perfect Weather." In *110 Stories: New York Writes After September 11*,
ed. Ulrich Baer, 47–48. New York: New York University Press, 2002.

Blanchot, Maurice. *L'Écriture du désastre*. Paris: Gallimard, 1980.

Bloom, Harold, ed. *Don DeLillo*. Philadelphia: Chelsea House Publishers, 2003.

Booker, Christopher. *The Seven Basic Plots: Why We Tell Stories*. London: Continuum, 2004.

Borradori, Giovanna. *Philosophy in a Time of Terror: Dialogues with Jürgen Habermas and Jacques Derrida*. Chicago: University of Chicago Press, 2003.

Boxall, Peter. *Don DeLillo: The Possibility of Fiction*. London: Routledge, 2006.

Brooks, Peter. "If You Have Tears." In *Trauma at Home: After 9/11*, ed. Judith Greenberg, 48–51. Lincoln: University of Nebraska Press, 2003.

Burwick, Frederick. " 'Transcendental Buffoonery' and the Bifurcated Novel." In *Narrative Ironies*, ed. Raymond A. Prier and Gerald Gillespie, 53–71. Amsterdam: Rodopi, 1997.

Butler, Judith. *Precarious Life: The Powers of Mourning and Violence*. London: Verso, 2004.

Caldwell, Gail. "Gods and Monsters." *Boston Globe*, June 4, 2006. http://www.boston.com/ae/books/articles/2006/06/04/gods_and_monsters/. Accessed August 17, 2007.

Camus, Albert. *Le Mythe de Sisyphe. Essai sur l'absurde*. 1942. Paris: Gallimard, n.d.

Carpenter, Rebecca. " 'We're Not a Friggin' Girl Band': September 11, Masculinity, and the British-American Relationship in David Hare's *Stuff Happens* and Ian McEwan's *Saturday*." In *Literature After 9/11*, ed. Ann Keniston and Jeanne Follansbee Quinn, 143–160. New York: Routledge, 2008.

Caruth, Cathy. "An Interview with Robert Jay Lifton." In *Trauma: Explorations in Memory*, ed. Caruth, 128–47. Baltimore, Md.: Johns Hopkins University Press, 1995.

——, ed. *Trauma: Explorations in Memory*. Baltimore, Md.: Johns Hopkins University Press, 1995.

——. *Unclaimed Experience: Trauma, Narrative, and History*. Baltimore, Md.: Johns Hopkins University Press, 1996.

Cioffi, Frank L. "Disturbing Comics: The Disjunction of Word and Image in the Comics of Andrzej Mleczko, Ben Katchor, R. Crumb, and Art Spiegelman." In *The Language of Comics*, ed. Robin Varnum and Christina T. Gibbons, 97–122. Jackson: University of Mississippi, 2001.

Craps, Stef. "Conjuring Trauma: The Naudet Brothers' 9/11 Documentary." *Canadian Review of American Studies*, 37, no. 2 (2007): 183–204.

Cubilié, Anne. *Women Witnessing Terror: Testimony and the Cultural Politics of Human Rights*. New York: Fordham University Press, 2005.

Cunningham, Michael. *Specimen Days: A Novel*. New York: Farrar, Straus and Giroux, 2005.

de Certeau, Michel. "Walking in the City." In *The Practice of Everyday Life*. Trans. Steven Randall, 91–110. 1984. Berkeley: University of California Press, 1988.

DeLillo, Don. *Falling Man*. New York: Scribner, 2007.

———. "In the Ruins of the Future: Reflections on Terror and Loss in the Shadow of September." *Harper's Magazine* (December 2001): 33–40.

Derbyshire, Jonathan. "Towering Voices." *Financial Times*, August 27, 2004. http://www.ft.com/cms/s/0/fb35e7a4-f65d-11d8-a879-00000e2511c8.html. Accessed March 27, 2005.

Dewey, Joseph. *Beyond Grief and Nothing: A Reading of Don DeLillo*. Columbia: University of South Carolina Press, 2006.

Donadio, Rachel. "Amis and Islam." *New York Times Book Review*, March 9, 2008, 31.

Doody, Terrence. "John Updike Takes on Terror." *Houston Chronicle*, June 2, 2006.

Douglass, Ana, and Thomas A. Vogler. Introduction to *Witness and Memory: The Discourse of Trauma*, ed. Douglass and Vogler, 1–53. London: Routledge, 2003.

Dwyer, Jim, Eric Lipton, Kevin Flynn, James Glanz, Ford Fessenden, Alain Delaqueriere, and Tom Torok. "102 Minutes: Last Words at the Trade Center; Fighting to Live as the Towers Died." *New York Times*, May 26, 2002. http://query.nytimes.com/gst/fullpage.html?res=9F00E6DC153BF935A15756C0A9 649C8B63. Accessed March 25, 2005.

Eaglestone, Robert. *Ethical Criticism: Reading After Levinas*. Edinburgh: Edinburgh University Press, 1997.

Edkins, Jenny. "The Absence of Meaning: Trauma and the Events of 11 September." *Infointerventions*, October 5, 2001. http://www.watsoninstitute.org/infopeace/911/article.cfm?id=27. Accessed January 25, 2005.

Erikson, Kai. "Notes on Trauma and Community." In *Trauma: Explorations in Memory*, ed. Cathy Caruth, 183–99. Baltimore, Md.: Johns Hopkins University Press, 1995.

Faludi, Susan. *The Terror Dream: Fear and Fantasy in Post-9/11 America*. New York: Metropolitan Books, 2007.

Felman, Soshanna, and Dori Laub. *Testimony: Crisis of Witnessing in Literature, Psychoanalysis, and History*. New York: Routledge, 1992.

Foer, Jonathan Safran. *Extremely Loud and Incredibly Close*. Boston: Houghton Mifflin, 2005.

Fonagy, Peter, and Mary Target. "Evolution of the Interpersonal Interpretive Function: Clues for Effective Preventive Intervention in Early Childhood." In

September 11: Trauma and Human Bonds, ed. Susan W. Coates, Jane L. Rosenthal, and Daniel S. Schechter, 99–113. Hillsdale, N.J.: Analytic Press, 2003.

Forster, E. M. *Aspects of the Novel*. 1927. London: Edward Arnold, 1961.

Freud, Sigmund. *On Murder, Mourning, and Melancholia*. Trans. Michael Hulse. London: Penguin, 2005.

Frost, Laura. "*Falling Man*'s Precarious Balance." *American Prospect*, May 11, 2007. http://www.prospect.org/cs/articles?article=falling_mans_precarious_balance. Accessed October 28, 2007.

Gathman, Roger. "Novelist Trapped in Post-9/11 Tale." *Chicago Sun-Times*, April 3, 2005.

Géniès, Bernard. "September 11, the Novel: Possible or Not?" *World Press Review* 50, no. 11 (November 2003). http://www.worldpress.org/article_model.cfm?article_id=1698&dont=yes. Accessed September 16, 2004.

Gilbert, Sandra M. "Writing Wrong." In *Extremities: Trauma, Testimony, and Community*, ed. Nancy K. Miller and Jason Tougaw Miller, 260–70. Chicago: University of Illinois Press, 2002.

Gilloch, Graeme. *Myth and Metropolis: Walter Benjamin and the City*. Cambridge: Polity Press, 1996.

Gioia, Dana. "'All I Have Is a Voice': September 11th and American Poetry." In *Disappearing Ink: Poetry at the End of Print Culture*, 163–67. Saint Paul, Minn.: Graywolf Press, 2004.

Glejzer, Richard. "Witnessing 9/11: Art Spiegelman and the Persistence of Trauma." In *Literature After 9/11*, ed. Ann Keniston and Jeanne Follansbee Quinn, 99–119. New York: Routledge, 2008.

Gordon, Joan. "Surviving the Survivor: Art Spiegelman's *Maus*." *Journal of the Fantastic in the Arts* 5, no. 2 (1993): 81–89.

Greenberg, Judith, ed. *Trauma at Home: After 9/11*. Lincoln: University of Nebraska Press, 2003.

Greer, R. W. "Disaster Recovery." ReviewsOfBooks.com, n.d. http://www.reviewsofbooks.com/extremely_loud_and_incredibly_close/review. Accessed December 2, 2005.

Gurwitch, Robin H., Betty Pfefferbaum, and Michael J. T. Leftwich. "The Impact of Terrorism on Children: Considerations for a New Era." In *Trauma Practice in the Wake of September 11, 2001*, ed. Steven N. Gold and Jan Faust, 101–24. New York: Haworth Maltreatment and Trauma Press, 2002.

Hajdu, David. "Homeland Insecurity." Review of *In the Shadow of No Towers*, by Art Spiegelman. *New York Times Book Review*, September 12, 2004, 13–14.

Hamill, Pete. *Forever*. Boston: Little, Brown, 2003.

Harris, Adrienne. "Relational Mourning in a Mother and Her Three-Year-Old After September 11." In *September 11: Trauma and Human Bonds*, ed. Susan W. Coates, Jane L. Rosenthal, and Daniel S. Schechter, 143–63. Hillsdale, N.J.: Analytic Press, 2003.

Harvey, David. "Cracks in the Edifice of the Empire State." In *After the World Trade Center: Rethinking New York City*, ed. Michael Sorkin and Sharon Zukin, 57–67. New York: Routledge, 2002.

Haspiel, Dean. "91101." In *9-11: Emergency Relief*, ed. Jeff Mason, 92–97. Gainesville, Fla.: Alternative Comics, 2002.

Hass, Aaron. *In the Shadow of the Holocaust: The Second Generation*. Ithaca, N.Y.: Cornell University Press, 1990.

Hatley, James. *Suffering Witness: The Quandary of Responsibility After the Irreparable*. Albany: State University of New York Press, 2000.

Herman, Judith Lewis. *Trauma and Recovery*. New York: Basic Books, 1992.

Heyen, William, ed. *September 11, 2001: American Writers Respond*. Silver Spring, Md.: Etruscan Press, 2002.

Hirsch, Joshua. "Post-traumatic Cinema and the Holocaust Documentary." In *Trauma and Cinema: Cross-Cultural Explorations*, ed. E. Ann Kaplan and Bang Wang, 93–121. Hong Kong: Hong Kong University Press, 2004.

Hirsch, Marianne. "Editor's Column: Collateral Damage." *PMLA* 119 (2004): 1209–15.

——. "Family Pictures: *Maus*, Mourning, and Post-Memory." *Discourse* 15, no. 2 (1992–93): 3–29.

Houen, Alex. "Novel Spaces and Taking Place(S) in the Wake of September 11." *Studies in the Novel* 36 (2004): 419–37.

Hughes, Robert. *Culture of Complaint: The Fraying of America*. New York: Oxford University Press, 1993.

Hungerford, Amy. *The Holocaust of Texts: Genocide, Literature, and Personification*. Chicago: University of Chicago, 2003.

Hutcheon, Linda. "Literature Meets History: Counter-Discoursive 'Comix.'" *Anglia* 117 (1999): 4–14.

Huyssen, Andreas. "Of Mice and Mimesis: Reading Spiegelman with Adorno." *New German Critique* 81 (2000): 65–82.

Jameson, Fredric. *Postmodernism; Or, the Cultural Logic of Late Capitalism*. London: Verso, 1991.

Janet, Pierre. *La Médecine psychologique*. New ed. Paris: Flammarion, 1980.

Junod, Tom. "The Falling Man." *Esquire*, September 2003. http://www.esquire.com/features/ESQ0903-SEP_FALLINGMAN. Accessed January 8, 2008.

———. "The Man Who Invented 9/11." *Esquire*, May 16, 2007. http://www.esquire .com/fiction/book-review/delillo. Accessed October 10, 2008.

Kakutani, Michiko. "A Boy's Epic Quest, Borough by Borough." *New York Times*, March 22, 2005. http://www.nytimes.com/2005/03/22/books/22kaku.html. Accessed August 27, 2005.

———. "John Updike's 'Terrorist' Imagines a Homegrown Threat to Homeland Security." *New York Times*, June 6, 2006. http://www.nytimes.com/2006/06/06/ books/06kaku.html. Accessed August 17, 2007.

———. "Portraying 9/11 as a Katzenjammer Catastrophe." Review of *In the Shadow of No Towers*, by Art Spiegelman. *New York Times*, August 31, 2004. http:// query.nytimes.com/gst/fullpage.html?res=9C05E5DD1731F932A0575BC0A9 629C8B63. Accessed September 16, 2004.

Kalfus, Ken. *A Disorder Peculiar to the Country*. New York: HarperCollins, 2006.

Kaplan, E. Ann. "A Camera and a Catastrophe: Reflections on Trauma and the Twin Towers." In *Trauma at Home: After 9/11*, ed. Judith Greenberg, 95–103. Lincoln: University of Nebraska Press, 2003.

Kaplan, E. Ann, and Bang Wang. "From Traumatic Paralysis to the Force Field of Modernity." In *Trauma and Cinema: Cross-Cultural Explorations*, ed. Kaplan and Wang, 1–22. Hong Kong: Hong Kong University Press, 2004.

———, eds. *Trauma and Cinema: Cross-Cultural Explorations*. Hong Kong: Hong Kong University Press, 2004.

Kaplan, Lawrence F. "American Idle." *New Republic*, September 1, 2005. http://www.tnr.com/politics/story.html?id=87d10aaf-3e6d-4c7c-b2b1- 9ff064e5492c. Accessed September 2, 2005.

Karen, Robert. "Terror and Forgiveness." In *Living with Terror, Working with Trauma*, ed. Danielle Knafo, 533–63. Lanham, Md.: Jason Aronson, 2004.

Kavadlo, Jesse. *Don DeLillo: Balance at the Edge of Belief*. New York: Peter Lang, 2004.

Kearney, Richard. *Strangers, Gods, and Monsters: Interpreting Otherness*. London: Routledge, 2003.

Keniston, Ann and Jeanne Follansbee Quinn, eds. *Literature After 9/11*. New York: Routledge, 2008.

Kermode, Frank. *The Sense of an Ending: Studies in the Theory of Fiction*. New York: Oxford University Press, 1967.

King, Nicola. *Memory, Narrative, Identity: Remembering the Self*. Edinburgh: Edinburgh University Press, 2000.

Kingsbury, Karen. *One Tuesday Morning*. Waterville, Maine: Thorndike Press, 2003.

Kingsbury, Karen, with Gary Smalley. *Remember*. Wheaton, Ill.: Tyndale House, 2003.

Kirn, Walter. "Everything Is Included." *New York Times*, April 3, 2005. http://www.nytimes.com/2005/04/03/books/review/0403cover-kirn.html. Accessed April 4, 2005.

Kirsch, Adam. "DeLillo Confronts September 11." *New York Sun*, May 2, 2007. http://www.nysun.com/arts/delillo-confronts-september-11/53594/. Accessed June 20, 2007.

Knopp, Josephine Zadovsky. *The Trial of Judaism in Contemporary Jewish Writing*. Urbana: University of Illinois Press, 1975.

Kremer, Lillian. *Witness Through the Imagination: Jewish American Holocaust Literature*. Detroit: Wayne State University Press, 1989.

LaCapra, Dominick. *History and Memory After Auschwitz*. Ithaca, N.Y.: Cornell University Press, 1998.

——. *Writing History, Writing Trauma*. Baltimore, Md.: Johns Hopkins University Press, 2001.

Lang, Luc. *11 Septembre mon amour*. n.p.: Stock, 2003.

Langer, Lawrence L. *Preempting the Holocaust*. New Haven, Conn.: Yale University Press, 1998.

Lanham, Fritz. "Wistful Novel Still Brings Smiles." *Houston Chronicle*, March 18, 2005.

Laub, Dori. "September 11, 2001—an Event Without a Voice." In *Trauma at Home: After 9/11*, ed. Judith Greenberg, 204–15. Lincoln: University of Nebraska Press, 2003.

——. "Truth and Testimony: The Process and the Struggle." In *Trauma: Explorations in Memory*, ed. Cathy Caruth, 61–75. Baltimore, Md.: Johns Hopkins University Press, 1995.

Lee, Stan, Marie Severin, and Ken Bruzenak. "The Sleeping Giant: A Hitherto Undiscovered Aesop's Fable." In *9-11: The World's Finest Comic Book Writers and Artists Tell Stories to Remember*, ed. Paul Levitz, 177–80. New York: DC Comics, 2002.

Leslie, Esther. *Walter Benjamin: Overpowering Conformism*. London: Pluto Press, 2000.

Levinas, Emmanuel. *Alterity and Transcendence*. Trans. Michael B. Smith. New York: Columbia University Press, 1999.

——. *The Levinas Reader*. Ed. Sean Hand. Oxford: Basil Blackwell, 1989.

——. *Otherwise Than Being; Or, Beyond Essence*. Trans. Alphonso Lingis. 1981. Pittsburgh: Duquesne University Press, 2004.

Leys, Ruth. *Trauma: A Genealogy*. Chicago: University of Chicago Press, 2000.

Luckhurst, Roger. *The Trauma Question*. London: Routledge, 2008.

Mars-Jones, Adam. "As His World Came Tumbling Down." *Observer*, May 13, 2007. http://observer.guardian.co.uk/review/story/0,,2078190,00.html. Accessed May 24, 2007.

Mason, Wyatt. "The Holes in His Head." Review of *In the Shadow of No Towers*, by Art Spiegelman. *New Republic*. September 21, 2004. Septemberhttp://www.tnr.com/docprint.mhtml?i=20040927&s=mason092704. Accessed September 22, 2004.

——. "Like Beavers." *London Review of Books*, June 2, 2005, 23–24.

Matthews, Charles. "9/11 Trauma Spurs Brainy Boy's Quest." *Mercury News*, April 3, 2005.

McDonell, Nick. *The Third Brother*. New York: Grove Press, 2005.

McEwan, Ian. *Saturday*. London: Jonathan Cape, 2005.

McGlothlin, Erin. "No Time Like the Present: Narrative and Time in Art Spiegelman's *Maus*." *Narrative* 11, no. 2 (2003): 177–98.

McGrath, Charles. "A Cautious Novelist, a Dangerous Subject; John Updike's Latest, a 'Loving Portrait of a Terrorist.'" *New York Times*, May 31, 2006. http://www.nytimes.com/2006/05/31/books/31updi.html. Accessed August 17, 2007.

McInerney, Jay. *The Good Life*. London: Bloomsbury, 2006.

Messud, Claire. *The Emperor's Children*. New York: Knopf, 2006.

Metcalf, Stephen. "'Windows on the World': French Twist." *New York Times Book Review*, April 17, 2005. http://www.nytimes.com/2005/04/17/books/review/17METCALF.html. Accessed April 20, 2005.

Metzger, Lothar. "Bombing of Dresden." May 1999. http://timewitnesses.org/english/%7Elothar.html. Accessed 5 May 2006.

Meyers, Jeff, ed. *September 11: West Coast Writers Approach Ground Zero*. Portland, Ore.: Hawthorne Books and Literary Arts, 2002.

Michaels, Walter Benn. "'You Who Was Never There.' Slavery and the New Historicism—Deconstruction and the Holocaust." In *The Americanization of the Holocaust*, ed. Hilene Flanzbaum, 181–97. Baltimore, Md.: Johns Hopkins University Press, 1999.

Miller, Laura. "Terror Comes to Tiny Town." *New York*, April 4, 2005. http://nymag.com/nymetro/arts/books/reviews/11574/index.html. Accessed December 2, 2005.

Miller, Nancy K. "'Portraits of Grief': Telling Details and the Testimony of Trauma." *Differences: A Journal of Feminist Cultural Studies* 14 (2003): 112–35.

Mishra, Pankaj. "The Politics of Paranoia." *Observer*, September 1, 2006. http://books.guardian.co.uk/departments/politicsphilosophyandsociety/story/0,,1874132,00.html. Accessed May 25, 2007.

Morrison, Toni. "The Dead of September 11." In *Trauma at Home: After 9/11*, ed. Judith Greenberg, 1–2. Lincoln: University of Nebraska Press, 2003.

Nietzsche, Friedrich. *Die Geburt der Tragödie. Der Griechische Staat.* Sämtliche Werke. Stuttgart: Alfred Kröner Verlag, 1964.

O'Neill, Joseph. *Netherland.* New York: Pantheon, 2008.

Orvell, Miles. "Writing Posthistorically: *Krazy Kat, Maus*, and the Contemporary Fiction Cartoon." *American Literary History* 4 (1992): 110–28.

Pinsker, Sanford. *The Schlemiel as Metaphor: Studies in the Yiddish and American Jewish Novel.* Carbondale: Southern Illinois University Press, 1971.

Plate, Liedeke. "The *Poethic* Turn: Writing, Poetry, and Politics After Nine Eleven." *Contemporary French Civilization* 29, no. 2 (2005): 23–49.

Portraits: 9/11/01. The Collected "Portraits of Grief" from The New York Times. 2nd ed. New York: Henry Holt, 2003.

Price, Reynolds. *The Good Priest's Son.* New York: Scribner, 2005.

Raban, Jonathan. "The Good Soldier." *New York Review of Books*, July 13, 2006. www.nybooks.com/articles/19132. Accessed July 17, 2006.

Reese, Jennifer. "'Loud' Narrator a Treasure." *Entertainment Weekly*, March 25, 2005. http://www.cnn.com/2005/SHOWBIZ/books/03/23/ew.books.loud/index.html. Accessed December 2, 2005.

Rich, Frank. "The Clear Blue Sky." *New York Times*, May 27, 2007. http://www.nytimes.com/2007/05/27/books/review/Rich-t.html. Accessed January 8, 2008.

Riemer, Andrew. "Terrorist." *Sidney Morning Herald*, August 5, 2006. http://www.smh.com.au/news/book-reviews/terrorist/2006/08/04/1154198307988.html. Accessed August 17, 2007.

Rinaldi, Nicholas. *Between Two Rivers.* New York: HarperCollins, 2004.

Román, David, et al. "A Forum on Theatre and Tragedy in the Wake of September 11, 2001." *Theatre Journal* 54 (2002): 95–138.

Rosenbaum, Thane. "Art and Atrocity in a Post-9/11 World." In *Jewish American and Holocaust Literature: Representation in the Postmodern World*, ed. Alan L. Berger and Gloria L. Cronin, 125–36. Albany: State University of New York Press, 2004.

Ruigrok, Jennifer Alina. "A Poem for America." Poetry.com n.d. http://www.poetry.com/us_tragedy/display.asp?ID=9. Accessed February 4, 2007.

Said, Edward W. *Orientalism.* New York: Pantheon Books, 1978.

Samuels, David. "Crossing Over." *American Scholar* 73, no. 4 (2004): 85–92.

Santner, Eric L. "History Beyond the Pleasure Principle: Some Thoughts on the Representation of Trauma." In *Probing the Limits of Representation: Nazism and the "Final Solution,"* ed. Saul Friedlander, 143–54. Cambridge, Mass.: Harvard University Press, 1992.

Sass, Louis. "Lacan and 9/11." *Raritan* 23, no. 1 (2003): 162–66.

Schwartz, Lynne Sharon. "Near November." In *110 Stories: New York Writes After September 11*, ed. Ulrich Baer, 260–62. New York: New York University Press, 2002.

——. *The Writing on the Wall*. New York: Counterpoint, 2005.

Scott, A. O. "Pinned Under the Weight of Shattered Towers, and 9/11 History." *New York Times*, August 9, 2006.

Serlin, Ilene, and John T. Cannon. "A Humanistic Approach to the Psychology of Trauma." In *Living with Terror, Working with Trauma: A Clinician's Handbook*, ed. Danielle Knafo, 313–30. Lanham, Md.: Jason Aronson, 2004.

Shainin, Jonathan. "The Plot Against America." *Nation*, July 10, 2006. http://www.thenation.com/doc/20060710/shainin. Accessed August 17, 2007.

Shreve, Anita. *A Wedding in December*. New York: Little, Brown, 2005.

Siegel, Lee. "The Imagination of Disaster." *Nation*, April 11, 2005. http://www.thenation.com/doc/20050411/siegel. Accessed September 16, 2008.

Simmel, Georg. "The Metropolis and Mental Life." 1903. Trans. H. H. Gerth with C. Wright Mills. In *Classic Essays on the Culture of Cities*, ed. Richard Sennett, 47–60. New York: Meredith, 1969.

Simpson, David. *9/11: The Culture of Commemoration*. Chicago: University of Chicago Press, 2006.

Slade, Andrew. "*Hiroshima, mon amour*, Trauma, and the Sublime." In *Trauma and Cinema: Cross-Cultural Explorations*, ed. E. Ann Kaplan and Bang Wang, 165–81. Hong Kong: Hong Kong University Press, 2004.

Smiley, Jane. *Thirteen Ways of Looking at the Novel*. New York: Knopf, 2005.

Sorkin, Michael. *Starting from Zero: Reconstructing Downtown New York*. New York: Routledge, 2003.

Sorkin, Michael, and Sharon Zukin, eds. *After the World Trade Center: Rethinking New York City*. New York: Routledge, 2002.

Spiegelman, Art. *The Complete Maus: A Survivor's Tale*. 1996. London: Penguin Books, 2003.

——. *In the Shadow of No Towers*. New York: Pantheon Books, 2004.

——. "Re: Cover. How It Came to Be." *New Yorker Online*, September 24, 2001. http://www.newyorker.com/printable/?online/011008on_onlineonly01. Accessed October 29, 2004.

Stein, Ruth. "Evil as Love and as Liberation." *Psychoanalytical Dialogues* 12, no. 3 (2002): 393–420.

Stevenson, Jane. "Ghost Machines." *Guardian*, August 7, 2005. http://books .guardian.co.uk/reviews/generalfiction/0,,1543435,00.html. Accessed January 22, 2008.

Stone, Robert. "Updike's Other America." *New York Times Book Review*, June 18, 2006, 1, 8.

Stow, Simon. "Portraits 9/11/01: *The New York Times* and the Pornography of Grief." In *Literature After 9/11*, ed. Ann Keniston and Jeanne Follansbee Quinn, 224–41. New York: Routledge, 2008.

Tchen, John Kuo Wei. "Whose Downtown?!?" In *After the World Trade Center: Rethinking New York City*, ed. Michael Sorkin and Sharon Zukin, 33–44. New York: Routledge, 2002.

Terrell, Kenneth. "9/11: The Comic Book." *U.S. News and World Report*, September 13, 2004.

Tomoyasu, Kinue. "Testimony of Kinue Tomoyasu." n.d. http://www.atomic archive.com/Docs/Hibakusha/Kinue.shtml. Accessed May 8, 2006.

Trilling, Lionel. *The Liberal Imagination*. Garden City, N.Y.: Doubleday, 1953.

Updike, John. "Mixed Messages." *New Yorker*, March 14, 2005. http://www.new yorker.com/archive/2005/03/14/050314crbo_books1. Accessed December 2, 2005.

——. *Terrorist*. London: Hamish Hamilton, 2006.

——. "Tuesday, and After." *New Yorker*, September 24, 2001, 28–29.

——. "Varieties of Religious Experience: A Short Story." *The Atlantic* (November 2002): 93–104.

Van Alphen, Ernst. *Caught by History: Holocaust Effects in Contemporary Art, Literature, and Theory*. Stanford, Calif.: Stanford University Press, 1997.

Van der Kolk, Bessel, and Onno van der Hart. "The Intrusive Past: The Flexibility of Memory and the Engraving of Trauma." In *Trauma: Explorations in Memory*, ed. Cathy Caruth, 158–82. Baltimore, Md.: Johns Hopkins University Press, 1995.

Versluys, Kristiaan. "Art Spiegelman's *In the Shadow of No Towers*: 9/11 and the Representation of Trauma." *Modern Fiction Studies* 52 (2006): 980–1004.

——. "'Nakedness' or Realism in Updike's Early Short Stories." In *The Cambridge Companion to John Updike*, ed. Stacey Olster, 29–42. Cambridge: Cambridge University Press, 2006.

——. "9/11 as a European Event: The Novels." *European Review* 15, no. 1 (2007): 65–79.

———. "Voyages Into the Dark: The Subway Motif in Pound, Eliot, Tate, and Crane." *Thought* 62, no. 246 (1987): 329–38.

Vonnegut, Kurt. *Slaughterhouse-Five*. 1969. Reprint, New York: Dell, 1991.

West, Edda. "The Dresden Bombing." *Current Concerns* no. 3 (2003). http://www .currentconcerns.ch/archive/2003/02/20030230.php. Accessed May 8, 2006.

Wigley, Marc. "Insecurity by Design." In *After the World Trade Center: Rethinking New York City*, ed. Michael Sorkin and Sharon Zukin, 69–85. New York: Routledge, 2002.

Wisse, Ruth. *The Schlemiel as Modern Hero*. Chicago: University of Chicago Press, 1971.

Wood, James. "Black Noise." *New Republic*, July 2, 2007, 47–50.

———. "Jihad and the Novel." *New Republic*, July 3, 2006. http://www.tnr.com/doc print.mhtml?i=20060703&s=wood070306. Accessed August 6, 2007.

Young, James E. "The Holocaust as Vicarious Past: Art Spiegelman's *Maus* and the Afterimages of History." *Critical Inquiry* 24 (1998): 666–99.

Žižek, Slavoj. "On 9/11, New Yorkers Faced the Fire in the Minds of Men." *Guardian*, September 11, 2006. http://www.guardian.co.uk/commentisfree/2006/ sep/11/comment.september11. Accessed January 24, 2008.

———. *Welcome to the Desert of the Real*. London: Verso, 2002.

INDEX

Abel, Marco, 167–68, 196n. 1
Abell, Stephen, 40
abnormality, as linguistic condition, 101–2
Adorno, Theodor, 11, 60, 195n. 6
aesthetics, 9–10, 154
Agamben, Giorgio, 97
agency, 4, 15, 43, 49, 119, 123, 186–88
"Age of Horrorism, The" (Amis), 158–59
alienation, 31–32, 51–52, 96–97, 152–53, 166
allegory, 14, 16, 65, 93, 105–6, 108, 145
Alterity and Transcendence (Levinas), 163
America, as category, 138–40
American Beauty (film), 135
Amis, Martin, 16, 157–59, 181; "The Age of Horrorism," 158–59; "The Last Days of Muhammad Atta," 159–63
"Among the Missing"/"Portraits of Grief," 8–9
anamorphosis, 13–14, 183
animal metaphors, 58, 63
apathy, 20
apocalyptic sensibility, 53, 56, 144–48
art, as redemptive, 30–31
"Art and Atrocity in a Post-9/11 World" (Rosenbaum), 11

Atta, Muhammad (Mohamed), 44, 167, 168–69
audience, 62, 91–92, 196n. 6
Aufhebung (sublation), 153
Auster, Paul, 16, 152–53
authenticity, 15, 62

Babel analogy, 16, 140–44
Babylon analogy, 16, 144–48
Baer, Ulrich, 80, 127
Barthes, Roland, 130
Barton, Nina (*Falling Man*), 22, 30, 41
Bassin, Donna, 1–2
Baudelaire, Charles, 143
Baudrillard, Jean, 4, 45, 124–25, 143
Bee, Caroline, 136
Begley, Adam, 51
Beigbeder, Frédéric, 15, 28, 121–48, 196n. 8; as character, 134–37
Benjamin, Walter, 132
Berger, Alan L., 52
Berger, James, 2, 22–23, 73, 145
Berger, Naomi, 52
Berman, Marshall, 8
Between Two Rivers (Rinaldi), 155–56
biblical analogies: Babel analogy, 16, 140–44; Babylon analogy, 16, 144–48
bin Laden, Osama, 44, 77; as "Bill Lawton," 29, 40–41

Eaglestone, Robert, 149, 181, 182
"Eiffel Tower, The" (Barthes), 130
empathy, American lack of, 157
Empire State Building, 81, 132–33, 141
end-determined fiction, 123
entropy, 35, 110
epiphany, negative, 106
Erikson, Kai, 68–69
erotics of knowledge, 129
ethics, 7, 149, 156; aesthetics as form of,
    154; poetics as form of, 9–10, 13; of
    responsibility, 16–17
Europe, parallelism with United States,
    136–37
Everything Is Illuminated (Foer), 82
Extremely Loud and Incredibly Close
    (Foer): bedtime story about Sixth
    Borough, 104–5; compensatory
    imagination, 99–100, 102–3, 119; con-
    striction in, 83–87; darkened page
    metaphor, 95–96; Dresden passages,
    82–100, 199n. 7; Grandpa's letter to
    Thomas Jr., 94–96; history in, 81–82,
    92; Internet sources, 94; language
    and Americanness, 96–97; magic-
    realist styling, 105–6; marriage of
    Grandpa and Grandma, 83–85; quest
    in, 100–119; reviews, 81, 105; void,
    theme of, 96–100

fall, as metaphor, 47–48
"Falling Man, The" (Drew), 22
Falling Man (DeLillo), 14–15, 19–48, 183,
    186; Alzheimer's in, 34–37; "Bill Law-
    ton" (Bin Laden), 29, 40–41; comfort
    denied, 21, 28; dispersed style of,
    40, 41; dystopia in, 30–34; evapora-
    tion of meaning, 39–43; Falling Man

character in, 22, 23, 24, 31–32; fall
    of man theme, 21, 24; flimsiness of
    existence, 35–36; future-oriented,
    45–46; geopolitical stalemate in,
    43–46; indirectness in, 26–28; inter-
    ruptions in, 40, 44; medical person-
    nel in, 32–33; melancholia in, 20–24;
    modern democracy as theme, 19,
    21–22, 32–34; as narrative of retreat,
    44; noninvolvement, 24–30; poker
    metaphor, 38–39, 42–43; reviews of,
    23, 39–40, 43–44, 196–97n. 6; stream-
    of-consciousness technique, 41–42;
    unrelieved gloom in, 46–48
Faludi, Susan, 23, 29–30
family relations, trauma and, 28–32,
    79–119, 145–46
Felman, Susan, 75–76
fetishistic narratives, 14, 196n. 8
flat character, 87, 199n. 5
Florence (*Falling Man*), 25–26
Foer, Jonathan Safran, 15, 28, 79–119,
    196n. 8; *Everything Is Illuminated*,
    82; Internet sources and, 94. *See also*
    Extremely Loud and Incredibly Close
Fonagy, Peter, 108
Forever (Hamill), 196n. 8
formulaic plots, 13
Forster, E. M., 87, 199n. 5
France, 136–40
Freud, Sigmund, 20
Frost, Laura, 39–40, 41
future, 111, 157, 183, 190–91; ruined by
    September 11, 19, 54, 146–47, 157,
    197n. 1; terrorist orientation toward,
    46–47

gendered discourse, 98

saying, 181–82; interruption of said by, 192–93

Schell, Grandma (*Extremely Loud and Incredibly Close*), 96–100

Schell, Oskar (*Extremely Loud and Incredibly Close*), 100–119

Schell, Thomas, Jr. (*Extremely Loud and Incredibly Close*), reading of Grandpa's letter, 94–95

Schell, Thomas, Sr. (Grandpa) (*Extremely Loud and Incredibly Close*): letter to Thomas, Jr., 94–96; marriage to Grandma, 83–85

Schwartz, Lynne Sharon, 11–12, 200n. 1

Scott, A. O., 1

self: as hostage, 164–65; Other as projection of, 172–73

self-absorption, 87–96

self-censorship, 22

self-othering, 26–27

self-projection, 26

semiosis, 67

September 11, 2001, 1–2; afterlife of, 127; as apocalyptic event, 15–16, 132, 140, 144–45; appropriation of, 11, 13, 73–76, 122–23; children, effect on, 28–29; commodification of, 64; cultural impact of, 29–30; as day of de-Enlightenment, 158; destruction of fiction, 124; discursive responses to, 3–7, 10–11, 143; dispatchers and telephone messages, 5–6, 55; future ruined by, 19, 54, 146–47, 157, 197n. 1; Holocaust and, 50–59; as limit event, 1, 49; missing-person signs, 7–8; photographs of, 22–23; political recuperation of events, 3, 6, 13–14, 22–23, 76, 82–83; precoding vs. recoding,

4–5; as semiotic event, 2, 64; as shattering of language, 140–41; similar incidents, 188–89; strict timeline of, 127; as transfigurative experience, 147; as unpossessable, 1–3; as utopian moment, 8–9, 71–73

September 11, 2001: American Writers Respond (ed. Heyden), 12

September 11 consciousness, 142

September 11: West Coast Writers Approach Ground Zero (ed. Meyers), 12

Serlin, Ilene, 23–24

short story collections, 12, 127

Shreve, Anita, 16, 184–87

Siegel, Lee, 201n. 3

signification, network of, 4

silence, 15, 80, 84, 87, 94, 98–99, 142, 153, 183, 199n. 8; mimetic approximation, 60–66; as only response, 11–12, 28

Simmel, Georg, 108, 153

Simpson, David, 150, 195n. 5

Skarbakka, Kerry, 22, 23

Slade, Andrew, 63

Slaughterhouse-Five (Vonnegut), 199n. 9

Smiley, Jane, 184

space, spectral, 128–34

species consciousness, 157–58

spectacle, terrorism of, 4–5

Spiegelman, Art, 15, 28, 49–77, 127, 196n. 8, 198nn. 11, 20; Jewish identity, 53; *Maus*, 49–50, 53, 57–58, 63, 197n. 4; as narrator-protagonist, 51–52; *New Yorker* cover, 76; paranoid Jew role, 55–56; as son of Holocaust survivors, 49. See also *In the Shadow of No Towers*

Stanley, Alessandra, 195n. 1

Stein, Ruth, 16, 151, 156, 162–63